Henry Charles Banister

A Text-book of Music

Henry Charles Banister

A Text-book of Music

ISBN/EAN: 9783337084646

Printed in Europe, USA, Canada, Australia, Japan

Cover: Foto ©Thomas Meinert / pixelio.de

More available books at **www.hansebooks.com**

A TEXT-BOOK OF MUSIC

GEORGE BELL AND SONS
LONDON : YORK ST. COVENT GARDEN
CAMBRIDGE : DEIGHTON, BELL & CO.
NEW YORK : THE MACMILLAN CO.
BOMBAY : A. H. WHEELER & CO.

A TEXT-BOOK

OF

MUSIC

BY

HENRY C. BANISTER

*Late Professor of Harmony and Composition at the Royal Academy of Music,
at the Guildhall School of Music, and at the Royal Normal College
and Academy of Music for the Blind.*

LONDON
GEORGE BELL AND SONS
1903

First Published, December 1872.
Reprinted, 1873, 1874, 1875, 1877 (twice), 1878, 1879, 1881, 1882, 1883, 1885, 1887, 1890, 1892, 1895, 1899, 1903.

PREFACE TO THE FIRST EDITION.

THIS book has been prepared *primarily* to supply the want, long expressed, of a compendious manual of musical knowledge, for the use of candidates for the Middle-Class Examinations, in connection with the Universities, &c. In the course of my experience in preparing candidates for such examinations, and in superintending classes for the Study of Musical Theory, the need of some such handbook has been very apparent, and I have repeatedly been urged to write one; it being difficult for students to remember *oral* instructions on a subject quite new to them; and there being no book sufficiently combining the two necessary elements of comprehensiveness and conciseness. I have endeavoured to compress within the limits of one small volume, all the information respecting Musical Theory, requisite for such students, so far as, in the nature of the case, such information could be supplied didactically. The book comprehends the entire range of theoretical knowledge.

I cannot but hope, therefore, that it will be found useful to Musical Students generally, beyond the class for whose use it was originally designed. It furnishes a guide to their studies, and a body of instruction, succinct indeed, but not, I trust, meagre or superficial, such as may help them to recall the more detailed instructions imparted orally by their professors; and serving, by its systematic arrangement, and its copious Index, together with the Glossary, as a book for ready reference in the course of their studies. It may answer, in this way, to some extent, the purposes of a Dictionary of Music, with the great advantage that everything that is referred to, by means of the Index, will be found in its proper logical connection.

This latter feature, indeed, induces me to hope still further, that the book will be found a convenient and useful manual of reference for general readers who do not systematically pursue the study of musical theory; whether performers, or simple lovers of music; forming a handy compendium of musical knowledge. It is mainly on account of this collateral purpose of rendering the book one for *reference* as well as for *study*, that so many *technical terms* are mentioned in it. Approval of them is by no means intended by their insertion, nor any wish that very many of them should be used; but, as they *are used*, by various writers, it is desirable that the student should know what they mean, when he meets with them.

The work being a *Text Book* rather than a *Treatise*, the discussion of controverted points must not be looked for in it. Such discussions would have been beyond its scope, and frustrated its purpose, with respect to those for whose use it is specially intended. Generally, those views are given which are most widely accepted by musicians not holding extreme or special opinions. Occasionally, different theories on the same subject are mentioned, when it is thought that they may be understood by an ordinarily intelligent student. It is hoped that it is never done in such a way as to bewilder or perplex him.

I have to offer a few suggestions as to the *order of study* which I think advisable; my opinion, of course, not being binding on any professor who may honour me by using the book.

First of all, *every* student is strongly urged to master Part I. Upon the elementary matters of which it treats, most uncertain and unsatisfactory notions are prevalent among those, even, who have attained considerable proficiency in the practice of music.

Respecting *Harmony* and *Counterpoint*, I have (§ 81) given my opinion that the two "should be studied conjointly" (see § 248). Of course, if any one wishes to obtain only a moderate acquaintance with Musical Structure, he need only study as far as chapter xxvi.; and then read chapter xxxiii. on Modulation, and any other portions of the book in which he may feel interested.[1]

But those who purpose to master the entire volume may pursue the following course. Study in order as far as chapter xvi.; then chapter xxvii., and chapter xxviii., 1st division, on the First Species of two-part Counterpoint. Some teachers think it desirable for the student of Counterpoint to study the First Species, in two, three, four, and even more parts, before proceeding to the other species in two parts; and, in like manner, to study the Second Species, in all the numbers of parts, before proceeding to the Third Species at all; and so on. The more usual course, however, is to go through the entire five species, in two parts, before proceeding to three-part Counterpoint at all · and so on. Each method has its advantages, perhaps; and I have, at different times, adopted each. Whichever course is taken, however, the study of Counterpoint may, from the point above indicated, be pursued in conjunction with that of the chapters on Harmony. The bearing of chapter xxii. on the *Fourth* Species of Counterpoint, and of chapter xxiii. on the *Second* and *Third* Species, is pointed out in the proper places (§§ 216, 224, &c.). In conjunction with chapter xvii., § 168, the early part of chapter xxxiii., on *Natural Modulation*, may be studied as far as § 340. The writing of the Exercises on Modulation may, however, be deferred till the whole of the chapters on *Harmony* (*i. e.*, as far as chapter xxvi.) have been studied. After chapter xx., §§ 341 and 348 of chapter xxxiii. may be studied, the Exercises being again deferred.

In conjunction with chapter xxxiv., chapters iii. and xiv. should be studied.

The study of chapters xxxv., xxxvi., and xxxvii., will appropriately follow that of the whole of the preceding chapters; but they may be fairly understood, if read at a somewhat earlier period. Chapter xxxviii. may be read at any time, or referred to as occasion requires.

---

[1] *Junior* candidates for the *Cambridge* Examinations are only required to understand as far as the inversions of the Dominant 7th; but I strongly advise them to study at least as far as chapter xx.

Preface.

All the Examples on Simple Counterpoint are on one Canto Fermo, by Fux and in many cases, which I have indicated, the Counterpoint also is his. Where this is not indicated, however, I am alone responsible for it. Fux does not give a complete series, in all the Species, on this Canto Fermo; and I have supplied the deficiency.

It only remains for me to tender my best thanks to the Rev. Professor Sir F. A. Gore Ouseley, to Professor Sir W. Sterndale Bennett, and to the Council of the College of Preceptors, for permission to insert the several Examination Papers in the Appendix.

H. C. B.

London, 1872.

PREFACE TO THE SIXTH EDITION.

I AVAIL myself of the opportunity presented by the issue of a sixth edition to offer a few remarks on some of the subjects treated of in this work, respecting which some further elucidation may be helpful to Students. It is for their benefit that the work has been written; and as, in carrying out this purpose, I have avoided introducing anything of a polemical, and therefore distracting nature, so in these remarks, I merely wish to meet difficulties, or answer inquiries that may naturally, and, to my knowledge, do often arise in their minds.

Taking the subjects in the order in which they are treated, the first matter to refer to is the *Mezzo-Soprano* Staff. As I have said, in the foot-note to p. 258, this term was formerly applied to the Staff with the C clef on the *second line*. That Staff, however, being now obsolete, it seemed to me that the term might now be applied to that generally termed the *Soprano* Staff, with the C clef on the *first* line; inasmuch as that fairly represents the compass of a Mezzo-Soprano voice, and the anomaly is thereby avoided of applying the term *Soprano* (from *superannus*, high), to that which is *not* the highest Staff; leaving the term *Treble* (from *tres*, three — that being the *third* part above, or including, the Tenor—see § 250), for the highest Staff. I enclosed the prefix, however, within brackets, in Fig. 2. I still think that this use of the term might prevent some confusion.

The subject of *Pitch* (see p. 6) is still engaging the attention of acousticians and musicians. The most recent discussion of the matter may be found in a paper read by Mr. Ellis before the Society of Arts, and printed in the *Journal* of that Society for May 25, 1877.

To the Chapters on *Time*, on *Embellishments*, &c., and on the *Chromatic Scale*, I have made several additions.

The *General View of the Chords* in Chapter xi. exhibits them according to the System of Harmony known as that of *Added Thirds*. System—be it observed—not *Theory*: a convenient *conspectus*, showing, as it seems to me, the simplicity of the subject, when the student is just starting. The different *Theories* of Harmony—of the derivation and origin of Chords, &c.—should hardly occupy the attention of students at first; and, therefore, I have not entered upon them. I think that if the student masters the most obvious and practical matters about which there is but little dispute among musicians, he will be the better prepared to enter, subsequently, upon those controversies which more or less engage advanced theorists. Possibly at some future time I may endeavour to furnish students with some help and guidance in the consideration and comparison of more or less conflicting theories.

In the mean time, students may rest assured that the *practical result* remains, for the most part, the same, whichever of the various theories now in vogue among good musicians be adopted and studied. One theory may be more clear, or more comprehensive than another : may seem to explain more completely and fully the origin and nature of chords, harmonies, and progressions : to account for and justify much that otherwise seems exceptional or questionable in acknowledged music : to furnish a more logical basis of principles, from which to deduce guiding rules; and, therefore, according to the soundness of the theory studied may the student's progress be more or less, consciously to himself, satisfactory—the laying hold of irrefragable truth, imparting confidence, **instead of constant uncertainty** and timidity. This *may* be: **though** there **is no** one of these various theories that **has not** been much questioned and controverted. But the practical result of all, so far as any directions or *rules* for students are concerned, is much the same. I have said this respecting **the** theories *now in vogue:* for, undoubtedly, the gropings after truth **of** Mersenne, **Zarlino, Rameau,** &c., resulted **in** little that could otherwise than *fetter*, **rather** than practically guide or help **a** student. So much was forbidden and unrecognised **in** former **times**, which by theorists **of all** shades **is now** freely admitted **and** permitted (see §§ 169, 249, 262, &c.), that **the** efforts **of** these later theoretical writers **have** been directed towards the reduction to principles **and** *formulæ* of that which artistic perception, as evidenced in **the works of the acknowledged** great modern composers, thus accepts.

Therefore, while theory should not be deduced **from rules**, neither, for the most part, should rules be regarded as **deductions** from theories or ascertained truths. They should, rather, be regarded as *friendly directions—guiding* rules, as I have above termed them—*for the **use and** help of students*, while they are *training for musicianship*. I am persuaded that, for practical purposes, this is **the** right way of viewing them. And herein lies a ready answer **to** the inquiries so frequently put **by** anxious students—" May I write this progression ? "— **" Is that** *wrong?* **is it** *forbidden?* " There is no senate, or parliament of musicians, with any power or right to *enact laws* for musical composers. But there are, happily, good, artistic, honest labourers *for Students*, who endeavour to arrange and classify for them the general principles which should regulate their procedure—as illustrated **in** the works **of fine** writers. This fraternity of helpers is that in which I wish **to** be considered as enrolled. When, therefore, a student makes such inquiries **of me,** my reply **in substance is,** "such and such **a** progression **or** combination is not allowed *for you* in your *exercises:* you are in your pupilage : the cases when it **is** good in effect **you** must judge of when your discerning and discriminating powers are matured by experience. *Then,* if you write **this** in your *compositions,* no longer as **a** mere learner, you will **act on** your own responsibility, **and** your decision will be judged on its merits." For, surely, **no** set of theoretical writers has any right **to** lay down *rules* as to what composers may or may not write, **when** they are out of their pupilage !

There are, indeed, certain rules given to students, which embody so much of truth, and are so unmistakeably founded on principles of beauty, that, if any composer habitually violates them, musicians detect him to be *untrained*—or else *defiant*. But occasional infringements of these, even, may be the result of deliberate judgment. And who, among theoretical writers, —or rather compilers of rules—has any right to condemn or gainsay such departures from prescription?

This leads me to make a few remarks upon what are termed *Licenses* (§ 168). It has been the fashion, latterly, to sneer at this term, as applied to exceptional departures from the ordinary rules; as though the admission of them implied that the rules were too stringent; or else, as though the *license* itself were an admission of that which is confessedly bad. But, without adducing the admission of *poetical licenses* (the nature of which I need not specify) in justification of the application of the term to musical writing, I may say, firstly, that in many cases the surroundings of an ordinarily forbidden progression,—the circumstances under which it is introduced,—render it either wholly unobjectionable, or even positively grateful to the ear, or the mind through the ear (see, for example, § 139, &c.). Secondly, that, in other cases, that which is licensed is for the avoidance of some other progression or effect, undeniably and perhaps invariably objectionable; or the *obtaining* of some special effect. The question may be one of a *choice of evils*, or a balancing of effects. And still further, be it again observed, the *License* is granted to *Students*, to whom alone the *Rules* are given. And, as the rules are guides as to how generally to proceed, so the licenses are guides as to how, and when, perhaps under great stress, not of *bad* laws, but of *good* ones, they may be departed from with little, or at all events the least, ill-effect: *perhaps* none at all. A *pedant* can enunciate laws, and frown even on good music which infringes them. A good *musician*, and wise teacher, can alone advise a learner as to when the acknowledged law can with good effect, or may, under pressure, be broken. But the rules should be stringently enforced on learners, at first: the licenses and exceptions only sparingly allowed until the student has made some advancement: or the result will be (I speak from some thirty years of experience as a teacher), these latter will be much more observed than the former, and *at the wrong times*.

There is one department, however, from which all thought

of license must be rigorously excluded : that, namely, of *strict composition*, canonical and fugal. This **is**, confessedly, a scholastic arena, into which none should **enter** but those who comply with its conditions. Be it admitted, for a moment, that the **whole structure of** such compositions is arbitrary. Still, **once let any one** attempt **to write in that** style, and infringement of **the rules is a** confession of weakness, except under **rare** circumstances, when such an infringement *may* be a declaration of power. But it **would not** be difficult to show that a Fugue, written as generally prescribed, **is a** very microcosm of all that is logical and powerful in musical structure. And it is only with the *structural* that **laws** have to do : not with the *imaginative*.

There are those who urge that the rules—few though they really be—curb and fetter the imagination ; and plead the example **of** such daring geniuses as Beethoven. Well, grant that the rules that Beethoven the *student* learned from Albrechtsberger were not binding on Beethoven the *mature genius*. But Beethoven himself, however independently and even **defiantly** he may sometimes have expressed himself **with** regard to *pedantic* rules, **said to** my revered master, Cipriani Potter, "*I have* not studied enough." Let students lay this to heart.

H. C. B.

London, 1877.

PREFACE TO THE SEVENTH EDITION.

In this Edition, besides various minor emendations, **I have** made considerable alterations in the Examples of Counterpoint in Chapters xxviii.—xxx. **In** the original preparation of this work, I thought to give interest and authority by introducing examples from so eminent a master as Fux (or Fuchs), whose *Gradus* **ad** *Parnassum* has for so long held a high position among works on Counterpoint. But, as I have remarked in § 249, the early writers were largely empirical in their treatment of this subject; there being, at the time when they wrote, no formulated system of Harmony,—no classification of chords,—to be referred to in justification of the Contrapuntal rules given. Still further, even up to the time of Fux, the modern tonality was so little fixed (see §§ 62, 263), that many of the Examples in his *Gradus* are far from being models for Students now-a-days. On consideration, therefore, I have thought it advisable to make more extensive alterations than in previous editions,—in some instances amounting to rewriting,—of the Examples given; especially as some of them infringed the rules. It has been, indeed, alleged that Counterpoint treatises in general are open to the charge of this inconsistency; and, with shallow logic, and unphilosophical musicianship, it has been intimated, not merely *implicitly*, but rather *explicitly*, that Counterpoint is a study more interesting historically than useful practically. In order to warn the Student against any such notion, I simply refer him to my remarks upon the true philosophy of Counterpoint in Chapter xxvii. If the exposition therein given be valid, it will be unaffected by any defects, real or supposed, in Contrapuntal Treatises. But, at all events, I have endeavoured to free the chapters on Counterpoint in this work from any charge such as has been alluded to. And the alterations that I have now made are, I trust, such as to commend the combinations and progressions to ears accustomed to modern harmonies.

But still these Examples conform to the rules of *Strict* Counterpoint: they are *Diatonic*, and are built upon the *Triad* and its *first inversion*. In a work like the present, designed to meet the requirements of those who are studying according to existing methods, it would have been inappropriate to attempt the inauguration of any revolutionary course. But there is nothing revolutionary in suggesting the enlargement of the basis of Contrapuntal study, in conformity with the wider range of harmonies now recognized. There is really no justification for the perpetual and rigid exclusion, *all through the Student's Contrapuntal course*, of the Chord of the 7th and its inversions. Or,—to put the matter in another way:—if, as I have urged (§ 81), the study of Harmony,—so called, by distinction,—be pursued in conjunction with that of Counterpoint, there is no valid reason why the rules should not be so far elasticized as to be progressively adapted to the further insight of the Student into the various essential chords. If, properly enough, in his early exercises, the only chords admitted are the

Preface to the Seventh Edition.

Triad and its first inversion, all other harmonies being excluded, and discords,—even the anomalous perfect 4th from the lowest part,—being taken only by transition, in the second and third species, or by preparation, in the fourth and fifth species; then, when the Student advances to the Fundamental Chord of the 7th, let that harmony be admitted, freely, as essential, and essential dissonances be taken, not only at the beginning of the bar, but even by skip, in such manner as shewn in Figs. 125 (*a*), 133 (*a*), &c. The subsequent application of the rules respecting Passing-notes, Suspensions, &c., need be of no practical difficulty under a judicious Teacher. The great matter is to keep the Student in mind, firstly, of the general laws of part-writing,—laws of melody, and laws of combined progression; and, secondly, of the important point that, in Two-part Counterpoint, a complete harmony is to be reduced, and represented as efficiently as possible: as, for example, in the opening Counterpoint to a Fugue answer. And it may be made very interesting to shew how the same Subject may be treated progressively with consonant and dissonant harmonies; as illustrated in Exercises 8, 20, 27. And, if all this is done, with a wise, *progressive Conservatism*, there will be no real provocation of the frequent complaint of Students against the stringent exclusion of dissonant harmonies from their early exercises. By the time, moreover, that they arrive at Chromatic Chords, even these, and Chromatic alterations, may be incorporated. (See §§ 249, 317.)

In connection with this branch of study, I may give it as a strong recommendation that Students should *figure* the lowest part of their Counterpoint exercises; especially those in only two parts, where the harmony is less clearly or completely defined.

The attention of the Student is directed to the close resemblance in the succession of harmonies of Exercise 83, p. 286, and that available for the Unfigured Bass, No. 13, p. 289. From the latter, he may obtain suggestions for Passing-notes to be introduced in the former.

H. C. B.

London, 1878.

TABLE OF CONTENTS.

PART I.
NOTATION.

		PAGE
INTRODUCTORY. MUSICAL SOUNDS: THEIR PRODUCTION, PITCH, FORCE, AND QUALITY		1

CHAP.
I.	THE NOTES, THE STAVE, AND THE CLEFS. THE OCTAVE	2
II.	SHARPS, FLATS, AND NATURALS	7
III.	THE LENGTH OF NOTES: RESTS: BARS, TIME: ACCENT	8
IV.	REPEATS: ABBREVIATIONS: EMBELLISHMENTS: MARKS AND WORDS INDICATING PACE, OR MANNER OF PERFORMANCE	14

PART II.
RUDIMENTS OF THEORY: HARMONY, AND COUNTERPOINT.

V.	THE DIATONIC SCALE: MAJOR MODE	21
VI.	THE DIATONIC SCALE: MINOR MODE	27
VII.	THE CHROMATIC SCALE	32
VIII.	INTERVALS	34
IX.	MELODY, HARMONY, THOROUGH-BASS, COUNTERPOINT, SCORE, CONCORDS, AND DISCORDS	40
X.	HARMONICS	42

CHAP.		PAGE
XI.	GENERAL VIEW OF THE CHORDS	44
XII.	ELEMENTARY LAWS OF PART-WRITING	46
XIII.	THE TRIAD, OR COMMON CHORD	56
XIV.	CADENCES	63
XV.	SEQUENCES	67
XVI.	INVERSIONS OF THE TRIAD	69
XVII.	CHORDS OF THE SEVENTH	76
XVIII.	INVERSIONS OF CHORDS OF THE SEVENTH	83
XIX.	THE CHORD OF THE DOMINANT $\frac{9}{7}$	86
XX.	CHORDS DERIVED FROM THE DOMINANT $\frac{9}{7}$	89
XXI.	THE CHORDS OF THE ELEVENTH AND OF THE THIRTEENTH	93
XXII.	DISCORDS BY SUSPENSION	94
XXIII.	UNESSENTIAL DISCORDS	104
XXIV.	CHROMATIC CHORDS, AND CHROMATIC ALTERATIONS OF CHORDS	109
XXV.	PEDAL-NOTES	112
XXVI.	ARPEGGIOS. GROUND BASS	115
XXVII.	GENERAL OBSERVATIONS ON COUNTERPOINT	117
XXVIII.	SIMPLE COUNTERPOINT IN TWO PARTS	120
XXIX.	SIMPLE COUNTERPOINT IN THREE PARTS	133
XXX.	SIMPLE COUNTERPOINT IN FOUR PARTS	144
XXXI.	COUNTERPOINT IN MORE THAN FOUR PARTS: FREE COUNTERPOINT	148
XXXII.	DOUBLE, TRIPLE, AND QUADRUPLE COUNTERPOINT	150

PART III.

ELEMENTS OF COMPOSITION.

XXXIII.	MODULATION	160
XXXIV.	RHYTHM	170

Table of Contents. xvii

CHAP.		PAGE
XXXV.	IMITATION AND CANON	176
XXXVI.	FUGUE	189
XXXVII.	FORM IN COMPOSITION	208
XXXVIII.	VOICES AND INSTRUMENTS	217
	GLOSSARY OF MUSICAL TERMS	231
	EXERCISES IN HARMONY AND COUNTERPOINT	255
	APPENDIX I.	301
	APPENDIX II.	309
	INDEX	316

LIST OF WORKS REFERRED TO.

ALBRECHTSBERGER, J. G. Douze Fugues pour le Clavecin. Op. 1. Berlin, 1778.
BACH, C. P. E. Versuch uber die wahre Art das Clavier zu spielen. Leipzig, 1787.
BACH, J. S. Das Wohltemperirte Clavier. (48 Preludes and Fugues.)
   „ The Art of Fugue.

(Not a didactic work; but a series of Fugues and Canons, illustrating the different methods of treating and combining the same subjects.)

   „ Fugue à deux voix, pour les commençans (in C Minor).
   „ Motet, "*I wrestle and pray.*"
   „ Thirty Variations on an Air in G Major.

BEETHOVEN. Studien im Generalbasse, Contrapuncte, und in der Compositions-Lehre. Vienna, 1832.

(An English translation by H. H. Pierson. Leipsic, 1853.)

   „ Two Preludes through all the Major keys. Op. 39.

BERARDI, ANGELO. Miscellanea Musicale. Bologna, 1689.
BERNARDI, STEFFANO. Porta Musicale: Parte 1ma. Verona, 1615.
CERONE, PEDRO. El Melopeo y Maestro. Naples, 1613.
COUSSEMAKER, C. E. H. de. Histoire de l'Harmonie au moyen age. Paris, 1852.
   „ L'Art Harmonique au xiie et xiiie siècles. Paris, 1865.

D'Ortigue, J. Introduction à l'Etude comparée des Tonalités. Paris, 1853.

D'Ortigue and Niedermeyer, L. Traité de l'accompagnement du plain chant. Paris, 1857.

Eberlin, G. E. ix Toccate e Fughe per l'Organo. Augusta, 1745.

Encyclopædia Britannica. 8th ed. Edinburgh, 1853, &c. (Article *Acoustics*.)

Encyclopædia Metropolitana. London, 1845. (Article *Sound*.)

Fétis, F. J. Traité complet de la théorie et de la pratique de l'Harmonie. 2nd ed. Paris, 1844.

Fux (or Fuchs), J. J. Gradus ad Parnassum. Vienna, 1725.

(There is an English abridgment, which is rather scarce. A similar abridgment appeared in successive numbers of *The Choir* for 1870.)

Handel. Suites de Pièces, or Lessons for the Harpsichord.

Hopkins, E. J., and Rimbault, E. F. (LL.D.). The Organ, its History and Construction. London, 1855.

Hullah, John. The History of Modern Music. A course of Lectures delivered at the Royal Institution. London, 1862.

„ A course of Lectures on the Third or Transition Period of Musical History. London, 1865.

Kiesewetter, R. G. History of the Modern Music of Western Europe. Translated by Robert Müller. London, 1848.

Lorente, Andres. El Porque de la Musica. Alcala de Henares, 1672.

Macfarren, G. A. Rudiments of Harmony. London, 1860.

„ Six Lectures on Harmony, delivered at the Royal Institution. London, 1867.

Marshall, J. (F.R.S.). Outlines of Physiology. 2 vols. London, 1867.

List of Works Referred to.

Martini, Giovanni Battista. Esemplare o sia Saggio Fondamentale Pratico di Contrapunto sopra il Canto Fermo. 2 vols. Bologna, 1779.

Morley, Thomas. A Plaine and easie Introduction to Practical Musicke. London, 1597.

Ouseley, Rev. Sir F. A. Gore, Bart. (M.A., Mus. Doc.). Treatise on Harmony. Oxford, 1866.

" Treatise on Counterpoint. Oxford, 1869.

Sala, Nicola. Regole del Contrapunto. Napoli, 1794.

Smith, Robert (D.D.). Harmonics, or the Philosophy of Musical Sounds. London, 1759.

Spencer, Charles Child. A concise explanation of the Church Modes. 2nd ed. London, 1846.

Tyndall, John (LL.D., F.R.S.). Sound. A course of Eight Lectures delivered at the Royal Institution. London, 1867.

Woolhouse, W. S. B. Essay on Musical Intervals, Harmonics, and the Temperament of the Musical Scale, London, 1835.

Zacconi, Lodovico. Prattica di Musica. Venetia, 1596.
" " Ditto. Parte 2^{nda}. Venetia, 1622.

TEXT BOOK OF MUSIC.

PART I.

NOTATION.

INTRODUCTORY.

MUSICAL SOUNDS: THEIR PRODUCTION, PITCH, FORCE, AND QUALITY.

1. MUSICAL SOUNDS are the result of *rapid* and *periodic* vibrations of the air. *Slow* vibrations do not affect the auditory nerve; *irregular* or *unperiodic* vibrations produce *noise*, not *music*.[1]

2. The PITCH—*acuteness* or *gravity*—of a musical sound depends upon the *rapidity* of the vibrations which produce it. The greater the number of vibrations in a given time, the more acute is the sound.[2]

3. The FORCE or *loudness* of a musical sound depends upon the *size* or *amplitude* of the vibrations: the greater their extent, the louder will be the sound. Moreover, sound is louder in proportion to the condensation of the air through which it is conveyed.[3]

4. The QUALITY or *timbre* of a musical sound depends partly upon the nature of the string, or other sonorous

---

[1] Tyndall on *Sound*, pp. 49, 50.   [2] *Ibid.* pp. 55—57.
[3] *Ibid.* pp. 11, 48; and Woolhouse on *Musical Intervals*, p 2.

body, employed in its production; and partly upon the form of the waves, and the varying intermixture of *Harmonics*,—the higher sounds produced, in conjunction with the principal or *fundamental* sound, by the vibration of parts of the length of such string.[1] (See chap. x. § 86, and *Note* at the end of that chapter.)

CHAPTER I.

THE NOTES, THE STAVE, AND THE CLEFS. THE OCTAVE.

5. MUSICAL sounds are named after the first seven letters of the alphabet. They are also designated by certain syllables, as follows:

    C. D. E. F. G. A. B.
    Do. Re. Mi. Fa. Sol. La. Si.

Formerly, Do was called UT; which term is still used by French musicians. (See also § 62, and Fig. 50.)

In Germany, B is termed H; and that which we term B *flat* is termed B.[2] (§ 263.)

The alphabetical names will be used, exclusively, throughout this work.

6. Musical characters are written upon a series of parallel lines, termed a STAVE or STAFF (Fig. 1), and upon

Fig. 1.

the intervening spaces; these being numbered from the lowest upwards.

---

[1] Tyndall, pp. 116, 117: also, article *Sound*, by Sir J. F. W. Herschel, in Encyclop. Metrop. vol. iv. p. 784, § 174.

[2] Thus J. S. BACH wrote Fugues on his own name:

The Stave, and Clefs.

In *modern* music, the stave generally consists of *five* lines; but this is not essential, nor was it the case in *early* music. Even now, some Ecclesiastical Chants are written upon staves of *four* lines.

7. To fix the position of the notes on the stave, three characters termed CLEFS are used; *viz.*:

𝄢 the F clef; 𝄡 the C clef; 𝄞 the G clef.

𝄡 represents the middle C on a Pianoforte. 𝄢 represents the F *below* and 𝄞 the G *above* this middle C.

Notes written upon a stave will bear no name, and represent no sound, till one or other of the clefs be placed upon it, to fix a standard wherefrom all the notes may be reckoned: the clef thus being a *key* (as its name implies) to the names of the notes. The clef used will depend upon the compass of the voice or instrument to be written for; the object being to include the music, as much as is practicable, within the limits of a five-line stave. The most frequent positions of the various clefs, in modern music,—in other words, the most frequently-used staves of five lines,—with their relations to one another, are shown in Fig. 2; but, in old music, they are found in other positions: *i. e.* on other lines of the stave.

Fig. 2.
(a) Bass Stave. (b) Tenor Stave. (c) Alto Stave. (d) [Mezzo-] Soprano Stave. (e) Treble, or Violin Stave.

(See Foot-note, p. 258.)

In modern Pianoforte music, two staves are used, braced (Fig. 3). Notes beyond the compass of these two staves are written upon short additional lines, called LEGER or LEDGER LINES, and on the spaces between them, as indicated. Were one more line inserted between these two staves, one continuous stave of eleven lines would be

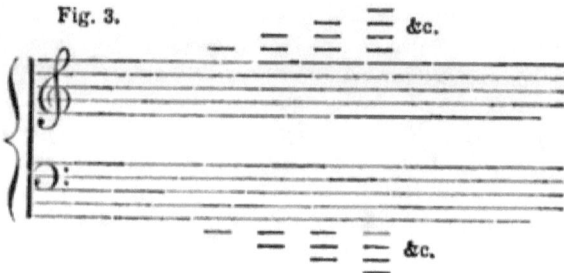

Fig. 3.

formed, termed the GREAT STAVE. The would be upon that middle line; and the names of the notes would be as in Fig. 4. Practically, however, it

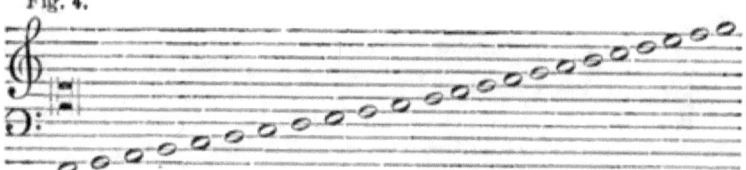

Fig. 4.

F G A B C D E F G A B C D E F G A B C D E F G

would be inconvenient to the eye to read so extended a stave; therefore it is broken by the omission of the middle line, as above (Fig. 3); and, when the intermediate C is required, a Ledger line is used (Fig. 5).

Fig. 5.

So that, in *modern music* for the Pianoforte, the Harp, &c., the C clef does not appear.[1] It is to be found, however, in old music for the instruments that preceded the Pianoforte: *e. g.* D. Scarlatti's *Lessons for the Harpsichord* (old edition).

When, however, it is desired to write for *voices*, or for instruments of more limited compass than the Pianoforte,

---

[1] It is used in J. B. Cramer's *Studio:* vol. ii. Ex. 35.

&c., a stave of five lines, forming a section of the *Great Stave*, is used, as in Fig. 1; and, for notes beyond the extent of such stave, Ledger lines, which form a continuation of the stave, are used.

The note in each of the Figs. 6 to 10 is, therefore, really the same note, written in apparently different ways.

In old music, the C clef was used on the second line; the G clef on the first line; and the F clef on the third line, in addition to the positions that they occupy above. More correctly speaking, other sections of the Great Stave were used.

The BASS STAVE (Fig. 6) is used for the *Bass*, or lowest voice of men, and for instruments of similar compass: *e. g.* the Violoncello, the Bassoon, &c. The TENOR STAVE (Fig. 7) is used for the *Tenor*, or high voice of men, and for the Tenor Trombone: sometimes for the higher notes of the Violoncello and Bassoon. The ALTO STAVE (Fig. 8) is used for the *Counter-Tenor*, the highest voice of men, or the *Contralto*, the lowest voice of women; and for the Alto Trombone and the Viola. The SOPRANO or MEZZO-SOPRANO STAVE (Fig. 9) is used for the *Mezzo-Soprano*, or medium voice of women, especially for the highest part in choruses; though not so much now, in England, as formerly. The TREBLE STAVE or VIOLIN STAVE (Fig. 10) is used for the *Soprano* or *Treble*, the highest voice of women, for the Violin, Flute, &c.

Fig. 6. Fig. 7. Fig. 8. Fig. 9. Fig. 10.

8. It will be seen, by Fig. 4, that the seven letters by which the notes are designated are repeated throughout the ascending series of notes. Each recurrence of the same letter indicates that the previous note *of the same name* is, at this recurrence, reproduced in a higher *register*, or *pitch*; and this reproduction is called the OCTAVE to the lower note. The nature of the resemblance between two sounds an octave apart; or, in other words, in what sense

the one is a reproduction or repetition of the other, it is impossible to express in words. With the fact—the effect—every one is familiar. The acoustical explanation is that the higher of two sounds an octave apart is produced by double the number of vibrations, which produce the lower sound. Thus, if Fig. 11 be the result of 256 vibrations in a second, Fig. 12, its octave, will have 512 vibrations.[1] (See § 88.)

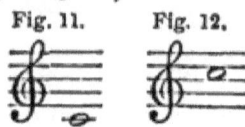

Fig. 11.   Fig. 12.

The term *Octave* is also applied to a complete series of notes, from any note to its octave: also termed DIAPASON. The notes included by Fig. 13 are termed the GREAT OCTAVE; those included by Fig. 14 the SMALL OCTAVE; those included by Fig. 15 the ONCE-MARKED OCTAVE, the notes being written of as c, d, &c.; those included by Fig. 16 the TWICE-MARKED OCTAVE: c, d, &c. The notes from Fig. 17 to the octave above are sometimes termed IN ALT.: those from Fig. 18 upwards are termed IN ALTISSIMO.[2]

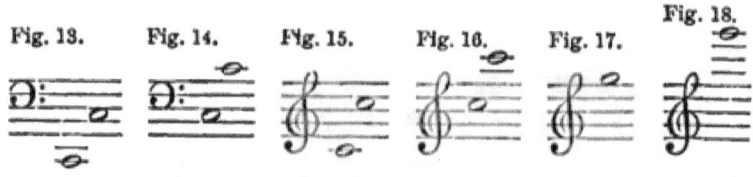

Fig. 13.   Fig. 14.   Fig. 15.   Fig. 16.   Fig. 17.   Fig. 18.

---

[1] This is lower than the modern pitch in England; which, however, is perhaps [1872] being modified. On the OCTAVE, see article *Acoustics*, Encyclop. Britan. p. 110; and Woolhouse, pp. 5 and 6.

[2] The octave of sounds *below* Fig. 13 is sometimes termed the CONTRA or DOUBLE OCTAVE, the notes being written of as C, D, &c. In *Organ* nomenclature, the lowest C of this Double Octave is written of as CCC, or 16ft. C (open pipe): that of the Great Octave, as CC, or 8ft. C: of the Small Octave, as C, or 4ft. C: of the Once-marked Octave, as 2ft. or Middle C or *c*: the Twice-marked, as 1ft. C, or *cc*: the C *in alt*, as 6 inches C.

CHAPTER II.

SHARPS, FLATS, AND NATURALS.

9. A Sharp, ♯, placed before a note, indicates that it is to be *raised* in pitch, one *semitone*,—the smallest interval, or difference of sound, recognized in Music (see § 40). More correctly speaking, perhaps, the note one semitone higher is to be *substituted* for the original note (§§ 66, 346).

10. A Flat, ♭, indicates the *lowering* of the note to which it is prefixed, one semitone; or, in other words, the substitution of the note one semitone lower, for the original note.

11. A Double-Sharp, ✕, raises the note to which it is prefixed *two semitones*.

12. A Double-Flat, ♭♭, lowers a note *two semitones*.

13. Either of the above signs of inflexion, applied to a note, will affect every note of the same name, and on the same stave, *throughout the measure*, or bar (§ 18), in which it occurs, unless *contradicted*. The contradiction of a Sharp or Flat is effected by a Natural, ♮, which restores the note to its original pitch. When it is desired to render a note [single] sharp which has been *double-sharpened*, in a previous part of the measure, it is marked ♮♯; sometimes only ♯. Similarly, when a note which has been *double-flattened* is to be rendered [single] flat, it is marked ♮♭, or, sometimes, simply ♭.

14. When the *last note in a measure* has been affected by either of these signs, and the next measure begins with the same note, that note will be similarly affected, and continue to be so, if repeated, until another note appear, which will terminate the power of the sign. It is more usual, however, to repeat the sign, in the new measure, to prevent mistake.

In old music, the ♮ was used *only* for contradicting a ♭, *not* for contradicting a ♮, which was effected by a ♭. A ♯ was also used to *naturalize* a *flat* note.

When certain notes are to be sharpened or flattened *throughout* a composition, a SIGNATURE is employed, as explained in chap. v. § 51.

In Germany, the syllables *is* and *es* are respectively affixed to the letter to denote the sharpening or flattening of the note: thus *Fis* signifies F sharp; and *Des*, D flat.

CHAPTER III.

THE LENGTH OF NOTES: RESTS: BARS, TIME: ACCENT.

15. THE *relative duration* of notes is determined by their *shape*. The following are the forms of the notes in use in modern music, in the order of their time value, each note being *twice the length* of that which follows it.

Breve.   Semibreve.   Minim.   Crotchet.   Quaver.   Semiquaver.

Demisemiquaver.   Semidemisemiquaver.

The stems may be turned either up or down, as seen above. Several Quavers, Semiquavers, &c., may be *grouped*, thus:—(Fig. 19.)

Fig. 19.

In old music two notes of greater length were used; viz. the LARGE ▭ and the LONG ▭, in contrast with which, the Breve (*Briefe*) received its name. In the present day, even the Breve is only used in Church Music; the Semibreve being the longest note in general use. (See § 24.)

16. A DOT after a note, 𝅗𝅥 · lengthens it one half; a *second dot*, 𝅗𝅥 ·· has half the value of the first dot. Thus, a *dotted minim* is equal in length to *three crotchets*; a *double-dotted minim* is equal to *three crotchets and a quaver*. Very rarely, a *third* dot is used, which has half the value of the second dot.

17. Characters called RESTS are used, denoting *silence* during a corresponding time to that of the notes whose names they bear. (Fig. 20.) *Dots* are placed after *Rests*, as well as after notes, though less frequently.

Fig. 20.
Breve Rest.   Semibreve Rest.   Minim Rest.   Crotchet Rest.   Quaver Rest.

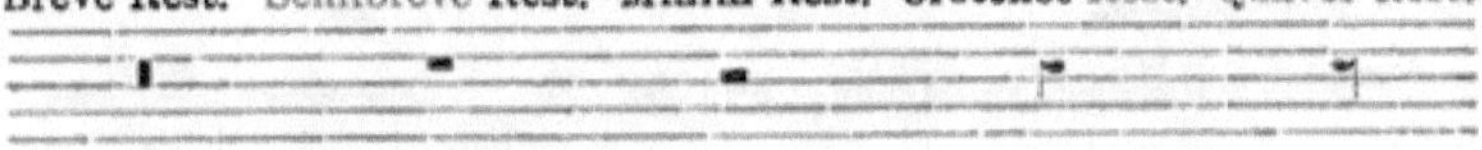

Semiquaver Rest.   Demisemiquaver Rest.   Semidemisemiquaver Rest.

Silence during a whole *measure* or *Bar* (see § 18) is indicated by a *Semibreve Rest*, whatever the length of the measure. Silence during several measures is indicated by the appropriate Rests; and, usually, by the number of measures being marked, as at Fig. 21, in which the *Breve Rest* and the *Semibreve Rest*, together, indicate silence for three measures. In *Breve* time, $\frac{4}{2}$ (§ 24), however, silence during a whole bar is often appropriately indicated by a *Breve rest*. Sometimes a bar's silence in $\frac{3}{2}$ time is indicated in like manner.

It may here be remarked that one of the commonest faults in musical performance—one of the most frequent ways of playing or singing *out of time*—is the *clipping*, not waiting the full length, of *dots* and *rests*.

18. Musical compositions are divided into short sections, of equal value, termed MEASURES, by perpendicular lines, termed BARS (Fig. 22). The portion of music between two of these is also spoken of as a *Bar of Music*, instead of a *Measure*.

At the end of a composition, or of an important section thereof, two thicker lines are placed, termed a DOUBLE-BAR (Fig. 23); this *Double-bar* not necessarily

Fig. 21.   Fig. 22. Bar. 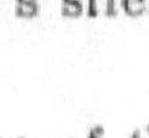   Fig. 23. Double-Bar.

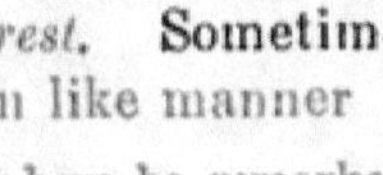

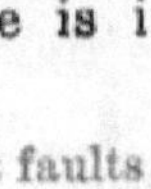

occurring at the termination of a *measure*, and in no way affecting the time, or the disposition of the *Single-bars*.

19. Every measure or bar is divisible into equal portions, termed BEATS: the commencement of such por-

tions being the place where, in indicating the time for a body of performers, the elevation, depression, or other movement of the hand (or *bâton*) is made.

20. When there is an *even* number of beats—two, or four—in a measure, the composition is said to be in COMMON TIME.

> The terms *Duple*, or *Binary*, and *Quadruple* Time are also used.
> Some writers apply the term *Common Time* to *Quadruple* Time *only* (C, see § 24); *not* to *Duple* Time.

21. When there are *three* beats in a measure, it is said to be in TRIPLE TIME, or *Ternary Measure*.

22. When the beats are of the value of an *aliquot part* of a Semibreve,—a Minim, Crotchet, Quaver, or Semiquaver (the latter very rarely), the time is termed SIMPLE. Thus, four Crotchets, or their equivalents, in a measure, constitute *Simple Common Time*; three Crotchets, or their equivalents, in a measure, *Simple Triple Time*.

23. When, on the other hand, the beats are of the value of *dotted notes*,—not, therefore, *aliquot* parts of a Semibreve, the time is termed COMPOUND. Thus, four dotted Crotchets in a measure constitute *Compound Common Time;* three dotted crotchets in a measure, *Compound Triple Time*.

24. The *Time* of a composition—*i. e.* the *value of the measures* in it—is indicated at the commencement by what is termed a TIME-SIGNATURE. In former times, *Triple Time* was called *Perfect Time*, and was signified by a Circle, O, as the symbol of perfectness; and *Common Time*, as *Imperfect Time*, was signified by a Semi-circle, C. The Circle, as indicative of triple time, is obsolete. The Semi-circle has assumed the form of C, which is the signature for *Quadruple Time ; i. e. Simple Common Time* with *four beats* in a measure, termed, also, *Tempo ordinario*. All other kinds of time, or measure, are denoted by figures indicating the number of aliquot parts of a Semibreve which each measure contains; the Semibreve being the standard of measurement, in modern music. (See § 15.) Thus $\frac{2}{4}$ signifies *two fourths* of a Semibreve,—*two Crotchets* in a measure,—or their *equivalents* in other notes, dots, or rests. $\frac{3}{8}$ signifies *three eighths* of a Semi-

breve—*three quavers*, or their equivalents—in a measure.

The *Breve measure* is signified by C, or $\frac{4}{2}$ (*four Minims, halves* of a Semibreve), or ₵, or C; or 2, or ₵. As has been intimated (§ 15), the Breve is in little use in the present day; and the Breve measure, which is *quadruple*, is more frequently **divided into** *two duple* measures; and this is, appropriately, indicated by ₵. This is termed ALLA BREVE TIME, or TEMPO A CAPPELLA (being much used for Church music); the difference from C time being that this latter is *quadruple*, with *two accents*, while ₵ time is *duple*, with *one accent* in the measure (see next paragraph). Usually, **moreover,** ₵ time is more **rapid in pace** than C time.

The following is a table of the *Time-signatures* in most frequent use; the above signs for the Breve **measure being omitted.**

	Simple.	Compound.
Duple.	₵ (alla Breve) Two Minims. $\frac{2}{4}$ Two Crotchets. $\frac{2}{8}$ Two quavers (*very rare*).	$\frac{6}{4}$ Two dotted minims. $\frac{6}{8}$ Two dotted crotchets. $\frac{6}{16}$ Two dotted quavers.
Quadruple.	C or $\frac{4}{4}$ Four crotchets.	$\frac{12}{8}$ Four dotted crotchets. $\frac{24}{16}$ Eight dotted quavers.* $\frac{12}{16}$ Four dotted quavers. $\frac{12}{4}$ Four dotted minims (*rare*).
Triple.	$\frac{3}{2}$ Three minims. $\frac{3}{4}$ Three crotchets. $\frac{3}{8}$ Three quavers.	$\frac{9}{4}$ Three dotted minims (*rare*). $\frac{9}{8}$ Three dotted crotchets. $\frac{9}{16}$ Three dotted quavers.

* See Cramer's *Studio*, vol. 1, No. 4, comparing Time-signatures of R. H. and L. H.

A very few instances occur of compositions with *five crotchets* in a measure, indicated by $\frac{5}{4}$. It is obvious that such exceptional time eludes classification. An irregular measure of five crotchets occurs in Mendelssohn's "*Rivulet*" Rondino, which is in C time.

25. In all measures, certain beats are *accented*, and the others *unaccented*. In simple Duple time, and simple Triple time, the *first* is the *accented* beat. In simple Quadruple time, the *first* (chiefly) and the *third* (subordinately) are the accented beats. In *compound* times, Duple, Triple, and Quadruple, the *principal* accents are also as above; but, in addition, a *subordinate* accent occurs at the *first note* of *each beat*. When *any* beat contains more than one note (in *any* time), there will be rather more emphasis to the *first* than to the others.

26. The *grouping* of Quavers, &c., is regulated by the time, beat, and accent. Thus, a measure of $\frac{3}{4}$ time and a measure of $\frac{6}{8}$ time both contain the value of six quavers, and may alike consist actually of six quavers; but the *division* of such measures is totally different: the first consisting of three beats, each of the value of two quavers; the second of two beats, each of the value of three quavers. They would, therefore, be grouped, accented, and accompanied, quite differently, as exemplified in Fig. 24.

Fig. 24. (*a*)   (*b*)

Quavers in $\frac{3}{4}$ time may be grouped as at either of the measures at (*a*); in $\frac{6}{8}$ time, *only* as at (*b*). In this latter, the *subordinate* accent (§ 25) will occur at the first note in the second group of each measure.

27. When a note is commenced on the *unaccented* part of a measure, or the middle of a beat, and prolonged during the succeeding *accent*, or commencement of beat, the accent is *thrown back* to the beginning of the note, and

SYNCOPATION is produced. The *syncopated* note is usually accented with additional emphasis: Fig. 25, in which the

Fig. 25. BEETHOVEN.

syncopated notes are indicated by >. (*For explanation of* ⌢ *see* § 33.)

28. *Three* notes are sometimes compressed into the time of *two* of the same kind: *e. g.* three quavers (instead of two) in the time of one crotchet. Such notes are usually grouped, and marked ͡3, as in Fig. 26 (*a*). A

Fig. 26. (*a*)

(*b*)

(*c*)

group of notes thus compressed is called a TRIPLET, or TRIOLET. A triplet may consist partly of rests, as at (*b*) and (*c*).

Other irregularities of the same kind also occur; such as *four* notes for *three*, termed a QUADRUPLET; *five* for *four*, a QUINTUPLET, &c.; and, sometimes, *less* than the full number of notes, as *two* for *three*, &c.

CHAPTER IV

REPEATS: ABBREVIATIONS: EMBELLISHMENTS: MARKS AND WORDS INDICATING PACE, OR MANNER OF PERFORMANCE.

29. A PORTION of a composition included between two *Double-bars, with dots* (Fig. 27), is to be *repeated*. When the dots precede the first Double-bar in the composition, the repeat is to be *from the beginning*. Sometimes an alteration of the termination of a repeated portion has to be made: this is indicated as at Fig. 28, in which the

measure marked 2*nd time* (sometimes simply 2, or 2*nda volta*) is, on the repetition, to be *substituted* for that marked 1*st time* (1, or 1*ma volta*).

When only a very short portion, as a single measure, is to be repeated, it is sometimes marked BIS (Fig. 29).

30. The words DA CAPO (from the beginning) placed at any point in a composition, indicate that a return is to be made to the beginning, and the repetition continued till the word FINE occurs, or a PAUSE, ⌢ (see § 31).

Sometimes the term AL SEGNO, or DAL SEGNO, or *D. C. sino al segno*, is used; indicating the return to a sign, :𝄋:, or similar character (*Le Renvoi*), either at the beginning, or at some other point in the piece. In all such

Abbreviations. 15

cases, the repeated portion is to be performed *without the observance of any repeat marks* that may occur in it.

Sometimes instead of D. C. or *Al Segno*, the 𝄋 itself is written.

Abbreviations, etc.

31. The PAUSE, ⌢ (§ 30), indicates that the performer is to wait, longer than the regular time, on the note or rest over which it is placed. The words "*lunga pausa*" are sometimes used, as a caution against the prevalent custom of shortening such pauses. (See § 17.)

32. Marks of ABBREVIATION, besides those already explained, are used. ·/· or // indicates the repetition of the preceding measure or half measure. Sometimes the word SIMILI is used in such a case. See Fig. 30, in which various abbreviations are exhibited. 8va ⁓⁓⁓ (*ottava*) written over a passage signifies that it is to be performed an octave higher than written, as long as the ⁓⁓⁓ is continued, at the end of which the word *loco* is usually written; 8va *sotto*, *under* a passage, signifies an octave *lower*. (Fig. 31.)

33. Certain marks are used to indicate the *manner of performance*. The SLUR, ⌢ or ⌣, indicates that the

passage over which it is placed is to be performed in a *smooth, connected* manner, Fig. 32 (*a*); the word LEGATO being also used for the same purpose, in a long passage. DOTS (*b*) and DASHES (*c*), on the other hand, indicate that the notes are to be *short, crisp, disconnected;* the word STACCATO being also used for the same purpose. The slur *with* the dot or dash (*d*) indicates the MEZZO-STACCATO,—detached but not crisp. ⸛ over a single note indicates a certain gentle pressure, with detachment.

The older writers seem to have used the *dash* to indicate the *Staccato*, and the *dot* to indicate the *Mezzo-staccato*. But there is uncertainty and ambiguity about the matter; and good taste must often determine the manner of performance. The *method of producing* these various effects belongs to the technicalities of different instruments.

The *slur*, when it occurs between two notes in *unison*,—*i. e.* on the same degree of the stave, and uninflected, is termed a TIE, BIND, or LIGATURE; and indicates that the second note is *not to be repeated*, but *sustained*, joined to the first. (Fig. 33, *a*.) When, however, the

Fig. 33. (*a*)   (*b*)   &c.

dots are associated with such slur, the notes are *not tied*, but *mezzo-staccato*, as above (*b*).[1]

34. When the notes of a *chord* (see § 79) are marked as at Fig. 34 (*a* or *b*) they are to be played, not

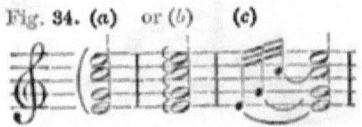

Fig. 34. (*a*)   or (*b*)   (*c*)

quite simultaneously, but in ARPEGGIO (see § 157)—or *spread* obliquely, as it is termed, as at (*c*).

35. The marks ⪡ and ⪢ signify, re-

---

[1] Some years ago, Sir Sterndale Bennett introduced the ⌐ in place of the ⌒ for tied notes, to prevent confusion. It is much to be regretted that the example was not followed.

spectively, a gradual *increase* or *decrease* of *tone*, or loudness in the passage. The words CRESCENDO and DIMINUENDO, or DECRESCENDO, are used for the same purpose.

36. *Emphasis* on a note is indicated by > or ^. A strong emphasis is indicated by *sf.* or *sfz.* (*sforzato*). *Reinforcement* of strength, after some little subsidence, is indicated by *rinf.* or *rf.* (*rinforzando*).

37. *p.* and *f.* signify, respectively, *piano* (softly), and *forte* (strong or loud). These two words gave name to the Pianoforte, from its capability of producing the gradations of tone, in contrast with its predecessors.

38. Certain EMBELLISHMENTS, or *ornaments*, are indicated in Fig. 35. The SHAKE (*a*); the TURN (*b*), fre-

quently, though not always, **used at** the termination **of a** shake; the INVERTED TURN (*c*); the TRILL (*d*); the *pincé simple* or *mordent* (*e*); *pincé double* or *double-mordent* (*f*); with prefixes, &c. (*g, h, i, k*); *passing shake* (*l*); *tierce coulée en montant* (*m*); *tierce coulée en descendant* (*n*); the latter nine being peculiar to old music, such as that of **Couperin, Bach, &c.;** in which **may** be **found various** other embellishments, **now obsolete.** Many such were introduced into the keyed-instrument music of that period, apparently to make up for the lack of sustaining power in the instruments then in use,—the precursors of **the** Pianoforte.

Other embellishments **are expressed by small** notes, not **by** signs; **as** the APPOGGIATURA (*o*), or *leaning-note* (from *appoggiare*, to lean), which takes half the length from the note which it precedes, except when preceding **a** *dotted* note, from which it takes one third: the ACCIACCATURA (*p*), or *crushing-note* (from *acciaccare*, to crush), which is played as a very short note, instantly proceeding to the principal note; **the** embellishment at (*q*) is **also** called *acciaccatura*, or *double-appoggiatura:* the PORTAMENTO (*r*): the BEAT (*s*).

The similarity in form of the *appoggiatura* and the *acciaccatura* renders it sometimes uncertain when the one or the other is intended. The **older masters** wrote the *appoggiatura* as a small note, because of its being *unessential* (see chap. xxiii.). In modern times, **this** practice has been abandoned, and it is generally written **as played.** Therefore, when such small note appears in modern music, **it is to be** understood as an *acciaccatura*. In music by **the old masters, the** question must be determined by the character of the composition, the form of the passage, and some considerations about the harmony; **for** which experience and knowledge are required. It may, however, be laid down, that when a small note precedes a group of even **notes, or a group of** three notes in which the first two are equal in length to the last one, as at (*p*), it is to be played as an *acciaccatura*. When, on the contrary, the group is of the reverse form to this latter, **as at** (*o*), the small note is an *appoggiatura*. (See § 226.)

It is generally prescribed that when an *appoggiatura* precedes a *dotted* note, it shall take *two thirds* from the length of that note; but Clementi, in his "*Instructions*," directs that *one* or *two* thirds be taken, "*as it best suits the passage.*"

Words indicating Pace.

39. The *pace* at which a composition is to be performed, and its general character, are approximately indicated by certain words placed at the beginning. Composers vary, somewhat, in their use of these words; but the following may be taken as the order in which they may be understood, beginning with those indicating the slowest pace.

GRAVE; very slow, gravely.
ADAGIO (*leisurely*).   LARGO (*large*); LENTO; slow.
                    LARGHETTO (diminutive of *Largo*).
ANDANTINO.   ANDANTE (*going, walking*).
                    ALLEGRETTO, ALLEGRINO (diminutives of *Allegro*).
ALLEGRAMENTE.   ALLEGRO (*gay, merry*).
PRESTO.   PRESTISSIMO.

The terms *Adagio* and *Largo* differ rather in their customary application with regard to the *character* than the *pace* of the composition to which they are applied. (Compare the slow movements of Beethoven's Sonatas, Op. 7, and Op. 22, &c.)

Andantino, being the diminutive of *Andante*, properly means *less going;* but seems more frequently used, by composers, to signify *less slowly* (than *Andante*).

Allegro, albeit that it means *gay*, is applied to compositions of a quick pace which have none of that character about them; being sometimes used in conjunction with words of quite an opposite tendency, such as *Maestoso, Serioso*, &c. Therefore, in its musical use, the word must simply be understood to mean quickly.

All these words, moreover, are often used in conjunction with other qualifying or intensifying terms, indicating the character of the movement; such as *molto*, very (*Allegro molto*); *non tanto*, or *non troppo*, not too much (*Allegro non troppo*); *con moto*, with movement, or impulse (*Andante con moto*); *assai*, decidedly (*Presto assai*), &c. Many more of these terms are explained in the GLOSSARY.

Composers have the means of indicating still more precisely the rate at which they wish their compositions performed, by the use of the *Metronome*. Thus ♩ = 124 would indicate that when the regulator on the pendulum is placed opposite 124 on the dial, each beat of the pendulum indicates the length of a crotchet in the composition. But, however useful such contrivances may be, and however carefully a composer may mark his compositions, by words, or otherwise, it should never be forgotten that musical compositions should, and good ones do, to a large extent, tell their own tale,—indicate their own character; and it must be left to the performer's appreciative judgment to execute them accordingly.

PART II.

RUDIMENTS OF THEORY: HARMONY, AND COUNTERPOINT.

CHAPTER V.

THE DIATONIC SCALE: MAJOR MODE.

40. If the student plays upon the Pianoforte the four notes (Fig. 36), he will perceive that between the first and

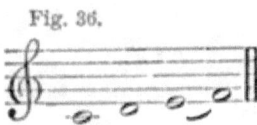

Fig. 36.

second keys there is a black key, as also between the second and third; but not between the third and fourth. The reason of this is that there is no sound in music between E and F, as there is between C and D, and between D and E: in other words, E and F are nearer together, in pitch, than are C and D, and D and E.

The distance from C to D, and from D to E, is termed a TONE: that from E to F is termed a SEMITONE,—'the smallest interval recognized in music' (§ 9),—the distance from one note to that *immediately* next to it on the Pianoforte, whether represented by a black key or a white.

It must be remarked that the word *tone* is here used in its *strictly technical* sense, to denote the *distance* between two sounds having *only one* sound between them. The word also signifies simply *sound;* as when we speak of the *tone* of an instrument. And it also is used to denote *tune;* as when the Ecclesiastical or Gregorian *Tones* are spoken of: certain short fragments of melody, appropriated by St. Ambrose [*cir.* 374—397] for the chants of the Church; and, subsequently, added to by Gregory the Great [*cir.* 590—604]. The term *tone*, in this last case, having reference to the relation of the notes of the chants to certain notes as *Tonics* (§ 45), (to use our modern phraseology,) seems somewhat equivalent to our term MODE, hereafter explained (see §§ 46, 62).

41. The four sounds represented above constitute a TETRACHORD (τέτρα, *four;* χορδή, *string*)—a series of four notes, including two tones and a semitone; the extreme notes, therefore, forming the interval of a *perfect* 4th[1] (§ 73). In the above Tetrachord, the two tones *precede* the semitone, which, however, is not always the case in a Tetrachord.

42. If the succeeding four notes (with white keys) to those of the above Tetrachord be played (Fig. 37), a

Fig. 37.

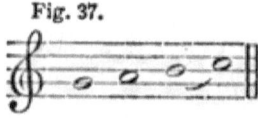

similar result will be obtained: a Tetrachord, with the same order of the tones and semitone. Even a moderately cultivated ear will perceive the correspondence of *effect* in the two Tetrachords, arising from the correspondence of *relation* between their respective sounds, although a difference of *pitch*.

43. If these two Tetrachords be united, they constitute a DIATONIC SCALE (διά, *through;* τόνος, *a tone, i. e.* through the *tones* or *sounds*, see § 40,[2]) consisting of two precisely similar Tetrachords. (Fig. 38.)

Fig. 38.

The semitones are indicated by the slurs.

44. A *Diatonic scale* may be defined as a series of eight

---

[1] Also termed, formerly, DIATESSARON.
[2] Macfarren's *Lectures*, p. 36.

notes, proceeding alphabetically from any note to its octave by five tones and two semitones.

The student will recognize a certain *completeness* of effect in the above scale; arising partly from the correspondence of the *final* with the *initial* note. (See § 8.)

45. The first or initial note of a Diatonic scale is termed its TONIC, or KEY-NOTE; also its FINAL.

46. When the semitones and tones succeed each other in the order at Fig. 38, the scale is said to be in the MAJOR MODE; or, briefly, is termed a MAJOR SCALE.

The term *mode* signifies the *order* of the tones and semitones in a Diatonic scale. Formerly the term had reference to *time*.[1]

47. A MAJOR SCALE, then, is a Diatonic scale (*i. e.* having five tones and two semitones), in which the semitones occur between the third and fourth, and between the seventh and eighth *degrees*, or notes. It is so termed on account of the interval from the 1st note to the 3rd being a *major* 3rd (§ 73).

48. Any note may be taken as the Tonic of a scale. If, however, a scale of *natural* notes—(*white keys* on the Pianoforte) be formed, commencing with any other note than C, the *order* of the tones and semitones will vary; the scale will not be a *Major* scale.

Thus the scale at Fig. 39 (*a*) has the semitones between the 2nd

and 3rd, and the 6th and 7th degrees; that at (*b*) has them between the 1st and 2nd, and the 5th and 6th; while at (*c*) they are between the 4th and 5th, and the 7th and 8th. All these scales—and the student can exemplify the same thing by commencing scales on other natural notes—are in different modes: modes which are *now* obsolete, though *formerly* recognized and used. (See § 62.)

---

[1] See Morley's *Introduction*, p. 12, &c.

49. To conform these scales of natural notes to the *model* scale (Fig. 38),—in other words, to constitute them *Major* scales—*sharps* or *flats* are requisite, as is shown in Fig. 40. The same necessity will present itself if *sharp*

Fig. 40.

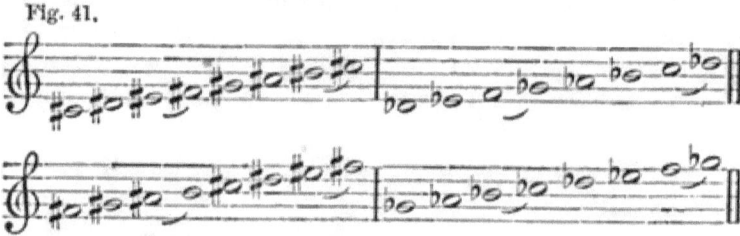

or *flat* notes be taken as Tonics. C♭, C♯, D♭, E♭, F♯, G♭, A♭, B♭, are, as well as *all* natural notes, taken as Tonics of Major scales.

The scales of C♯ and D♭ are, on keyed instruments, identical, as are those of F♯ and G♭. The *names* and *positions on the stave*, when written, are, in each case, different; as a Diatonic scale is an *alphabetical* series of notes. (§ 44.) Thus:—

Fig. 41.

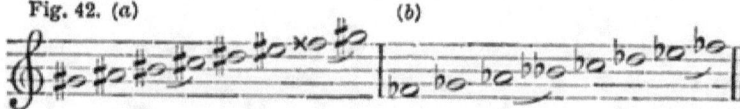

Scales commencing on any other notes than those above specified would require more than *seven* sharps or *flats*, *i. e. double-sharps*, or *double-flats*. They are not generally written, therefore, as they can be more simply represented by a different notation. Thus, the two scales at (*a*) and (*b*), Fig. 42, are identical, on keyed instruments, with

Fig. 42. (*a*)   (*b*)

the scales of A♭ and E, respectively. So the scales of D♯, E♯, B♯, would be identical with those of E♭, F, and C, respectively; and the latter notation is preferred.

50. All the notes in any scale, taken collectively,

constitute what is termed a KEY, which is named after the *Tonic*, or *Key-note* of such scale. Thus, if a musical composition is formed of *natural* notes, it is in the *Key of C;* and so on.

There may be, however, in a composition some notes introduced, foreign to the key in which it is written, by the use of ACCIDENTALS —sharps, flats, or naturals, not belonging to the scale. These *may* effect a modulation (change of key); or *may* be simply *auxiliary*, or *chromatically altered* notes. This will be explained further on (chap. xxiv. xxxiii.).

51. The sharps or flats proper to any scale or key are customarily written, once for all, at the commencement of a composition; and, thus written, affect every note of their respective names, throughout the piece, unless contradicted. These sharps or flats, so arranged, constitute the KEY-SIGNATURE (or SCALE-SIGNATURE); which is placed *after* the clef, and *before* the time-signature. Fig. 43 is a table of the signatures for Major scales; *i. e.* of the sharps or flats in the respective scales, and of the *order* in which they are written in the signature; which order, it will be observed, is to *add* the *last* sharp or flat required to the previous signature.

Fig. 43.

Frequently, in old music, the *last* sharp or flat was *omitted* from the signature.

52. Every degree of the Diatonic scale has a technical name, as indicated in the following table, and in Fig. 44.

1st degree .. the TONIC, KEY-NOTE, or FINAL.
2nd ,, .. . the SUPER-TONIC.
3rd ,, ... the MEDIANT.
4th ,, ... the SUB-DOMINANT.

5tl. degree .. .. the DOMINANT.
6th   „   .. .. the SUB-MEDIANT.
7th   „   .. .. the LEADING-NOTE, SUB-TONIC,
             or LA NOTE SENSIBLE (Fr.);
             also the SUB-SEMITONE.

Fig. 44.

Thus, the *Super-tonic* of the scale of D is E; the *Dominant* of that scale is A, &c.

The term MEDIANT, indicating that the 3rd of the scale is midway between the Tonic and the Dominant, is not in common use; nor is that of SUB-MEDIANT, indicating that the 6th of the scale is midway between the Tonic and the Sub-dominant below it. The term SUPER-TONIC sufficiently explains itself.

The DOMINANT is so called because of the *governing, influential* character of the harmony proper to that degree of the scale, especially in determining the key, as will be explained subsequently (§§ 113, 162, 166, &c.).

The term was formerly applied to the *reciting-note* of Ecclesiastical Chants.

The SUB-DOMINANT may have been so termed as being a 5th *under* the Tonic, whereas the *Dominant* is a 5th *above* it; but, more probably and reasonably, as being the note *under* the Dominant.

The LEADING-NOTE is so termed because, in a peculiar sense, it *leads* to the octave. If the scale be played or sung, in ascending, as far as the 7th note, an irrepressible desire will be felt to hear the octave; whereas, if a pause be made on any other note of the ascending scale, though the effect will not be *terminal*, it will not be, in this way, suggestive—even provocative—of the ascent to the succeeding note. The 7th note is, therefore, emphatically a *Leading-note;* and specially appropriate, and expressive of its character, is the term *La note sensible*, the SENSITIVE NOTE. (See § 57.)

53. Two scales which have a *Tetrachord in common* are termed RELATIVE scales. Every Tetrachord belongs to *two* Major scales; every Major scale having one Tetrachord in common with the scale which *precedes* it, in the series of scales; and another Tetrachord in common with that which *succeeds* it. This is exemplified in Fig. 45, which might be extended throughout the entire series

Major Mode. 27

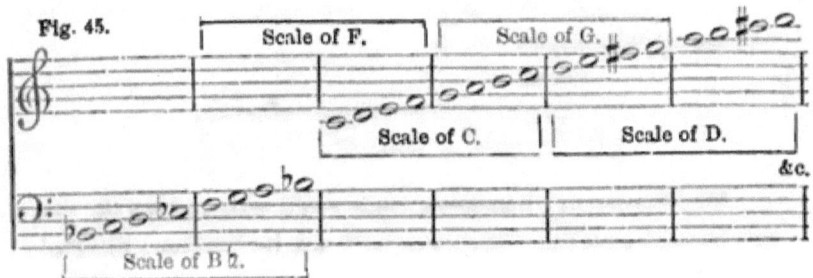

Fig. 45.

of scales. It will be seen that, in the series of scales with *sharps*, the second Tetrachord of one scale is the first Tetrachord of the next scale in order; and that, in the series of scales with *flats*, the first Tetrachord of one scale is the second Tetrachord of the next in order. This possession of a Tetrachord in common, constitutes the relationship between the two scales.

The importance of this relationship will be shown in treating of modulation (chap. xxxiii.); where it will be seen that to modulate to either of the *relatives* of a given key is the most natural and easy modulation.

It will be seen by Fig. 45 that the relatives to any given Major scale are the scales commencing with its *Dominant* and its *Subdominant*. Other relatives will be treated of further on (§§ 54, 56, 61).

Two Tetrachords, in which the last note of one is the first note of the other, *e. g.* the 2nd Tetrachord of the scale of C, and the 2nd Tetrachord of the scale of F,—are termed *Conjunct* Tetrachords. Two Tetrachords *adjoining* one another, but not thus connected—as the two Tetrachords of any scale—are termed *Disjunct* Tetrachords.

CHAPTER VI.

THE DIATONIC SCALE: MINOR MODE.

54. Two scales containing the same notes are said to be *relative* scales.

Thus, the scale at Fig. 46, consisting entirely of *natural* notes, is *relative* to the scale of C major.

Fig. 46.

55. Obviously, however, such scale will not be in the *Major mode*, as the semitones will not be between the 3rd and 4th, and between the 7th and 8th degrees. Moreover if the above scale be examined, it will be seen that from the Tonic to the Mediant there are only a tone and a semitone, which constitute the interval of a *minor* 3rd, in contradistinction from a *major* 3rd, which consists of two tones (§ 73). The scale at Fig. 46 is therefore termed a MINOR SCALE; or a Diatonic scale in the MINOR MODE.

56. The *sixth note* of a Major scale is taken as the Tonic of its *Relative Minor* scale.

This is often expressed conversely, thus: the Tonic of a Minor scale is a minor 3rd below that of its Relative Major scale.

57. If a similar experiment be made with the scale (Fig. 46), to that suggested in § 52, with regard to the 7th note, the result will not be found to be the same; the note G will by no means suggest the progression to the 8ve, nor will the effect, to modern ears at least, of the termination G A be at all satisfactory or conclusive as that of B C in the scale of C major. In other words, G is not a *leading-note* to A.

This results from G being a *tone* below A; whereas the 7th note of a scale awakens desire for the 8ve—in other words, is a true *leading-note*—*only* when it is a *semitone* under that 8ve (as one of its names, *Sub-semitone*, implies).

58. Formerly, scales without leading-notes were used. In modern times, a scale without a leading-note is considered unsatisfactory; and much of the modern system of harmony depends upon that note, its relation to certain other notes of the scale, and its consequent suggestiveness (§§ 113, 124, 128, &c.). Therefore, it is now customary to

raise the 7th note of the Minor scale one *semitone*, accidentally, to obtain a true leading-note (Fig. 47).

Fig. 47.

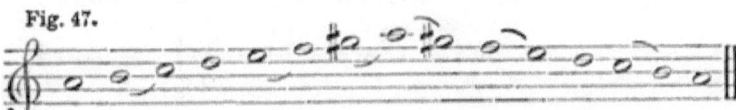

59. The scale, as thus altered, ceases to be purely *Diatonic;* having three tones, three semitones, and one distance of a tone and a half: F to G♯. To avoid this last large interval, the 6th note of the ascending Minor scale is sometimes raised a semitone, accidentally, as at Fig. 48. When both notes are thus altered, however, in

Fig. 48.

ascending, it is usual to contradict these accidentals in *descending;* there being no requirement of a leading-note in descending; and, the 7th note being restored to its original pitch, the necessity for the *raised* 6th note no longer existing.

The scale, in this form, does consist of five tones and two semitones; the semitones, in *ascending*, being between the 2nd and 3rd, and the 7th and 8th degrees; in *descending*, between the 6th and 5th, and the 3rd and 2nd; the degrees being, in all cases, reckoned from the lower or commencing, not from the upper or terminal Tonic. The relation of the Minor scale to its relative Major is seen in its *descending* form, when it is taken as at Fig. 48.

The effect of both the 6th and the 7th notes being raised in the *descending* scale, is far from agreeable, generally; but examples of even this form are found in the best old masters:—Handel, D. Scarlatti, Mozart, &c.

Both forms of the Minor scale—that at Fig. 47, and that at Fig. 48—are of frequent occurrence; the greatest musicians, notably Mozart, adapting the scale passages in their works to the accompanying harmony.[1]

---

[1] See the different minor scales in Beethoven's Sonatas, Op. 2, No 1 (1st movement); Op. 10, No. 1 (1st movement), Op. 13 (last movement); Op. 57 (last movement), &c.

Performers should practise the **Minor scale** in both forms.

In the above examples, the alterations, in ascending, have been effected by *sharps*, as the notes to be altered were natural; and, in consequence, the contradictions, in descending, by *naturals*. This, of course, will not always be the case, as will be seen from the following examples (Fig. 49, *a, b, c*).

Fig. 49. (*a*)

60. The following is a list of the Relative Minor scales to the different Major scales. The *signatures* of the Minor scales are the same as those of their Relative Majors, so that every signature represents two keys: a Minor and a Major.

C	Major,	relative	to A	Minor.
G	„	„	E	„
D	„	„	B	„
A	„	„	F♯	„
E	„	„	C♯	„
B	„	„	G♯	„
F♯	„	„	D♯	„
C♯	„	„	A♯	„
F	„	„	D	„
B♭	„	„	G	„
E♭	„	„	C	„
A♭	„	„	F	„
D♭	„	„	B♭	„
G♭	„	„	E♭	„
C♭	„	„	A♭	„

61. Some eminent musicians of the present day deny the relationship of the Major and Minor scales, as above explained, and repudiate the very term *Relative Minor*, or would apply it to the Minor scale with the *same Tonic* as a given Major scale, regarding *C minor*, for example, as properly the relative minor to *C major*. In most theoretical books, the Minor scale is not mentioned as relative or attendant to the Major scale with the same Tonic, though the close connection between the two is obvious and undeniable, the second Tetrachord being common to the two scales, when the Minor scale is as at Fig. 48.

The explanation above given is that which is generally accepted by musicians; the differences among whom, on this and various other points, have reference, principally, to *theory*,—the way of accounting for, or explaining certain matters; not as to *effect*, or as to what is good or bad in composition. (See Appendix I.)

62. Formerly, other modes were in use than those here explained, consisting of Tetrachords differently arranged. (See §§ 40, 48.)

Every natural note, except B, was taken as the Tonic or *Final* of a scale. These modes, from the Final to its 8ve, were termed AUTHENTIC; and were those adopted by St. Ambrose, it is said, from the Greek. They were named as follows :—

        1st mode, from C, the *Ionian*.
        2nd mode, from D, the *Dorian*. (All naturals.)
        3rd mode, from E, the *Phrygian*. ,,
        4th mode, from F, the *Lydian*. ,,
        5th mode, from G, the *Mixolydian*. ,,
        6th mode, from A, the *Æolian*. ,,

The *numbering* of these modes differs in various lists.

Subsequently, subordinate forms of these, commencing a 4th below the authentic modes, were introduced by St. Gregory, and were termed PLAGAL (πλάγιος, oblique, transverse); apparently as lying *athwart*, or *across* the authentic scales (Αὐθεντέω, to possess or assume authority). The *Authentic* modes were also termed *Hyper*-Ionian, *Hyper*-Dorian, &c.; the *Plagal* being termed *Hypo*-Ionian, &c.; (Ὑπό, under the influence of, subordinate).[1] See § 40.

---

[1] Those who wish for further information respecting the Ecclesiastical Modes, can consult the works of L. Niedermeyer, Joseph D'Ortigue, and C. C. Spencer. (See list of works at the beginning.)

Subsequently, the notes were arranged in HEXACHORDS, named as follows (Fig. 50). It will be seen that the notes were named accord-

Fig. 50.
Hard Hexachord.   Natural Hexachord.   Soft Hexachord.

Ut Re Mi Fa Sol La Ut Re Mi Fa Sol La Ut Re Mi Fa Sol La

ing to their order in the Hexachords, *Ut* being always the 1st note, and *Mi Fa* always representing the *semitone*. The lowest note, *Sol*, or G, is said to have been first adopted by *Guido* of *Arezzo* (supposed to have lived in the eleventh century), and to have been designated by him by the Greek Γ (gamma); and this, being the *Ut* of the hard Hexachord, gave rise to the term GAMUT (Gamma, Ut), applied to the series of sounds.

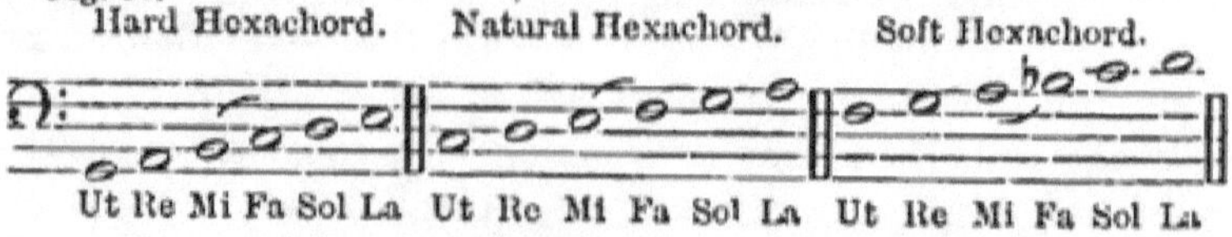

CHAPTER VII.

THE CHROMATIC SCALE.

63. THE distances between the notes that are a tone apart in the Diatonic scale, may be filled up by the insertion of the intermediate notes, thus producing a *scale of semitones*, termed the CHROMATIC scale (from χρῶμα, *colour;* the origin of the term, as applicable to this scale, being uncertain, however). Fig. 51.

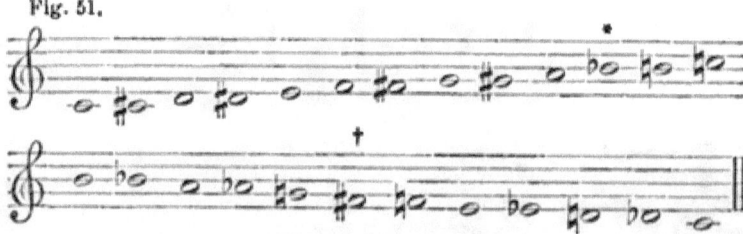

Fig. 51.

64. The raising or lowering the pitch of a note one semitone without changing its position on the stave, or its alphabetical name, is termed *Chromatic alteration.* The Chromatic scale is formed by inserting the chromatically raised notes of the *ascending,* and the chromatically lowered notes of the *descending* Major scale, with the exception of the notes marked * and †, which are usually noted as indicated, though sometimes written respectively as A♯ and

G♭. Thus, the Chromatic scale commencing on G♭ would be written as at Fig. 52 (a); and that from F♯ as at (b).

Fig. 52. (a)

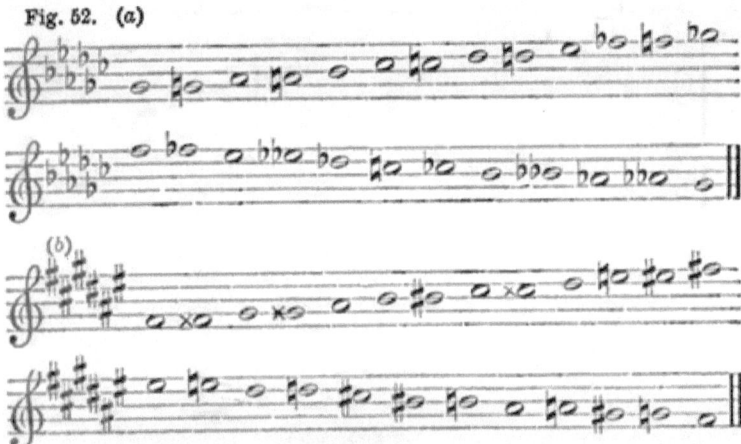

The reason for the exceptions indicated is that the *lowered* 7th note and the *raised* 4th note of the scale are more closely related to the key than the *raised* 6th note and the *lowered* 5th note, respectively, would be.

65. Some eminent musicians, however, adopt a different notation for the Chromatic scale, as at Fig. 53, it being founded on that of the *Minor*, instead of on the *Major* scale; or rather on the two combined.[1]

Fig. 53.

The notation at Fig. 53 is the same in *descending* as in *ascending*. The justification of the *Minor 2nd* from the Tonic, instead of the *Chromatic raising* of the Tonic, is that it combines with the Subdominant and Minor 6th, thus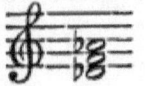

66. The semitone obtained by *Chromatic alteration*, occurring *only* in the Chromatic scale, and consisting, therefore, of two notes on the *same* position of the stave, is termed a CHROMATIC SEMITONE; whereas that which is

---

[1] See Macfarren's *Rudiments of Harmony*, p. 7.

found in a *Diatonic scale*, consisting of two notes on *different* positions of the stave, is termed a DIATONIC SEMITONE. Examples, Fig. 54.

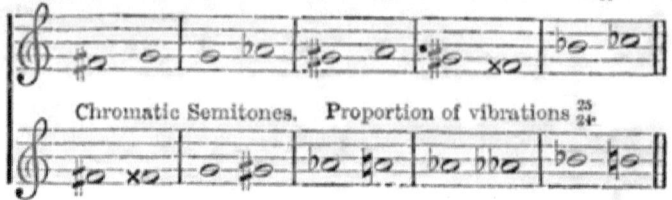

Fig. 54. Diatonic Semitones. Proportion of vibrations $\frac{16}{15}$.

Chromatic Semitones. Proportion of vibrations $\frac{25}{24}$.

The Chromatic semitone is also termed a *Minor semitone*,[1] and, likewise, a *Superfluous Prime*, and an *Augmented Unison*, or *Diminished Unison*, according as it is obtained by raising or lowering a note. The Diatonic semitone is also termed a *Major semitone;* likewise a *Minor 2nd*, as will be seen, § 73.

CHAPTER VIII.

INTERVALS.

67. An interval is the distance from one note to another; or the difference in acuteness and gravity between two sounds.

68. An interval is *named* according to the number of degrees of the stave included by the two notes which constitute it; *e. g.* from E to F is a 2nd, because there are two degrees of the stave included; from F to A is a 3rd, because there are three degrees of the stave included, and so on. This will be illustrated by the following table, in which the intermediate degrees of the stave are indicated by black notes (Fig. 55).

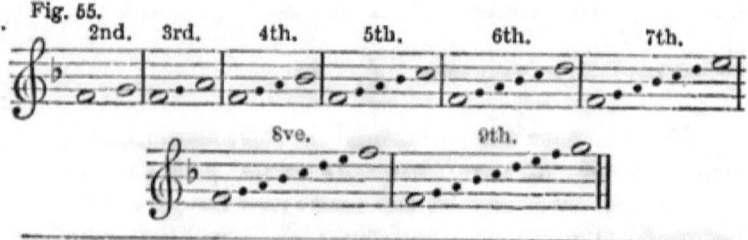

Fig. 55.

---

[1] Formerly, *Apotome*.

Intervals.

69. The *Unison*, or identical sound, is not an interval, though generally reckoned among intervals, for convenience of classification.

70. Intervals beyond the 9th are usually considered as repetitions, and COMPOUND forms, of the intervals within the 8ve, which are called SIMPLE intervals. The 9th is sometimes considered as a compound 2nd, and sometimes as an independent interval. The 11th and 13th are also sometimes treated as independent intervals, and sometimes as a compound 4th, and compound 6th respectively. (Chaps. xx. xxi.)

71. No inflexion of either of the notes in the above table, by a sharp, flat, or natural, would affect the name of the interval as a 2nd, 3rd, &c., which depends *solely* on the position of the notes on the stave; the number of notes in alphabetical order, from one to the other. F to G♭ is a 2nd; F♯ to A is a 3rd, and so on.

72. Intervals which occur in an unaltered Diatonic scale are termed DIATONIC INTERVALS; *i. e.* the distance between any two notes in the same Diatonic scale is a Diatonic interval. Intervals that occur *only* in the Chromatic scale are termed Chromatic intervals. (See also § 66.) Diatonic intervals will first be considered.

73. If the Diatonic scale of two octaves, Fig. 56, be

Fig. 56.

examined, and the notes in it compared with one another, it will be found that the following intervals occur in it, to which the names attached are given (Fig. 57).

DIATONIC INTERVALS.

Minor 2nd,	1 semitone.
Major 2nd,	1 tone.
Minor 3rd,	1 tone and 1 semitone.
Major 3rd,	2 tones.
Perfect 4th,	2 tones and 1 semitone
Tritone 4th,	3 tones.

Intervals.

Fig. 57. (a) Minor. (b) Major. 2nds.
(c) Minor. (d) Major. 3rds.
(e) Perfect. (f) Tritone. 4ths.
(g) Imperfect. (h) Perfect. 5ths.
(i) Minor. (k) Major. 6ths.
(l) Minor. (m) Major. 7ths.
(n) Perfect. 8ves.
(o) Minor. (p) Major. 9ths.

Imperfect 5th,[1] 2 tones and 2 semitones.
Perfect 5th,   3 tones and 1 semitone.
Minor 6th,   3 tones and 2 semitones.
Major 6th,   4 tones and 1 semitone.
Minor 7th,   4 tones and 2 semitones.
Major 7th,   5 tones and 1 semitone.
Perfect 8ve,   5 tones and 2 semitones.

---

[1] Also Defective 5th.

Intervals.

> Minor 9th,   5 tones and 3 semitones.
> Major 9th,   6 tones and 2 semitones.

The *Tritone* 4th (or *Tritonus*) is also termed the *Augmented* 4th (though inappropriately, as will be explained § 75); the *Extreme*, *Superfluous*, or *Plu-Perfect* 4th, &c. (See also § 76.)

The *Imperfect* 5th is also termed the *Diminished* 5th, the *False* 5th, the *Flat* 5th, &c. (See § 75.)

The *Minor* 7th is also termed the *Flat* 7th.

These terms are here given, under protest, simply because they are in more or less common use.

It will be useful to observe that the Tritone 4th *only* occurs on the *Sub-dominant* of the Major scale; and the Imperfect 5th, *only* on the *Leading-note*. In the true Minor scale, these intervals will occur on the same degrees; and the *Imperfect* 5th will occur also on the *Super-tonic*, and the Tritone 4th on the *Sub-mediant*.

Obviously the same *Intervals* will be found in *every* Diatonic scale.

74. The CHROMATIC INTERVALS are obtained by *Chromatic alteration* of one of the notes of the Diatonic intervals, either *augmenting* or *diminishing* it, by one semitone. Thus a Major 2nd is *augmented* by *chromatically raising* the *upper* note. A Minor 3rd is *diminished* by *chromatically raising* the *lower* note (Fig. 58), &c. &c.

Fig. 58.
Major 2nd.   Augmented 2nd.   Minor 3rd.   Diminished 3rd.

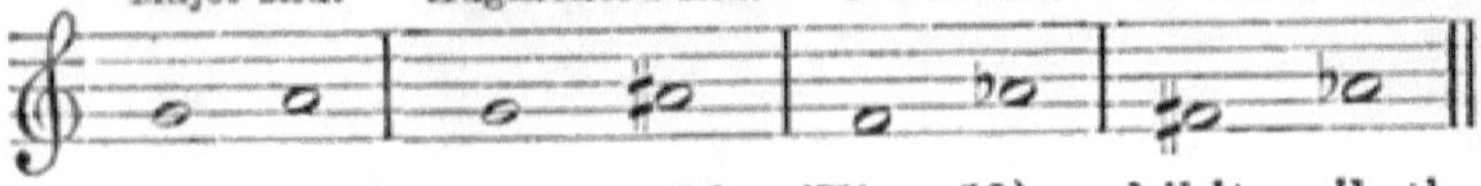

75. The following table (Fig. 59) exhibits all the intervals, Diatonic and Chromatic, in their relation to one another.

Some writers include an *Augmented* 3rd and a *Diminished* 6th, which, however, do not enter into any chords.

It will be understood that the *Augmented* and *Diminished* intervals are so termed because they are *augmentations* and *diminutions*, respectively, of Diatonic intervals. These terms, then, seem *misnomers*, when applied to the *Imperfect* 5th and the *Tritone* 4th, respectively, and are only inserted above, out of deference to prevailing custom among musicians.

76. The following is the list of Chromatic intervals, with their number of semitones.

All the Augmented intervals are also variously termed by different writers, *Extreme*, *Superfluous*, *Redundant*, *Sharp*, *&c.* The term *Augmented* appears the best, because embodying its own explanation.

Intervals.

CHROMATIC INTERVALS.
Augmented 2nd, 3 semitones.
Diminished 3rd, 2 semitones.
Diminished 4th, 4 semitones.
Augmented 5th, 8 semitones.
Augmented 6th, 10 semitones.
Diminished 7th, 9 semitones.
Diminished 8ve, 11 semitones.
Augmented 8ve, 13 semitones.
Augmented 9th, 15 semitones.

Fig. 59.

Intervals. 39

77. Intervals are subject to INVERSION; *i. e.* making the lower note the higher, as exhibited in Fig. 60.

Thus, by Inversion,
A 2nd becomes a 7th, and *vice versâ.*
A 3rd   „   6th,   „   „
A 4th   „   5th,   „   „
Minor intervals become Major, and *vice versâ.*
Diminished intervals become Augmented, and *vice versâ.*
Perfect intervals *remain* Perfect.

Only intervals within the 8ve are inverted; the inversion of an interval being its *complement*,—that which, added to it, would constitute it an 8ve; *e. g.* a 7th + 2nd = 8ve.

CHAPTER IX.

MELODY, HARMONY, THOROUGH-BASS, COUNTERPOINT, SCORE, CONCORDS, AND DISCORDS.

78. MELODY is a well-ordered *succession* of *single* sounds, popularly termed *Tune*. The highest part of a composition is often called *the melody*.

79. HARMONY is a proper *combination* of *simultaneous* sounds.[1] Any such combination of three or more sounds constitutes a CHORD. To study Harmony is to study the nature of chords, their varieties, and the laws which regulate their treatment.

The term, formerly, was used in the sense which we attach to *Melody*.

80. THOROUGH-BASS (also termed *General Bass, Basso-Continuo*,[2] *Basso-Cifrato,* or *Figured-Bass*) is the term applied to a Bass part of a composition, with figures,

---

[1] HARMONY-MUSIC is a term applied, in Germany, to music for *wind-instruments* only.

[2] The terms *Thorough-Bass* and *Basso-Continuo* were originally applied to a Bass part *continued throughout* a vocal composition, as an accompaniment or support. The *figuring* of such Bass was introduced subsequently; probably about 1600, or earlier. See Fétis' *Traité de l'harmonie*, chap. xii.

and some other signs, placed over or under it, indicating what chords should accompany it.

The practice of thus figuring a Bass was very general, formerly for the organ part of Church and Oratorio music; the accompaniment for keyed-instruments, of vocal music, and instrumental solos; for the Violoncello part in Recitatives, &c. The modern practice, however, is to write the Organ or Pianoforte part in full, and to write the accompaniment to Recitatives for more instruments than the Violoncello. So that Figured-Bass has fallen into desuetude, except as a useful adjunct to the study of Harmony, and a convenient system of musical short-hand. The use of Figured-Bass in connection with the study of Harmony has been so general, that the terms have almost been regarded as synonymous; whereas *Harmony* has to do with the musical combinations: *Figured-Bass* simply with the system of *signs*, as above explained.

81. COUNTERPOINT (*Punctum contra punctum*, the old notes having been termed *points*,)—formerly termed *Descant*, and, in its early, crude forms, *Diaphony*, *Organum*, *Faux-bourdon*, &c., is the art of adding one or more parts, or successions of notes, to another part, to be performed simultaneously with it. Briefly, it may be defined as *Part-writing*. It has also been defined, happily, as "*the art of combining melodies.*"[1]

This was the form in which musical composition with combined parts was studied and practised by the older musicians; the classification of Chords, and systematizing of their treatment and progression, as represented in our laws of *Harmony*, being of comparatively recent origin and growth.[2] The older musicians considered more the relation of part to part, and the progression of individual parts: we combine, with these considerations, the further one of the *succession of combinations*. In modern times, *Harmony* is usually studied before *Counterpoint*. The two should not be dissociated so entirely, but should be studied conjointly.

82. When the parts assigned to the different voices or instruments in a composition are written one over another, on separate staves, the music is said to be in SCORE (*Partitur, Partition*). When they are written in two

---

[1] Ouseley on *Counterpoint*, p. 2.

[2] Coussemaker: *Histoire de l' Harmonie au moyen age ;* and *l' Art Harmonique aux xii*[e] *et xiii*[e] *siècles.* *See also* Kieswetter, Hullah' *Lectures*, &c.

staves, as in most modern Psalm-tune books, &c., it is said to be in SHORT SCORE, *Compressed*, or *Condensed Score*, *Pianoforte*, or *Organ Score*.

83. Combinations of sounds which are satisfactory to rest on, not requiring any other combination to follow them, are termed CONCORDS, or CONSONANCES.

84. Combinations which suggest and require another combination to follow them, not being satisfactory to dwell on, finally, are termed DISCORDS, or DISSONANCES. Following a Discord by the combination which it suggests to the ear is called *Resolving* it. A Discord, then, is a combination requiring RESOLUTION.[1]

85. The *Concords*, or Consonant combinations, are

The Perfect 8ve, ⎫
The Perfect 5th, ⎬ Perfect Concords.
The Perfect 4th, ⎭

The Minor and the Major 3rd, ⎫
The Minor and the Major 6th, ⎬ Imperfect Concords.

All other combinations are Dissonant. (See § 88.)

Many musicians of high authority have classed the Perfect 4th among *Discords*. Being the inversion of the Perfect 5th, however, which is undeniably Consonant, it is inconsistent so to class it; as well as for other reasons, which will appear. Undoubtedly, however, in some chords, it has to be *treated* as a *Discord*, on account of the dissonance of one of its notes with regard to another note (expressed or implied) in the harmony. (See chap. xxii.)

CHAPTER X.

HARMONICS.

86. IF a stretched string, fastened at both ends, be made to vibrate, communicating its vibrations to the air,

---

[1] See Sir J. F. W. Herschel on *Sound;* Encyclop. Metrop. vol. iv. p. 791.

the whole length of the string vibrates alone only momentarily; its divisions also vibrate, producing certain sounds, in rapid succession, called its HARMONICS, UPPER PARTIALS, or OVERTONES; the sound of the whole length of the string being termed the PRIME, FUNDAMENTAL, or GENERATOR.

Thus the vibration of the whole length of the string is followed by that of half its length, producing the 8ve to the Prime; then by one third of its length, producing the 5th; then by one quarter, producing the double 8ve; then by one fifth, producing the Major 3rd to that double 8ve; and so on. All these Harmonics, taken together, constitute the HARMONIC CHORD or *Series;* exhibited, sufficiently for our present purpose, in Fig. 61. The 3rd, 6th, 9th, and 12th partials are a little sharper, the 5th, 7th, 10th, and 15th considerably flatter than the sounds here represented; as will be seen by the under figures, which represent the proportion of double-vibrations per second.

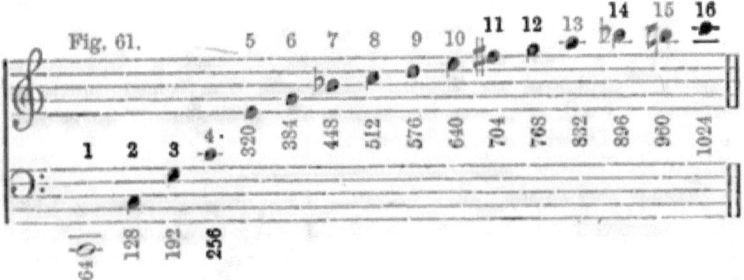

The case is supposed, above, of a stretched cord, as of a Violoncello or Pianoforte string. The same holds good of a column of air vibrating in a pipe or tube, as an Organ pipe, a Horn, &c. But the vibrations vary in extent, and consequently the Harmonics in completeness, under varying circumstances, which is one cause of the difference of *quality* or *timbre* in the tone of different instruments.

These Harmonic notes are the *natural* notes produced by instruments such as the Horn, &c. (*tubes without pistons or valves*); these notes, termed the *open* notes of the instrument, being produced simply by the propelling of the air, with varying force, through it. Whereas the intermediate notes, termed the *shut* notes,—not nearly equal in quality to the open notes—are produced by means of the insertion of the hand in the *bell* of the instrument.

87. Those Harmonies or Chords used in music, which are derived from the *Harmonic chord*—Nature's chord,—are termed *Fundamental Harmonies* or *Chords.*

88. Combinations are *consonant* or *dissonant* according to the order in which the intervals of which they are

formed are produced or generated in the Harmonic chord. Thus the first Harmonic is the Perfect 8ve, the most perfect of Consonances (§ 8). Then follow the Perfect 5th, with its inversion, the Perfect 4th, completing the *Perfect* Consonances. Afterwards, the Major and the Minor 3rd, with their inversions, the Minor and the Major 6th; the *Imperfect* Concords. Then, the Minor 7th and the Major 9th, *Fundamental Discords* (§ 85).

Attempts have been made to construct the entire system of Harmony upon the principles of Harmonics; and to account for the scale and for every chord thereby. The subject cannot be here entered into at length. So much of it as appears to have a practical bearing upon music is briefly stated above. Further consideration of it belongs to the science of Acoustics; for information on which, the student is referred to recognized treatises; among which may be mentioned the articles in the *Encyclopædia Britannica*, and the *Encyclopædia Metropolitana;* Professor Tyndall's *Lectures on Sound;* Woolhouse on *Musical Intervals;* Dr Robert Smith on *Harmonics;* and, for some elucidation of the bearing of the subject on music, to Ouseley on *Harmony.*

NOTE. "A musical note, far from being only a repetition of the same simple sound, should be considered as the conjunction of subordinate sounds reiterated at proportionate intervals. The sweetness of this compound effect on tone appears to depend on the frequent recurrence of interior unison. The secondary sounds which accompany the fundamental note are repeated only two, three, or four times faster; nor does the science of music admit of any proportions but what arise from the limited combinations of those very simple numbers. . . . At the same time, in fact, that the whole cord oscillates, its simpler proportions, the half, the third, and the fourth of its length, actually perform a set of intermediate vibrations."—*Article* ACOUSTICS, part ii, by Prof. Leslie, in *Encyclop. Brit.* pp. 108, 109.

CHAPTER XI.

GENERAL VIEW OF THE CHORDS.

89. A NOTE with its 3rd and 5th constitute a TRIAD, or COMMON CHORD,—the first combination of three notes in the Harmonic chord (Fig. 62, *a*).

General View of the Chords.

Fig. 62.

90. To this, if a 7th be added, the *Chord of the 7th* is obtained (*b*).

91. If to this a 9th be added, the *Chord of the 9th*, or 9th and 7th, is obtained (*c*).

Both of these additions are authorized by the Harmonic chord.

92. To this, the 11th (*d*), and the 13th (*e*), are, by some theorists, added, the results being the *Chord of the 11th*, and the *Chord of the 13th*.

93. In the Minor key, these chords are as exhibited in Fig. 63.

Fig. 63.

94. These chords, with their *Mutations* or *Inflexions*, their *Inversions* and their *Derivatives* (all to be explained in their proper order), are all the chords used in music. The additional combinations are obtained by notes of *ornament*, &c., such as *Passing-notes* (chap. xxiii.), and by notes of *delay*, called *Suspensions* (chap. xxii.).

The above, then, is a comprehensive view of the ground to be traversed by the student of harmony.

95. The *Triad*, in Figs. 62 and 63, is *consonant*, consisting entirely of consonant combinations.

96. All the other chords are *dissonant*, containing discords.

97. It will be seen that the *Triad* is the basis of all the other chords, all of them being obtained by *adding* a 3rd (to the highest note of the previous chord), the dissonances being termed ADDED DISCORDS;[1] also, ESSENTIAL DISCORDS, belonging *essentially* (not ornamentally or transiently) to the chords.

---

[1] A term which has been differently used, however (see § 189).

98. Of all the above chords, which are in the keys of G major (Fig. 62) and G minor (Fig. 63), D is the ROOT, or FUNDAMENTAL BASS, *i. e.* the note on which they are founded; and, likewise, of all chords obtained from them, by *inversion*, or *derivation*, the term being used to denote the bass note of a chord from which others are obtained, by either process (§§ 140, 141, &c.).

The treatment of these chords will be the subject of the ensuing chapters.

CHAPTER XII

ELEMENTARY LAWS OF PART-WRITING.

99. THE term *Part-writing* is used here in a somewhat wider sense than in § 81. By it, here, is meant, the writing of successions of chords; and by *Laws of Part-writing*, therefore, is meant the principles which regulate the *position* of chords, or *distribution of parts;* the *relation of part to part*, and the *progression of individual parts.* In other words, laws of *combination*, and laws of *progression*, individual and simultaneous. Those here given are such as are *generally applicable;* not those which are *special* to particular chords.

Compare with this chapter the rules of Simple Counterpoint, chap. xxviii. &c.

100. The *highest* and *lowest* parts in a chord, or succession of chords, are termed the EXTREME PARTS. The others are termed the INNER PARTS.

101. The best *position* in which to write a chord—to superpose the parts—is that in which the parts are as nearly *equally distributed* as possible, *i. e.* the distances between *proximate* parts being nearly equal; the *larger* distances being between the *lower* rather than between

the *upper* parts, which may be at smaller distances from one another.

This law is justified by the arrangement of the *Harmonic Chord* (Fig. 61), in which the largest interval, an octave, is between the lowest **two** parts, and the distances *gradually diminish*, **till** between the highest two parts there is only a semitone. The law is also borne out by the fact that the *graver* sounds are less readily distinguished from one another by the ear than the acute; and, therefore, require more separation. Care should particularly be **taken** not to have the 3rd, especially the *major* **3rd of a** chord, near the Bass, except, of course, in **a composition for men's voices, or** instruments of low register.

Thus, **of the various positions of the same chord, in Fig. 64, that**

at. (*a*) is bad, because the smallest distance **is between** the lowest two parts, the upper **of** those two, moreover, **being** the *major* 3rd of the chord; and because of the great *inequality* **in** the distribution of the parts, there being so wide a separation between the two inner parts. Those **at** (*b*) **and** (*c*) **are likewise objectionable, on** account of inequality **of** distribution, though **the lowest parts are** well separated. Those **at** (*d*) **and** (*e*) are good, **because of the** comparative equality of the distribution of **the parts, there being no** great discrepancy between the distances of any proximate parts; and **because the lowest parts are** tolerably separated from one another. The position at (*e*) **is, in fact, a** section from the *Harmonic Chord*. If all these chords **be played, it** will be heard that, in the first three, the parts do not seem to *amalgamate;* they **lack** *cohesion*. The reverse will **be recognized in** the last two chords.

102. **When two parts rise or descend** together—not necessarily by the same interval—they are said, obviously enough, **to** proceed **by** SIMILAR MOTION; also termed DIRECT MOTION. Fig. 65 (*a*).

When **one part rises and** the **other descends, the** motion is termed CONTRARY, **or** INDIRECT MOTION (*b*).

When one part remains stationary, *retaining* or *repeat-*

48   Elementary Laws of Part-Writing.

Fig. 65.

ing the same note, while the other moves, the motion is termed OBLIQUE (*c*).

The term *Parallel motion* has been applied to the *repetition* of the same combination (*d*); also to *similar motion*.

103. Two, or more, *perfect* 5ths, *perfect* 8ves, or *perfect unisons*, are forbidden between the same two parts, whether by *skip*, or by *conjunct* movement—(movement by one degree); *especially* by *similar motion*. (Fig. 66.)

Fig. 66.

This, one of the most important *prohibitions* concerning part-writing, has been variously accounted for, and justified. The bad effect of consecutive perfect 5ths may perhaps arise from the suggestion of two different scales which they produce. The baldness of effect in consecutive 8ves and unisons doubtless results from the virtual reduction of the number of parts which they occasion, in a succession of chords. For it is in a *succession of chords*, or *progression of simultaneous parts*, that these consecutive intervals are forbidden; not in a passage which moves wholly in 8ves or unisons, as at Fig. 67. Nor is the *repetition* of the *same* 8ve, 5th, or unison, as

Forbidden Consecutives.

Fig. 67. MOZART.

&c.

at Fig. 68, forbidden; there being no *motion*, properly speaking, in such case; and no change of harmony.

Fig. 68.

There is special **danger of** these forbidden consecutives when all, or most of the parts, in a succession of chords, proceed by *similar motion;* when, moreover, the effect is specially bad. Thus, though both chords in Fig. 69 (a) are in good positions, the connection of the

Fig. 69. (a)   (b)   (c)   (d)

chords is bad, because of the consecutive 5ths between the *lowest two* parts, and the consecutive 8ves between the *extreme* parts. These may be avoided as at (b), where, though both chords have an 8ve and a 5th (to the Bass), those intervals are not in the *same parts* in both chords. Similarly, the consecutives at (c) may be avoided as at (d).

Consecutive 5ths are not forbidden where one is *Imperfect;* though even these should be avoided in the *extreme* parts.

(It must be understood that intervals in their *compound* forms (§ 70) are subject to the same laws as in their *simple* forms, and generally, are spoken of as though simple, the 12th being termed a 5th, the 15th (*double* 8ve) an 8ve, &c., and treated as such.)

The forbidden consecutives, though not so bad in effect, generally, between parts proceeding by *contrary* as by *similar* motion, require great caution in their introduction, and should be avoided by the student. See Fig. 70 (*a*), in which there are consecutive 8ves between

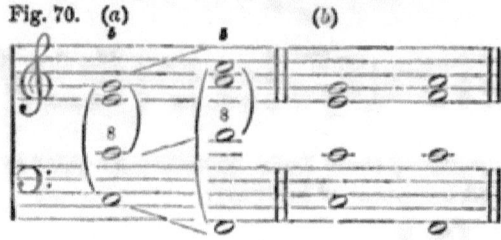

the *lowest* two parts, and consecutive 5ths between the *extreme* parts, by *contrary* motion; and consecutive 5ths between the *highest* (*Soprano*) part, and the part next the Bass (*Tenor*), by *similar* motion. These may be rectified as at (*b*). It will be seen that the consecutives are forbidden between *any two parts*; not only between the *Bass* and another part.

Some writers allow exceptions to the **prohibition** of consecutive 8ves and 5ths, **in** progressions between **the** *Tonic* **and the** *Dominant*, and between the *Tonic* and the *Sub-dominant*. These exceptions, however, require care, and had better be avoided by the student.

A *short rest* between two chords does not absolve **from** consecutives, or any other bad connection or progression.

104. It is generally productive of bad effect to proceed in the *extreme parts*, by *similar motion*, to a perfect concord (8ve, or 5th,) or a unison, as at Fig. 71, in which the

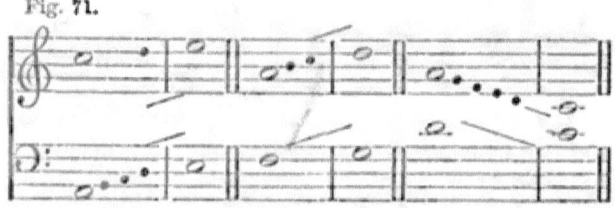

wider intervals (represented by the semibreves) are filled up by small notes, and it will be perceived that consecutives are *passed over*; *i. e.* would occur if the intermediate notes were performed. This effect is termed HIDDEN, or COVERED CONSECUTIVES. This prohibition gives rise to the general rule that a *Perfect Concord*, or a *Unison*, should, in the *extreme parts*, be approached by *contrary* or *oblique* motion (Fig. 72), the unison, moreover, being only so approached between *any* parts.

Exception to this rule is permitted when the *highest* part moves one degree (*conjunct* movement), and the lowest part skips a 4th or a 5th (Fig. 73); especially when proceeding from the chord on the

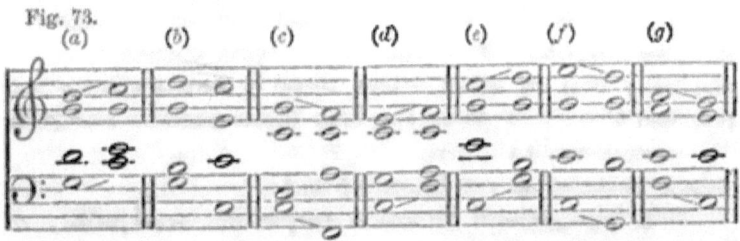

Dominant to that on the *Tonic* (*a*, *b*); or *vice versâ* (*e*, *f*); or from that on the *Tonic* to that on the *Sub-dominant* (*c*, *d*); or *vice versâ* (*g*); and in some cases where the *inversions* (to be subsequently explained) of these chords are used in juxtaposition.

Other exceptions will be noticed further on; and many cases will occur in which good cultivated taste must determine the advisability or otherwise of the progression.

Similar motion to the 5th is not objectionable, in proceeding from a chord to another position of the same harmony (Fig. 74.)

105. In writing chords in four or more parts, similar motion in *all* the parts is generally to be avoided; both because it is likely to cause the forbidden consecutives

(see Fig. 69, *a*, *c*), or some awkward contrivance to avoid them; and because the mixture of two, or of all three kinds of motion is more grateful in effect. Thus, at Fig. 69 (*b*), there is both *similar* motion and *contrary;* at (*d*), *contrary* and *oblique;* at Fig. 73 (*a*, *d*, *f*, *g*), *similar* and *oblique;* and at Fig. 73 (*b*, *c*, *e*) *similar*, *contrary*, and *oblique*.

106. In early attempts at part-writing, the student will do well to keep the parts as *tranquil* as possible; *i. e.* connecting the chords as *closely* as is consistent with the other rules. To this end, if any note is *common to two successive chords*, it is advisable to keep it in the *same part* in both chords, as at Fig. 69 (*d*), Fig. 70 (*b*), Fig. 73 (*a*, *c*, *d*, *e*, *f*, *g*); the note thus serving as a connecting link between the two chords. Two chords occurring successively are generally best in effect when there is such a connection between them; or when the first chord strongly suggests the second, as in the case of a *dissonant chord* suggesting, indeed *demanding*, resolution (§ 124).

107. The general direction respecting tranquillity of the parts, given in the last paragraph, is not, however, constantly to be observed, though desirable in the student's *early* exercises. Progression by the *smaller* intervals, 2nds and 3rds, is characteristic of softness and ease; progression by the *larger* intervals, especially the *Perfect Concords* (§ 85), is characteristic rather of boldness and power.[1] A due admixture—interchange—of these, then, in the various parts of a composition, will tend to the balance or equilibrium of the effect; and is one of the constituents of good melody, where no *specially characteristic effect* is desired. A wide skip in either direction

Fig. 75.

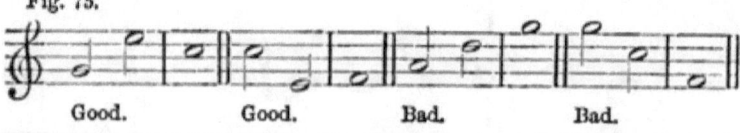

Good.   Good.   Bad.   Bad.

---

[1] Compare, for example, the opening of "*With verdure clad*," or "*Vedrai Carino*," with that of "*Rejoice greatly*," or "*They loathed to drink*."

should generally be followed by a progression in the opposite direction; two successive wide skips in the same direction being generally undesirable (Fig. 75).

That which has been said respecting the softness of small and the power of large intervals and Perfect Concords, in *progression*, or *melody*, is likewise applicable to *combination* or *harmony*. A chord is good in which the two kinds are found. (See § 101.)

108. Some intervals are more difficult to take accurately, in singing, than others; the difficulty being *mental* rather than *vocal*. That is, it is more difficult to apprehend, with the mind, one distance—or succession of notes—than another; and this apprehension by the mind *must precede* the taking of the notes by the voice. If comparatively difficult for the mind to apprehend, before it is sung, it is, more or less, correspondingly *unwelcome* to the mind, difficult to acquiesce in, when sung. Therefore, in vocal music, generally, and in other music, unless amply expounded and justified by surrounding or accompanying harmonies, such intervals should be avoided, as intervals of melody; not merely in *the melody*, but in *any* individual part. (See § 78.) These intervals are the *Tritone* 4th, 5th from the *Mediant*, the *Major* 7th, intervals beyond the 8ve, and *all the Chromatic Intervals* (Fig. 76).

Fig. 76.

The Augmented 2nd is not so objectionable, when occurring in a passage forming part of the *Minor scale*, as at Fig. 47, p. 29. (See Fig. 77.) **Nor are** some of these intervals forbidden when both the notes

Fig. 77.

form parts of the same harmony, in different positions. The student had better observe the prohibition strictly at first; leaving the exceptions till he has made some advancement.

The Imperfect 5th and the Minor 7th should, when taken as intervals of melody, be followed as at Fig. 78, for reasons which will appear further on (§ 262).

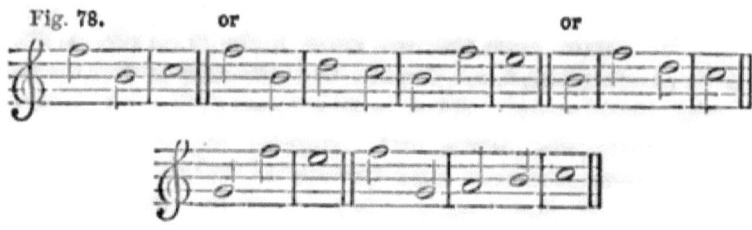

Fig. 78.

109. It has been shown (§ 52) that, in the ascending scale, the *Leading-note suggests* the *Tonic*, to follow it. From this results the desirableness of its being followed by the Tonic, in the same part, whenever a chord which has the Leading-note in it is followed by one which includes the Tonic. Briefly, the Leading-note should, when practicable, *rise* to the Tonic. This is especially desirable when it occurs in the *highest* part, as being more prominent than the under parts; and additionally so when it forms part of *Dominant* harmony. (§§ 124, 128, &c.) Fig. 79.

Fig. 79.

This is a *modern* law, not observed by the old masters, such as J. S. Bach, and his predecessors. Exceptions are permitted in cases where the Leading-note forms part of a *descending scale*, as in Fig. 80.

When the chord containing the Leading-note is not followed by a chord containing the Tonic, it is generally productive of better effect for that note to *rise* (though not to the Tonic), rather than to

False Relation. 55

Fig. 80.

descend. Thus, the progression at (*a*), Fig. 81, is better than that at (*b*).

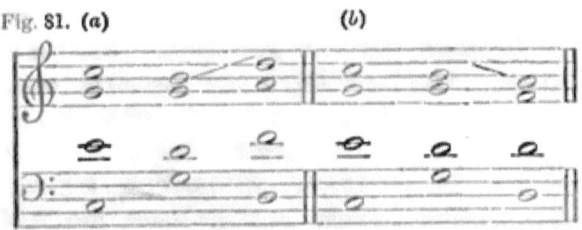
Fig. 81. (*a*)   (*b*)

110. When a chord in which any *natural* note occurs is followed by a chord containing that **same note** *sharpened* or *flattened*, or **vice versâ**, that note so altered should appear in the same part; or a FALSE RELATION between the parts is produced. The same principle obviously holds good with regard to a note inflected by a *double-sharp* or a *double-flat* (Fig. 82).

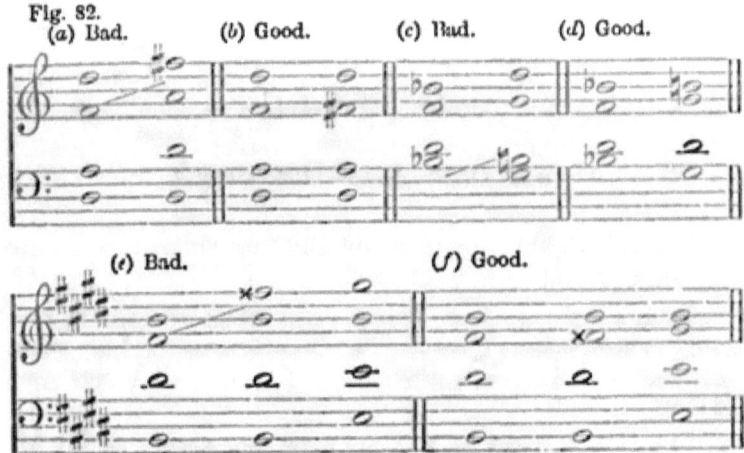
Fig. 82.
(*a*) Bad.   (*b*) Good.   (*c*) Bad.   (*d*) Good.

(*e*) Bad.   (*f*) Good.

When the altered note is *doubled* (*i. e. appears in two parts*, § 115), the change will be made in *one* part only, as at (*d*).

Generally speaking, *one* intermediate chord will not destroy the ill effect of a *False relation* between two chords.

In chromatic progressions, and many other cases, however, *False relations* between the parts are permitted; the ear must determine the desirableness, or otherwise, of the progression.

Another form of *False relation* is explained in chap. xxviii. § 252.

111. The laws of Part-writing must yield to one another: laws of *progression*, to laws of *position*, and *vice versâ*. It is rarely, if ever, possible to have successive chords in *absolutely* the *best position* and the *best connection* likewise. The laws here given are such as are most important for the student to observe at first; but, with the exception of the laws against consecutive 8ves, 5ths, and unisons, which are rarely infringed by any composers of repute, violations of most, or all of them, are to be found in the compositions of the greatest masters. Many seeming violations, however, are violations of the letter, not of the spirit of the laws, and are susceptible of ample explanation and justification, which, however, require ripe and complete theoretical knowledge.

CHAPTER XIII.

THE TRIAD, OR COMMON CHORD.

112. The TRIAD, or COMMON CHORD, consists of a note with its 3rd and 5th (§ 89).

Some writers only apply the term *Common chord* when the 8ve to the Bass note is added; others, when the 8ve to either of the notes in the chord is added, *i. e.* when the chord is in at least four parts (§ 115).

113. If a Triad be written upon every note of the Dia-

tonic scale (Fig. 83), it will be found that there are three varieties :—

Fig. 83. Major. Minor. Minor. Major. Major. Minor. Imperfect.

(1.) That with a *Major* 3rd and a *Perfect* 5th, which is termed a MAJOR TRIAD, occurring on the *Tonic*, the *Dominant*, and the *Sub-dominant* of the Major scale.

(2.) That with a *Minor* 3rd and a *Perfect* 5th, termed a MINOR TRIAD, occurring on the *Super-tonic*, the *Mediant*, and the *Sub-mediant* of the Major scale.

(3.) That with a *Minor* 3rd and an *Imperfect* 5th, termed an IMPERFECT TRIAD, occurring *only* on the *Leading-note* of the Major scale: not termed a Common Chord.

As the *Imperfect* 5th is most frequently termed *Diminished* (see §§ 73, 75), so the triad in which it occurs is generally termed the *Diminished Triad*. (See § 231, Fig. 187.)

The Triads on the *Tonic* and *Sub-dominant* of the *Minor* scale are *minor*, that on the *Dominant* almost invariably *major:* a Minor chord on that degree not being considered *Dominant harmony*, having no *governing* power, on account of the absence of the Leading-note. (See §§ 52, 123, 166.) The Triad on the 3rd of the true Minor scale (Fig. 47) is augmented (§ 231); and that on the Leading-note (as in the Major scale) *Imperfect* (or *Diminished*); the Imperfect Triad also having place on the *Super-tonic* of the Minor scale. (Compare with §§ 73, 123.) On the raised 6th, and on the Minor 7th, chords of the 6th (chap. xvi.), not Triads, are usually taken (§ 123).

It will be seen that the *Major* and *Minor* Triads differ in their 3rd, corresponding in their 5th; the *Minor* and *Imperfect* Triads differ in their 5th, corresponding in their 3rd (Fig. 84).

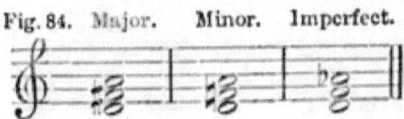

Fig. 84. Major. Minor. Imperfect.

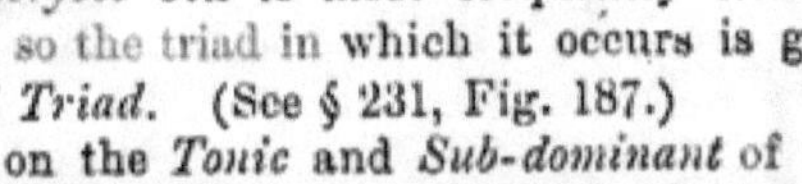

114. The *Major* and *Minor* Triads are *Consonant chords*, consisting entirely of *Consonant intervals*. The Imperfect Triad contains a *Dissonant interval*, and is, therefore, a *Dissonant chord*, requiring *resolution* (§§ 84, 121).

The Triad: Doubling.

115. When the Triad, a chord of three notes, has to be written in four (or more) parts, one (or more) of its notes must be written *twice*. This is termed *doubling* that note, which may be in 8ve or in unison.

By referring to Fig. 61, it will be seen that, in the Harmonic chord, within the limits of the Triad, the *fundamental* note occurs three times,—is *doubled twice;* the 5th occurs *twice*, is *doubled once;* the 3rd occurs only *once*, is *not doubled* at all. From these facts we gather the general principles that the *Bass-note*, or *root* of the Triad, is the *best* note to double; after that, the 5th, and *least of all*, the 3rd, especially when it is a *Major* 3rd, as is the case in the Harmonic chord.

In the three examples, Fig. 85, that at (*a*) is, therefore, the *best;*

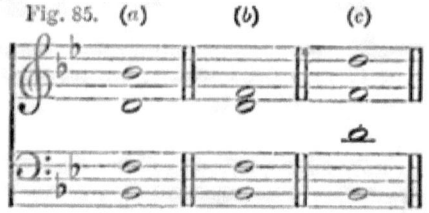

Fig. 85. (*a*) (*b*) (*c*)

that at (*c*) the *least desirable*, but not absolutely wrong. (The student should test these, *and all similar examples*, at the Pianoforte, that the ear may justify the axioms laid down.)

116. A Triad in four parts, then, most frequently consists of a note with its 3rd, 5th, and 8ve, it being understood that the *compound forms* of these intervals are used, as well as the simple (§ 70); and, as will be seen by the examples, that these notes of the chord may be variously superposed.

117. While the *principles* enunciated in § 115 are sound, it is more frequently found *expedient* to double the 3rd than the 5th of a chord, when the Bass-note cannot be doubled. To double the 5th increases the danger of *consecutive* 5ths. (See also § 119.)

Thus at Fig. 86 (*a*), the forbidden consecutive 8ves and 5ths occur; at (*b*), to avoid these, contrary motion to the Bass in all the upper parts is taken; but the effect of the *descending Leading-note*, B, in the highest part (*Soprano*), is unpleasant; at (*c*), both these faults

The Triad: Doubling.

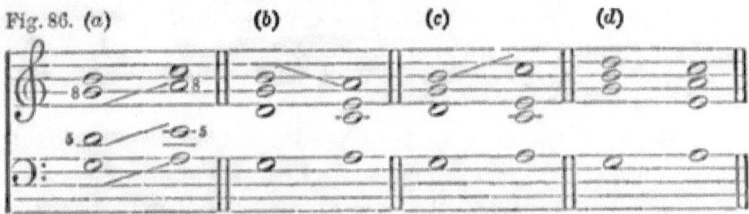

Fig. 86. (a) (b) (c) (d)

are obviated, by doubling the 3rd in 8ve, **in the** second chord. The chords might be written as **at** (*d*), where the descending Leading-note is not so objectionable, **being in an** *inner part* (the Alto). See also § 119, and Fig. 88.

118. The *Leading-note* **of** the **scale**, being peculiarly delicate, should never be doubled, **except in** the Imperfect Triad, little used ; and, occasionally, in *Sequences* (§ **139**), which furnish occasion and justification for various exceptions to **rules.** Therefore, in the **Dominant** *Major Triad*, the 3rd of the chord, **which is the** Leading-note of the scale, must not, on any account, **be doubled.**

Thus, at Fig. 87, to avoid the doubled **Leading-note in the third** chord, it is better to double the Bass **note in** unison, as at (*b*).

Fig. 87. (a)   Bad.   (b)

119. The accidentals occurring in the Minor scale render the danger of objectionable intervals of melody (§ 108) more likely to present itself in progressions in the Minor key than in the Major; and, to avoid such intervals, the doubling of the 3rd **in a chord is often expedient.**

Thus, at **Fig. 88,** which is in *A Minor* (indicated by the G♯; see

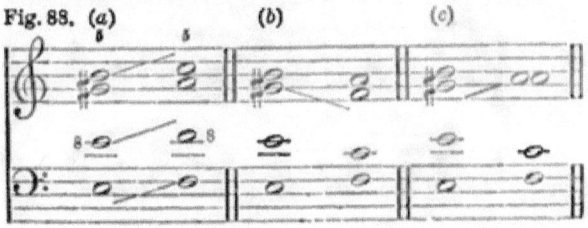

Fig. 88. (a) (b) (c)

also § 121), there are consecutive 8ves and 5ths at (*a*) ; at (*b*) there is an *Augmented 2nd*, G♯ to F, in the Alto ; these errors are both obviated at (*c*) by doubling the 3rd in unison (Soprano and Alto). (*Compare with* § 117, and Fig. 86.)

120. Sometimes a note of a chord has to be *omitted*, on account of some exigency of Part-writing. The note most usually omitted, in such a case, from the Triad, is the 5th ; the 3rd rarely (except for a special effect), as it determines the chord as major or minor. (See § 128, and Fig. 93 (*c*), chap. xiv.)

121. The *Resolution of a Dissonance* (§ 84) is usually effected by the dissonant note *descending* one degree, *i. e.* a 2nd, major or minor ; in other words, by the part which has the dissonant note proceeding to the note below (§ 164, &c.). Generally, this takes place in the succeeding chord ; occasionally the resolution is deferred (§ 168), or even interrupted by an intermediate progression (§ 139).

The 5th in the Imperfect Triad is the dissonant note (§ 114), and, therefore, should resolve by proceeding as at Fig. 89. On this account, the Imperfect Triad on the

Fig. 89. Imp. Triad.

Leading-note is generally followed by the *Tonic* Triad except in sequences. (Chap. xv. § 139, Fig. 102.) The Imperfect Triad on the *Super-tonic* of the *Minor* scale (§ 113) is usually followed by the *Dominant* Triad (Fig. 90, which is in F♯ *Minor*, as indicated by the E♯).

Fig. 90. Imp.

The reason why the *upper* note—not the *lower* note—in an Imperfect 5th is said to be the *dissonant* note of the combination, will be better understood subsequently (§ 147, and chap. xvii. §§ 162, 164).

122. The Triads on the 3rd and the Leading-note of the Major scale are little used, except in Sequences (chap. xv.). The Triads on the other degrees of the scale are freely used (in proper connection), especially those on the *Tonic*, *Sub-dominant*, and *Dominant*,—the three *Major* Triads, termed the *Fundamental chords* of the key; the *Major* Triad, as has been seen, being the *basis* of all the other chords, and the first chord generated in the Harmonic chord (§§ 86, 97). These three chords contain all the notes of the scale, the Dominant of the scale, moreover, being common to the Tonic and the Dominant Triads: the Tonic, common to the Tonic and the Sub-dominant Triads (Fig. 91). With these three chords, then, (or their inversions, chap. xvi.) the scale *may* be harmonized.

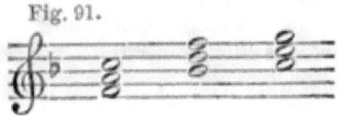

Fig. 91.

The Super-tonic chord, and that on the Sub-mediant, are valuable subordinate harmonies to relieve from the monotonous alternation of the Fundamental harmonies.

123. In the Minor key, the Imperfect Triads, on the *Super-tonic* and the *Leading-note*, are little used, *especially* that on the Leading-note.

The *raised* 6th note of the scale must never bear a Triad: the impression of a *Root* foreign to the key would be produced (§ 113).

On the other notes of the Minor scale, including the *unraised* 6th note, Triads may be freely used; the same remarks about the Tonic, Sub-dominant, and Dominant chords holding good, as were made in the last paragraph, it being borne in mind that the *true Dominant chord* in the Minor key is *major* (§ 113).

124. Two chords are most agreeable in succession, either when the first *suggests* the second, *e. g.* when it

contains a *Leading-note* or a *dissonant note*, having (with some exceptions) *fixed progressions*, or, when they have a note in common (§ 106). The two conditions sometimes combine.

It will follow that successive Triads are better when their Bass notes are a 3rd, a 4th, a 5th, or a 6th apart, than when they are distant a 2nd or a 7th (the latter very rare) ; except in the case of the *Dominant* Triad, which, containing the *Leading-note*, is generally followed either by the *Tonic Triad* (the Bass note of which is a 4th above or a 5th below the Dominant), or an inversion thereof (chap. xvi.), or by that on the 6th of the scale, a 2nd above the Dominant. (See §§ 128, 131, and Figs. 93, 100.)

Although the *Sub-dominant* Triad likewise contains the Tonic of the scale, to which the Leading-note tends, that chord does not agreeably follow the Dominant chord, two *Major* chords, with, of course, different *Fundamental* notes, having, generally, a harsh effect in succession, *unless there be a note common to the two chords* (see, however, Fig. 100, *b*), a condition which is fulfilled in the case of the Dominant and Tonic Triads.

Frequently, however, in approaching a cadence, the Sub-dominant chord is *followed by* the Dominant chord. The contrary motion seems to modify, and render acceptable, that which would appear to be a harsh succession, possibly by dismissing all suspicion of forbidden consecutives.

(*Compare with* §§ 252, 263.)

125. In a *Figured Bass* part (§ 80) the notes which are to be accompanied by Triads are not usually figured; it is understood that the unfigured notes bear Triads. Except (1.) when any other chord is to precede or follow the Triad on the same Bass-note, when *both* chords must be figured, the Triad being indicated, according to context, by 8, 5, or 3, or any combination of these, $\frac{8}{5}, \frac{8}{3}, \frac{5}{3}, \frac{8}{5}$;

(2.) when either note of the chord is to be affected by an *accidental ;* when the figure indicating that note must be written, preceded (or occasionally followed) by the requisite sign.

When the 3rd of *any* chord is to be thus affected, frequently the *accidental only* is written, it being understood that an accidental, standing alone in a Figured Bass, applies to the 3*rd* in that chord.

When any interval in a chord is to be *raised* one semitone, whether by a ♮, a ♯, or a ×, frequently it is indicated by an oblique mark *through* the figure, thus: $\sharp\!5$, $\sharp\!8$ (compare § 174), or by a × *before* the figure. The Imperfect 5th (and Triad) is, by some, figured ♭5, even when the *note* is ♮.

The 8ve to the Bass is always to be natural, sharp, or flat, like the Bass itself, that is, a *Perfect* 8ve, unless otherwise indicated.

All this is illustrated in Fig. 92, except the *contextual* figuring, which will be exemplified further on.

Fig. 92.

CHAPTER XIV.

CADENCES.

126. A CADENCE is the *close* of a musical phrase; the term being generally applied to the final two chords of such phrase.

The term is also applied to an ornamental passage, introduced by vocalists and soloists—sometimes written by the composer—towards the end of a piece, or at *pauses,* and other places. Also, to a somewhat extended and elaborate passage, of an improvised character, introduced, at an indicated point (sometimes termed *Point d'Orgue*, see also § 237), near the end of an instrumental concerto; in which the performer recapitulates, more or less, the subjects of the movement, with such diversified treatment as his knowledge and fancy may suggest. Such passage, commencing with a $^6_4$ chord (chap. xvi.), *precedes* the real cadence, in the sense first given above, in which sense alone the term is used throughout this chapter.

127. Cadences are of different kinds, more or less *conclusive,* or suggestive of repose; bearing, in this respect, some analogy to the different stops in reading. The principal cadences are the PERFECT, the PLAGAL, the IMPERFECT, and the INTERRUPTED.

128. The PERFECT (formerly termed AUTHENTIC) CADENCE, or FULL CLOSE, consists of the *Major Triad* on the *Dominant* (to which the 7th may be added, § 167 (1.)), followed by the Triad on the *Tonic*, which will be Major or Minor according to the mode in which the composition is written (Fig. 93). This is the cadence which is gener-

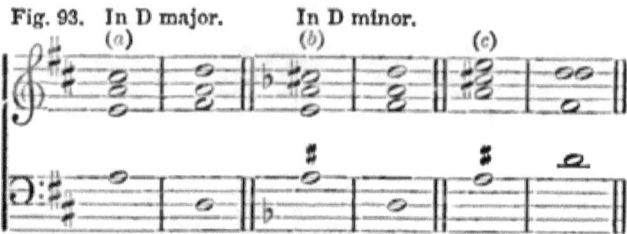

Fig. 93. In D major. In D minor.
(a) (b) (c)

ally used to terminate a composition, or an important section thereof; giving the most satisfactory impression of the key.

Sometimes, at the conclusion of a composition in the Minor key, the final chord is accidentally *Major*. This, however, more frequently occurs in the *Plagal* cadence, to be explained immediately. The 3rd, rendered Major, thus accidentally, has been termed the *Tierce de Picardie;* it being alleged that this termination had its origin in that province (§ 233).

The progression of the Leading-note to the Tonic is especially to be observed in the Perfect cadence; particularly when occurring in the highest part, as at (*a, b*). When the melody descends, as at (*c*), it may be desirable to omit the 5th in the final chord, doubling the bass-note twice. (See § 120, and § 294.)

Generally, the final chord of a Perfect cadence occurs at the beginning of the bar or measure: almost invariably at the *accented beat* (§ 25). To this, however, there are exceptions, especially in triple time, as in Fig. 94; the close of the slow movement of Beethoven's Sonata, Op. 7.

129. The PLAGAL CADENCE consists of the *Sub-dominant Triad,* followed by that on the *Tonic.* These chords will be Major or Minor according to the mode: the *Major* chord on the *Tonic* being, however, frequently and in

Cadences.   65

Fig. 94.   Perfect Cadence.

former times almost invariably, substituted for the Minor, even when the composition is in the Minor mode.

This cadence is not used as a *substitute* for the Perfect cadence, —not being nearly so indicative of the key; but as an *appendix* to it, especially in Church and Oratorio Music, in which its effect is sometimes very impressive. (Fig. 95.) It is sometimes called the *Church Cadence*. (See § 62.)

Fig. 95.

130. The IMPERFECT CADENCE (or HALF-CADENCE) ends on the *Dominant* Chord, most frequently preceded by the Tonic Chord (in which case it is the exact *reverse* of the Perfect Cadence); but sometimes by other chords.

This Cadence is not used to terminate a *Composition*, or *Movement*; but to terminate a *Phrase*, or *Section*. (See chap. xxxiv.)

Cadences.

It has not the effect of *finality* and *repose*, like the *Perfect Cadence*, which may be likened to a Period; but of *suspended* progress,—being somewhat analogous to a semi-colon. (Figs. 96, 97, 98, 99.)

131. An INTERRUPTED CADENCE, as its name implies, is really, in the strictest sense, not a cadence at all, but the interruption of one, by the appearance of some other than the Tonic Chord, when the progression has been such as to lead to the expectation of a Perfect Cadence. The varieties of form which such interruptions may assume are numerous; and the effect often most beautiful. A few are instanced in Fig. 100.

The terms False, Broken, Deceptive (Ital. *Inganno*, trick, deceit,) &c., are also applied to these Cadences; those at (*a*, *b*) being generally understood by a *False* Cadence.

132. Besides the above, there are *Inverted Cadences*,— *i. e.* inversions of the above; and other forms of close to musical phrases, to which no distinctive names are applied.

133. One of the first elements of musical construction is the proper management of the cadences; especially the avoidance of *tautology: i. e.* the too frequent and too proximate recurrence of the same form of cadence. In a short composition, such as a Chant or Psalm-tune, this is especially necessary.

CHAPTER XV.

SEQUENCES.

134. A *Sequence* is the repetition of the same *progression*, in Melody, or Harmony, or both, with different *notes* —degrees of the scale.

Thus, at Fig. 101, a sequence of Triads, the Bass alternately descends a 4th and rises a 2nd.

Fig. 101.

135. A Sequence is termed *Real* when all the Chords, or Intervals, are Major or Minor, &c., at each *recurrence* of the repeated progression, as at the original *occurrence* of it.

136. A Sequence is termed *Tonal* when the Chords or Intervals, at each recurrence, are according to the *key* in which the passage occurs; and, therefore, do not strictly resemble the original pattern. This is the more frequent kind of Sequence. Fig. 101 is a Tonal Sequence: two of the ascending 2nds are Major, one (from D to E♭) Minor: moreover, some of the *Chords* are Major: others Minor.

137. A Sequence may consist of the repetition of a progression of two, three, or more notes or chords: frequently it embraces a complete phrase (§ 359).

138. In harmonizing a Melody or Bass that progresses sequentially, the sequence should be preserved, both in the harmonies used and in the progression of all the parts.

Thus, in Fig. 101, in the first bar, when the Bass descends a 4th, the Tenor remains stationary, and the other two parts descend a 2nd. This connection of the chords is preserved in the succeeding three bars: the limit of the sequence.

Exceptions occur, sometimes, to obtain variety. Notably, a sequence of *harmonies* may be varied by a different superposition of the *parts:* an effective device, requiring, however, some contrapuntal skill.

139. The preservation of a sequential progression will often lead to, and justify, exceptional intervals. doublings,

&c.; the symmetry of the sequence outweighing the objections which might otherwise lie against such exceptional arrangements. *Design*—using the word in its artistic sense of *intelligent aim* at a *defined* and *desirable* effect, especially with regard to *form*—reconciles, and more than reconciles, the mind to details which, taken by themselves, would be questionable, or even positively objectionable. (See §§ 118, 121.)

In Fig. 102, for example, the Tritone 4th in the Bass, from C to

Fig. 102.

F♯; and the non-resolution of the Imperfect 5th in the Tenor, at *, till the next chord *but one*, are both justified by the sequential form of the passage. (See also § 170, Figs. 126, 127.)

Such exceptional progressions, however, though permissible in the *course of the sequence*, must not occur in the *original pattern*, in which the writing must be perfectly pure.

CHAPTER XVI.

INVERSIONS OF THE TRIAD.

140. CHORDS, like Intervals, are subject to *inversion*; *i. e.* taking another note of the chord than its *Root* (§§ 98, 141) as the lowest note, so that the Root is—not *changed*, but—*transferred* to an upper part.

141. By the ROOT of a chord, or its *Radical Bass*, is meant its Bass-note in its original, *uninverted* form.

Therefore, *Root* and *Bass-note* are not synonyms. The term *Fundamental Bass* is also used for *Root;* but is, by many theorists, confined to the Bass notes of *Major* Chords. The term *Prime* is applied *only* to the lowest note of the *Harmonic* Chord. (§§ 86, 87.)

142. The *Triad* has *two inversions*. The *first* inversion has the 3rd of the original chord for its lowest note: the *second* inversion has the 5th of the original chord for its lowest note. (Fig. 103.) Therefore the *Root* of the

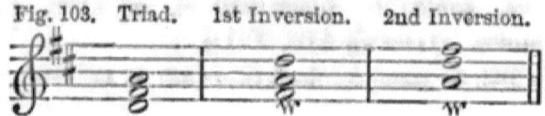

Fig. 103. Triad.   1st Inversion.   2nd Inversion.

first inversion is a 3rd below the Bass-note (or lowest note, by whatever voice sung); the *Root* of the second inversion is a 5th below the Bass-note. D is the Root of the chords in Fig. 103, as indicated by the *Direct*, ⋎.

143. The *first* inversion of the Triad, consisting of a note with its 3rd and 6th, is termed the CHORD OF THE SIXTH: the *second* inversion, consisting of a note with its 4th and 6th, is termed the CHORD OF THE SIX-FOUR (or 6th and 4th).

First Inversion of the Triad: the Chord of the Sixth.

144. In a *Figured-bass* part, a note that is to bear a *Chord of the Sixth* is usually figured simply 6 (Fig. 104),

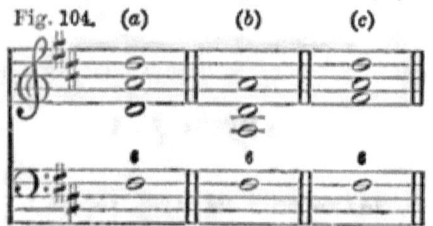

Fig. 104. (a)   (b)   (c)

the 3rd being understood. It is sometimes figured more fully, $\frac{6}{3}$, or (when the Bass-note is doubled) $\frac{8}{6}$.

It is an almost invariable practice, in a Figured-bass *signature* (as the figures, &c., are termed) to place the largest number at the top, and smallest at the bottom, as above; but such arrangement does not dictate the *superposition* of the parts: nor does the *succession* of the figures indicate the *progression* of the parts, except in a few instances of somewhat intricate **part-writing**.

Chord of the Sixth.   71

145. In the chord of the 6th, the 6th, being the *Root* of the chord, is the best note to *double*, in four-part-writing, all other things being equal (see § 115), as at Fig. 104 (*a*). The other notes of the chord may, however, and frequently *must*, be doubled, as at (*b, c*). In the first inversion of a *Major* Triad, the Bass-note, being the *Major* 3rd to the *Root*, is not so desirable to double as either of the other members of the chord; but it is sometimes inevitable to double it. In the first inversion of the *Dominant* Triad, the Bass-note, being the *Leading-note* of the scale, should never be doubled. (See § 118.)

The chord at (*a*), Fig. 104, is the best; and that at (*c*) the least desirable of the three. In Fig. 105, the harsh effect of the second

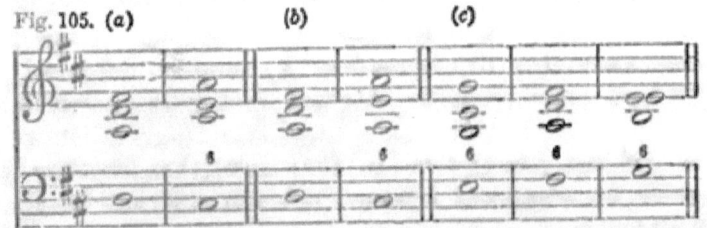

Fig. 105. (*a*)   (*b*)   (*c*)

chord at (*a*) will be felt, resulting from the doubled Leading-note. This is avoided at (*b*). The contrary and conjunct motion at (*c*) justify the doubled F.

146. The chord of the 6th on the *Super-tonic* of the scale (both Major and Minor) is the first inversion of the *Imperfect* Triad on the *Leading-note*. The chord of the 6th on the *Sub-dominant* of the *Minor* scale is the first inversion of the *Imperfect* Triad on the *Super-tonic*. The note which was the Imperfect 5th, to the Bass, in the original chord, is the 3rd in the first inversion. This note, being *dissonant*, should *rarely* be *doubled*. (§ 167 (1.).) In the chord of the 6th on the *Super-tonic*, the 6th, being the *Leading-note*, should not be doubled. Therefore, the Bass-note is to be doubled in this chord. In the chord of the 6th on the *Sub-dominant* of the Minor scale, the 6th may be doubled; though it is more usual to double the Bass-note.

147. Although, in the first inversion of the Imperfect Triad, the 3rd of the chord is a dissonant note,—(disso-

nant to the 6th, being either a Tritone 4th below it, or an Imperfect 5th above it,—compare with § 121)—that note is not rigorously subject to resolution; being often permitted to *rise*, especially in a *series* of chords of the 6th (see § 148), for contextual reasons.

148. If the 3rd in a chord of the 6th be in the highest part, the interval between the 6th and that note will be a 5th. (Fig. 106 (*a*).) This is perfectly good: but,

Fig. 106. (*a*) (*b*)

in a *succession* of such chords, the result would be consecutive 5ths (*b*). Therefore, in such a succession, on a Bass ascending or descending by conjunct degrees, the 6th had better be in the highest part (with possible exception at the beginning or end, according to context); and, if the passage be in four parts, the *doubling* had better be *alternated* between the 6th and the Bass-note, both to avoid consecutives, and to preserve a symmetrical progression. (Fig. 107.) See another method, Fig. 105, (*c*).

Fig. 107.

In this Example, the chord on E is the inversion of the Imperfect Triad; but, for symmetry, the dissonant note, G, rises. (§ 147.)

149. The chord of the 6th may be taken on any note of the scale. The 3rd of the scale, when in the Bass, bears that chord more frequently than any other. The Leading-note, also, generally bears the 6th (or the $^6_4$, § 176; or the 7th, § 190). So does the 6th, raised or unraised, and the descending 7th of the *Minor* scale.

150. When a Triad precedes or follows a chord of the

6th on the same Bass-note, that note is figured 5 6, or 6 5, according to the order of the chords: the 3rd, common to the chords, generally remains stationary, while the 5th rises, or the 6th descends. (Fig. 108 (*a*, *b*).) The

Bass-note had better be doubled, in four-part-writing, as at (*b*); but in a series, as at (*a*), the passage had better be in three parts, unless the student has acquired some contrapuntal facility.

Second Inversion of the Triad: the chord of the Sixth and Fourth.

151. A Bass-note that is to bear this chord is figured $^6_4$, or $^6_4$.

152. The notes of the scale on which the $^6_4$ most frequently occurs are the *Dominant*, *Tonic*, and *Super-tonic*; the inversions, respectively, of the *Tonic*, *Sub-Dominant*, and *Dominant Triads*. It rarely occurs on other degrees, and never on the *Sub-dominant*, except in sequences.

153. In four-part-writing, the 4th of the chord, being the *Root*, is good to double; but, for contextual reasons, the Bass-note is more frequently doubled: the 6th, least frequently, though it *may* be doubled. Fig. 109.

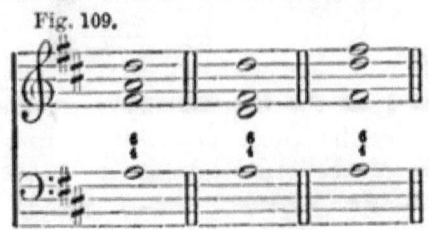

154. Quite the most frequent cases in which the $^6_4$

occurs are, (1.) in an Imperfect Cadence (§ 130), slightly varying it (Fig. 110 (*a*, *b*),) ; and (2.) to precede a

Perfect Cadence § (128,) (*c*); in both which cases it is followed by a Triad (or 7th) on the same note (or its 8ve), which is figured as shown.

When a Bass-note bears two or more successive chords, all those chords must be figured. Comp. § 125 (1.)

In this context, the ⁶⁄₄ occurs at the *accent*, forming a kind of *double appoggiatura* (§ 226) to the succeeding Triad; and the 6th will generally descend to the 5th, in the same part, and the 4th to the 3rd; the Bass-note being doubled. It is more convenient to double a *stationary* than a *changing* note. (See § 153.)

155. The ⁶⁄₄ on the Tonic is usually followed by the Triad on the same Bass-note, with similar part-writing to that just indicated. (Fig. 111.)

156. The ⁶⁄₄ on the Super-tonic is generally preceded and followed by the Tonic Triad, or its first inversion, as at Fig. 112. Moreover, any ⁶⁄₄ may be preceded and followed by chords on *proximate* Bass-notes. (Fig. 113, *a*, *b*.)

157. A ⁶⁄₄ is also preceded and followed by other positions of the *same harmony*, in a kind of *Arpeggio bass*

Chord of the Sixth and Fourth.

Fig. 112.

Fig. 113. (a)   (b)

(§ 244). Fig. 114. Such progressions may be *figured*, or indicated by the *line of continuation*, as shown. (See § 180.)

Fig. 114.

or

158. Except in the case just specified, the ⁶₄ is always followed by a chord either on the *same* or on a *proximate* Bass-note.

159. A ⁶₄ is rarely approached by similar motion in all the parts, except from another position of the same harmony; in which case, however, oblique motion is preferable, as in Fig. 114. When not preceded by another chord on the same Bass-note, if the Bass rises, the upper parts usually descend, to meet it (Fig. 110, *c*), especially if the Bass *skips*; and, if the Bass descends, the upper parts, or at least one of them, had better rise; unless there be *oblique motion* by the retaining of one note, as in Fig. 113 (*a, b*). The chord should *not* be approached

by *skip*, in the Bass, from the *inversion* of another chord (Fig. 115, *a*); *only* from a *fundamental* chord (*b*).

CHAPTER XVII.

CHORDS OF THE SEVENTH.

160. A CHORD OF THE SEVENTH consists of a *Triad*, with a 7th (to the lowest note) *added* (§§ 90, 97).

161. Fig. 116 exhibits a chord of the 7th on every

note of the Major scale. The chords on the Tonic and Sub-dominant consist of a *Major Triad* and a *Major 7th*: those on the 2nd, 3rd, and 6th degrees consist of a *Minor Triad* and a *Minor 7th*: that on the Leading-note consists of an *Imperfect Triad* and a *Minor 7th*; and that on the *Dominant* consists of a *Major Triad* and a *Minor 7th*.

162. The chord on the *Dominant* is expressly termed the CHORD OF THE DOMINANT SEVENTH. Occurring only on that degree of the scale, it *determines the Tonic*, wherever it appears; and, on this account, is of special importance, and claims prior attention. (See § 52.) The chord on G, in Fig. 116, is proved by the B♮ not to be in a key with *flats* (unless in *C minor*, with true Leading-

note); and, by the F♮, not to be in a key with *sharps*: therefore, C is the Tonic.

Similarly, the G♯, in the chord in Fig. 117 (*a*) shows that there

Fig. 117. (*a*)   (*b*)

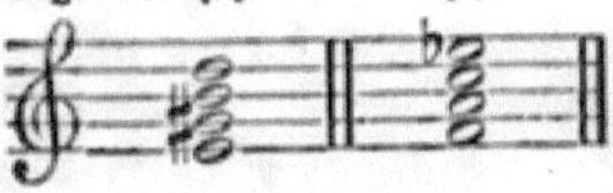

are *at least three* sharps in the key (unless in *A minor*, with Leading-note); and the D♮ shows that there are *not four*: therefore A must be the Tonic, of which E, the lowest note of the chord, is the Dominant.

In like manner, at (*b*), the E♭ and A♮ prove that there are *two*, but not *three* flats in the key (unless in B♭ *minor*); therefore B♭ is the Tonic, of which F is the Dominant. None of the chords of the 7th on other degrees of the scale will thus determine the key.

163. Chords of the 7th not on the Dominant are termed SECONDARY SEVENTHS, or, sometimes, *Simple Sevenths*. *Non-dominant* seems an appropriate because self-defining term.

164. The 7th, in all these chords, is the dissonance, and must be resolved, by descending one degree. (§ 121.)

165. A Bass-note on which a chord of the 7th is to be written (or played), is figured 7: sometimes, more fully, $^7_5$, $^7_3$, $^7_3$, $^9_7$, &c., according to context.

The Chord of the Dominant Seventh.

166. The chord of the DOMINANT SEVENTH, consisting of a *Major Triad* and a *Minor* 7th (§ 162), is the same in the *Minor* key as in the *Major:* the *Dominant Triad*, in the *Minor* key, being always made Major, by the accidental raising of the 3rd, when the 7th is added (see §§ 93, 113), except in Sequences.

The Chord at Fig. 118 (*a*) is not a *Dominant 7th*, having a *Minor* 3rd. That at (*b*) is Dominant.

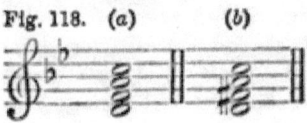

Fig. 118. (*a*)   (*b*)

The Dominant 7th, therefore, determines the *Tonic*, but not the *Mode*.

167. The Dominant 7th is usually followed by (1.) the Tonic Triad: (2.) the Triad on the 6th of the scale: (3.) the ♮ on the same Bass-note: (4.) one of its own inversions: (5.) a chord of the 7th on the 4th above (or 5th below) its own Bass note. In all these cases, the 7th must be resolved by descending one degree; and the 3rd, being the Leading-note, should generally rise to the Tonic, except in the last two cases.

(1.) When followed by the Tonic Triad, if in four parts, *one* of the two chords must be *incomplete*, the 5th being omitted. At (*a*) Fig. 119, the progression of the upper two parts is fixed; and the

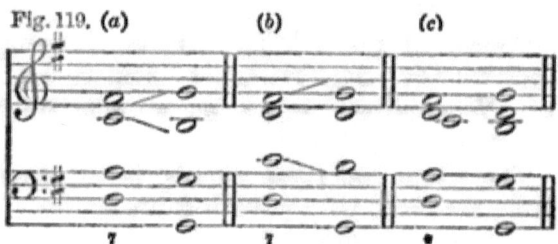

5th could not be in the Tenor of the second Chord, or consecutive 5ths would ensue. Therefore, the Bass-note is doubled twice, in the Tonic Triad. At (*b*) the fifth is omitted from the Dominant 7th, and the Bass-note doubled; the Tonic Triad being complete. If any note be *omitted* from the Dominant 7th, it should be the 5th, the other notes being *characteristic*,—determining the chord as *Dominant*. If any note be *doubled* it should be the *Bass-note*; or, occasionally the 5th: the *dissonant note* must *never* be doubled, in any chord (with the exception of the 3rd in the first inversion of the Imperfect Triad). At (*c*), both chords, being in *five parts*, are complete. (See Fig. 131 (*f*) with remarks thereon.)

The Chord of the Dominant 7th, followed by the Tonic Triad, is commonly used in the *Perfect Cadence*. (§ 128.)

(2.) When followed by the Triad on the 6th of the Scale, the Bass-note of the Dominant 7th must not be doubled, as consecutive 8ves would result, Fig. 120 (*a*), or else the awkward progression and doubling at (*b*). The chord of the 7th should be complete, and the 3rd be doubled in the succeeding chord (*c*). Frequently, when the Leading-note is in an *inner part*, it descends, as at (*d*).

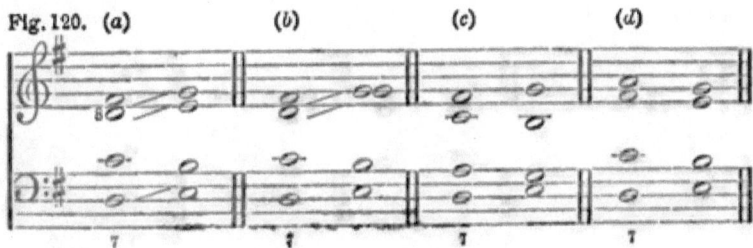

Fig. 120. (a)   (b)   (c)   (d)

(3.) The Resolution of the **Dominant 7th** on the $\substack{6\\4}$ on the same Bass-note is shown in Fig. 121.

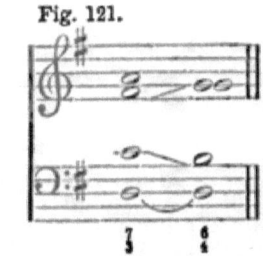

Fig. 121.

The other two methods of following the Dominant 7th are shown in §§ 170, 171, 179.

The Dominant 7th should never be followed by the *first inversion* of the Tonic Triad, on account of the hidden 8ves, as shown in Fig. 122. Indeed, *no part should ever proceed, by similar motion with a*

Fig. 122.

dissonant note, to the doubling, in **8ve or unison,** *of the note on which that dissonance resolves* (§ 205).

The Dominant 7th in G minor, with **its appropriate figuring and resolution,** is exhibited in Fig. 123.

168. A beautiful effect is sometimes obtained by *deferring* the resolution of **a dissonance**; a chord being interpolated,—or sometimes several chords,—in which the dissonant note appears as a consonant note. In all such cases, however, it must *ultimately* take its progression to

The Dominant Seventh.

Fig. 123.

the note below. (Fig. 124.) Occasionally it is *transferred*

Fig. 124.

to another part, in which it must be resolved. Fig. 125

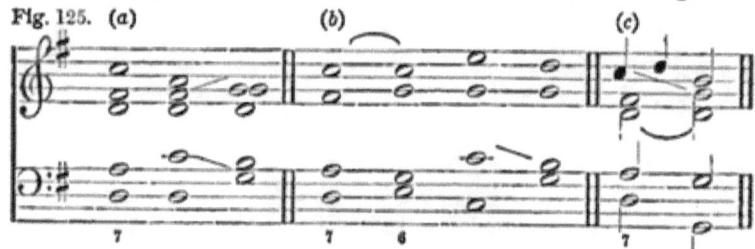
Fig. 125. (a)   (b)   (c)

(*a, b*). Sometimes another note of the harmony is interpolated, prior to the resolution (*c*). Such devices are termed *licenses*.

Secondary, or Non-Dominant Chords of the Seventh

169. The custom and the rules respecting the use of *Discords* have undergone considerable modification. Naturally enough, *consonant combinations* only would be used in the early stages of part-writing. Afterwards, *discords by transition*, or *Passing-notes; i. e.* notes to fill up the distance between two *essential* (and, in old times, consonant) notes, were used; and, likewise, *discords by*

prolongation, or *prepared discords; i. e.* notes which had appeared as *consonant* in one chord, appearing as *dissonant* in a second chord. *Essential discords* (§ 97) seem not to have been recognized. Therefore, it was the old rule, that all discords, except discords by transition, must be *prepared*. Subsequently, the rule was relaxed in favour of the *Dominant* 7th; the use of which, however, was at first considered an innovation. The requirement of preparation for all other discords (except transient notes) was still stringent. This was during the period when the *strict style* (§ 249) prevailed. Gradually, freedom asserted itself; and, now-a-days, discords are used with little—perhaps too little—restriction. No good writer leaves a dissonance *unresolved;* but many use dissonant combinations without *preparation*. In vocal music, however, it is, to say the least, *very desirable* that a *non-dominant discord* should be prepared; *or*, that the dissonant note should be approached from a *proximate note*. The preparation should be in the *same part* as that in which the note appears as a dissonance. Students are strongly urged to prepare them, invariably.

Some of the above statements are exemplified in the *five species of counterpoint* (chaps. xxvii.—xxx.); which, be it remembered, are the formula in which the principles of composition were first presented (§ 81).

170. SECONDARY CHORDS of the 7th are usually followed by a Triad, or a Chord of the 7th, on the Bass-note a 4th above, or a 5th below, that on which the Chord of the 7th has occurred; which permits of the dissonant note resolving by descent, which is imperative in all Chords of the 7th (with such exceptions as are specified in § 168). The 3rd in non-dominant 7ths has no fixed progression; not being a Leading-note, as in the Dominant 7th. (See also Appendix I.)

171. A *series* of Chords of the 7th, on a Bass proceeding *sequentially* (§§ 134, 138), as at Fig. 126, is frequent. If in *four parts* only, the chords will be alternately *complete* and *incomplete;* the 5th, in the latter,

Fig. 126. Prep.

being omitted, and the Bass-note doubled, to admit of the preparation and resolution of the dissonant notes. If in five parts, all the chords can be complete. (Fig. 127.)

Fig. 127.

Alternate Triads and 7ths on a similar Bass have a good effect. In all these examples the discord is prepared, as well as resolved. The last Chord of the 7th, Fig. 126, is *Dominant*.

The Sequence justifies the Tritone 4th, between E♭ and A, in the Bass of the 2nd and 3rd chords in these examples. (§ 139.)

The Chords of the 7th on the *Super-tonic* and *Sub-mediant* are the most frequently used of the Secondary 7ths.

172. An examination of any non-dominant Chord of the 7th will show that it does not, like the Dominant 7th, determine the Tonic (see § 162); not having a Major Triad and Minor 7th, which, combined, are the distinctive characteristics of a Dominant 7th.

Thus, the first chord, Fig. 128, may be in C, or in G, or in E

Fig. 128.

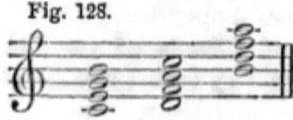

minor. The second chord may be in C, or in F, or in B♭. The

third chord may be in C, or in A minor. The first chord might be made a Dominant 7th by the B being flattened; the second chord, by the F being sharpened; and the third chord, by the F and D being sharpened.

CHAPTER XVIII.

INVERSIONS OF CHORDS OF THE SEVENTH.

173. CHORDS of the seventh have *three inversions*. The *first inversion*, with the 3rd of the original chord as the lowest note, consists of a note with its 6th, 5th, and 3rd (Fig. 129, *a*). The *second inversion*, on the 5th of

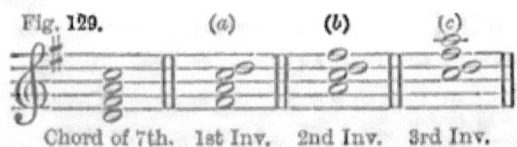

the original chord, consists of a note with its 6th, 4th, and 3rd (*b*). The *third inversion*, on the 7th of the original chord, consists of a note with its 6th, 4th, and 2nd (*c*). D is the *Root* of all the chords in Fig. 129.

174. The Bass-note of the first inversion of the Chord of the 7th is figured ⁶⁄₅, or, more fully, ⁶⁄₅₃: of the second inversion, ⁴⁄₃, or ⁶⁄₄₃; of the third inversion, ⁴⁄₂, or ⁶⁄₄₂: the omission of the figure for one of the intervals *not implying* the omission of that note from the chord.

The *first inversion* of the *Dominant* 7th is sometimes figured simply 5, or ♯. The *third inversion* of the *Dominant* 7th is sometimes figured simply 4, or 2. (Compare with § 125.) ♯ signifies a *raised* 5th : ♭ signifies an Imperfect 5th, and, on the Leading-note, a ⁶⁄₅.

175. The dissonant note, in the original chord, is the dissonance in all its inversions : *viz.* the 5th in the ⁶⁄₅ : the 3rd in the ⁴⁄₃ : the Bass-note in the ⁴⁄₂.

Inversions of the Dominant 7th.

176. The *first inversion* of the Dominant 7th occurs on the *Leading-note* of the scale. The 5th, being the dissonance, must resolve. The chord is, therefore, usually followed by the Tonic Triad (Fig. 130).

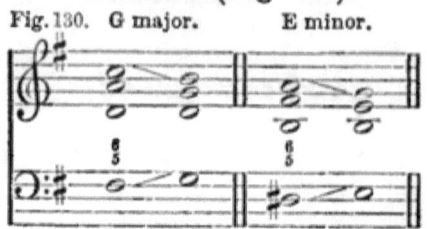

177. The *second inversion* of the Dominant 7th occurs on the *Super-tonic.* The 3rd, being the dissonance, must resolve. The chord is usually followed, either by the Tonic Triad (Fig. 131, *a*), or by the first inversion thereof

(*b*). In the latter case, the resolution of the dissonance leads to the doubling of the Bass-note in the second chord; that note being the 3rd to the Root. To obviate this, which is especially undesirable in a *Major* chord (§ 115), the dissonant note sometimes *rises*, by *license*, as at (*c*); the effect of the Bass-note being considered sufficiently powerful to satisfy the ear. This licensed progression is not so good when the 4th has been in proximity to the 3rd, as at (*d*): some writers, however, sanction even this.

Frequently, especially in the works of the Old Masters, the 4th in this chord is omitted, and the chord becomes simply a $\frac{6}{3}$ on the Super-tonic;—the first inversion of the Imperfect Triad on the Leading-note. In this case, the Bass-note is generally doubled, and the dissonance often rises (*e*). But sometimes the 3rd, albeit that it is dissonant, is doubled, and resolves, of course, in *one* part only (*f*). This is the only case in which a dissonant note may be doubled.

178. The *third inversion* of the Dominant 7th occurs on the *Sub-dominant*. The Bass-note, being the dissonance, must resolve. The chord is followed by the first inversion of the Tonic Triad (Fig. 132).

179. Either of the inversions of the Chord of the 7th may be followed by another inversion of the same chord, or by the original chord. (Compare § 168.) The dissonant note, whether retained or transferred, must ultimately resolve (Fig. 133, *a*).

The ⁴⁄₂ is not followed by the original chord, as the effect of the dissonant note rising one degree is bad (*b*).

180. A short horizontal line, —, over a Bass-note, indicates that the *note* represented by the figure which it follows is to be *retained*. When that figure is the *only* figure over the first Bass-note, the *whole chord* will be retained during the second Bass-note. When an *unfigured* Bass-note is followed by a note so marked, the notes of the Triad of that first note will be retained during the second note. Thus, a ⁴⁄₂ may be indicated as at Fig. 134.

86 *Inversions of Secondary Chords of the Seventh.*

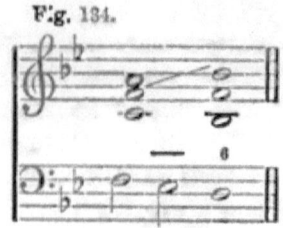
Fig. 134.

(See § 157.) This chord frequently occurs in this context; *i. e.* after a Dominant Triad.

Inversions of Secondary Chords of the Seventh.

181. The preparation and **resolution** of these inversions are exhibited in Fig. 135.

Fig. 135. (a) (b) (c)

The 1st inversion of non-dominant 7ths is in most frequent use. That on the Sub-dominant—the first inversion of the Super-tonic 7th—is often used as the ante-penultimate chord of a cadence, as at (*a*). The chord used to be called the *added 6th*, the 6th being considered as simply an addition to the Triad: a theory quite **untenable.** Beethoven's Sonata, Op. 31 (or 29), No. 3, commences with this chord. (See Appendix I., Example B, *q*.)

The 2nd inversion of non-dominant 7ths is disallowed by some theoretical writers. (See Appendix I., Example B, *r*.)

CHAPTER XIX.

THE CHORD OF THE DOMINANT $\frac{9}{7}$.

182. THE CHORD OF THE DOMINANT $\frac{9}{7}$ consists of the Dominant 7th, with the 9th added (§ 91, Fig. 62, *c*). The Chord of the Dominant 7th is *unchangeable*, whether

The Chord of the Dominant 7.

the key be *Major* or *Minor* (§ 166). The added 9th, however, is Major or Minor according to the key (§ 93): though sometimes *accidentally* Minor, in the Major key.

183. A Bass-note on which this chord is to be written is figured $\frac{9}{7}$; or, more fully, $\frac{9}{\frac{7}{5}}$, $\frac{9}{\frac{7}{3}}$, or $\frac{9}{\frac{7}{\frac{6}{3}}}$.

184. When this chord is written in four parts, the 5th is usually omitted.

185. In the *Major* key the 3rd should be *below* the 9th, especially in vocal writing. The effect of the inversion of these two notes of the chord is harsh. This restriction does not apply in the *Minor* key. (Compare the effect on the Pianoforte of the two chords, Fig. 136.)

Fig. 136. Harsh.   Good.

186. The 9th is a dissonance, as well as the 7th, and *must resolve* by descending one degree. It is also generally *prepared*. The 3rd, being the Leading-note, will rise to the Tonic. Therefore this chord is followed by the *Tonic Triad*, as at Fig. 137 (*a*); or, more agreeably, with the

Fig. 137. (*a*)   (*b*)

interposition of the Dominant 7th with the Bass-note doubled, as at (*b*), in which case the 9th resolves first, and the 7th subsequently. This obviates the doubling of the

3rd, in the Triad, as at (a); inevitable, in that case, to avoid consecutive 5ths.

Fig. 138 exhibits the chord in the Minor key, and in *four parts*.

Fig. 138.

187. The *interval* of the 9th is not inverted (§ 77); nor is it *contracted* to a 2nd, though a 2nd may be extended to a 9th, becoming a *compound* 2nd (§ 70).

188. The *Chord* of the Dominant $\frac{9}{7}$, however, is so far susceptible of inversion, that the 3rd, 5th, or even the 7th (but *not* the 9th), may be taken as the Bass-note; the *fundamental* note appearing in an upper part, with the 9th in a part above it. The dissonant notes must still resolve: the fundamental note, generally, remains stationary (Fig. 139). These inversions are not usual in vocal

Fig. 139.

music, however, except as explained in the next chapter.

189. The 9th may be added to non-dominant chords of the 7th, in which case it must always be prepared, as well as resolved. The non-dominant chord of the 9th is followed by a Triad, or a 7th, on the 4th above its Bass-note. Fig. 140. Some theorists have expounded such chords as formed by *adding* a 3rd *below* the Bass of a Dominant 7th. Fig. 141. (See note, p. 45.) Many theorists, however, consider all such chords, and even the Dominant $\frac{9}{7}$, as *discords by suspension*. (See chap. xxii.)

Chords Derived from the Dominant $^9_7$.   89

Fig. 140.

Fig. 141.

In connection with this chapter, see Appendix I.

CHAPTER XX.

CHORDS DERIVED FROM THE DOMINANT $^9_7$.

190. IF the Root be omitted from the Dominant $^9_7$, a chord of the 7th on the Leading-note will be the result. This chord, in the *Major* key, will consist of an *Imperfect Triad* and a *Minor* 7th (Fig. 142). This is called

Fig. 142.

the CHORD OF THE LEADING 7th. In the *Minor* key, the chord will consist of an *Imperfect Triad* and a *Diminished* 7th (Fig. 143). This is termed the CHORD OF THE

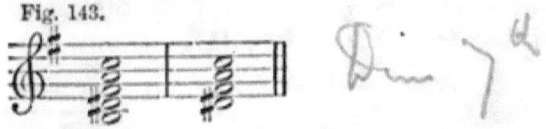

Fig. 143.

DIMINISHED 7th. The Dominant (eliminated) is the *Root* of both these chords; which are termed DERIVATIVES of the *Dominant* $^9_7$: by some writers, *Inversions*, being considered incomplete forms of the inversions described § 188.

90 Inversions of the Leading Seventh.

Sometimes, in the *Major* key, the 7th in the Chord of the Leading 7th is accidentally diminished. (Compare § 182.)

191. These chords are usually followed by the *Tonic Triad;* the $_5^6$ being sometimes interposed. (Compare § 186.) The 7th and 5th, being the 9th and 7th, respectively, of the original chord, must resolve, by descent. Figs. 144, 145. The ᴡ indicates that B is the *Root* of the chords under which it is placed.

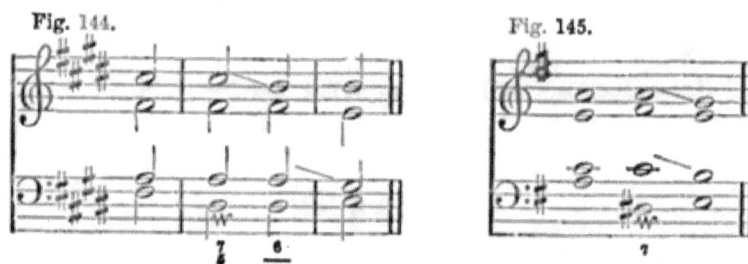

192. The chords of the *Leading* 7th and *Diminished* 7th are inverted, like other chords of the 7th. The 3rd inversion of the *Leading* 7th, however, is not much used; as the 9th to the Root would be in the Bass, and, therefore, below the 3rd (to the Root). (See § 185.) All three inversions of the Chord of the *Diminished* 7th are freely used. The dissonances in the original chord remain dissonant in the inversions, and must be resolved. These are the 5th and 3rd in the $_5^6$; the Bass-note and 3rd in the $_3^4$; and the 6th and Bass-note in the $_2^4$. In the inversions of the *Leading* 7th, the 9th and 3rd to the Root must be a seventh apart, as in the original chord (§ 185). These chords, with their resolutions, are exhibited in Figs. 146, 147.

Inversions of Leading 7th.

Inversions of Diminished 7th.

Fig. 147.

193. The chord of the 7th on the Leading-note of the Major scale may occur as a simple non-dominant 7th (see **Figs. 126, 127**), in which case it will *not* be followed by Tonic harmony, and the Bass-note may be doubled. When followed by Tonic harmony, the chord is to be regarded as derived from the $\frac{9}{7}$, and the Bass-note must not be doubled. The application of these remarks to the inversions of the chord is obvious.

194. The Chord of the 7th on the *Super-tonic* of the *Minor* scale is precisely the same as the *Leading* 7th in the *Major* key; consisting of an *Imperfect Triad* and a *Minor* 7th. The chord on the Super-tonic of the Minor scale will be followed by some form of *Dominant* harmony. The *Leading* 7th will be followed by Tonic harmony (Fig. 148). In the former case, the Bass-note may be doubled, but not in the latter.

Fig. 148. C Minor.   E♭ Major.

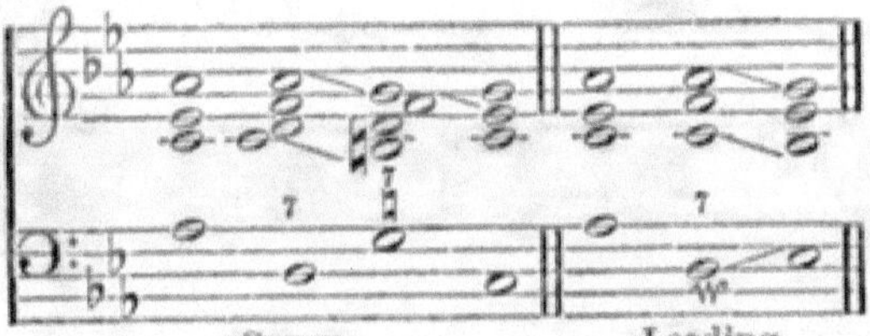

Super-Tonic.   Leading 7th.

195. The Chord of the Diminished 7th, in its simplest form, consists entirely of *Minor* 3rds. All three of its inversions, likewise, consist of *Minor* 3rds, and of *one Augmented* 2nd, which, like the Minor 3rd, contains *three semitones* (Fig. 149). By a change of notation, therefore, a chord of the Diminished 7th may become an

Fig. 149.

inversion of a Diminished 7th on some other note than its own Bass-note (Fig. 150). The chords in the upper

Fig. 150.

stave are inversions of those under them, which are all Diminished 7ths. The roots are indicated by the ᙎ. The 1st chord is in E minor; the 2nd in C♯ minor; the 3rd in A♯ minor; the 4th in B♭ minor; and the last in G minor. Obviously, different notes are the dissonances in these various chords, and the resolutions will, accordingly, differ; as in Fig. 151. (See Appendix I.)

Fig. 151.

On account of that which has been explained, this chord is sometimes called the *Ambiguous* Chord, also the *Enharmonic* Chord (see § 346); the sound alone will not determine which notation it bears. The use of this chord, with changed notation, in *Modulation*, will be illustrated further on (§ 348).

A fine effect is produced by introducing the fundamental note of the Diminished 7th, after the striking of the chord itself; and, subsequently, with changed notation, and the introduction of the changed root (Fig. 152).

Chords of the 11th and 13th.

Fig. 152.

CHAPTER XXI.

THE CHORDS OF THE ELEVENTH AND OF THE THIRTEENTH.

196. These chords, formed by adding 3rds to the Dominant $^9_7$ (§ 92, Fig. 62, *d, e*), are not considered as *essential* chords by some theorists, but as containing *Discords by Suspension* on that chord (chap. xxii.). Indeed, as has been said (§ 189), some consider even the 9th in that chord as a suspension of the 8ve in the Dominant 7th.

197. Neither of these chords will often be met with in its complete form. Generally, the third is omitted from the Chord of the 11th; and the 3rd and 5th from the Chord of the 13th (Fig. 153, *a, b*). Or, from the latter, the 5th, 9th, and 11th are omitted (*c*): sometimes, the 7th also, and the Bass-note is doubled (*d*). The 11th and 13th are generally prepared, and *resolved on the same root:* in this case they certainly have the character of suspensions, and are so exhibited in chap. xxii § 213, Fig. 169. Some writers of distinction, however, *approach* and *quit* the 13th by *skip*, neither preparing nor resolving it; but using it, in Cadences especially, as at Fig. 154

Fig. 154. (a) (b) (c) (d)

(*a*): or, more frequently, only *quitting* it by skip, as at (*b*). Those who do not recognize the 13th as an *essential* discord (§ 97) regard the B in these cases simply as ornamental. (Compare *c, d,* with chap. xxiii.)

Some theorists regard all chords of the 7th as derived from the *complete* Chord of the 13th; and, therefore, as having the *Dominant* for their *Root*. (See Chap. XI., Figs. 62, 63.)

In the *Minor* key, the 13th will be *Minor*. (See Appendix I.)

CHAPTER XXII.

DISCORDS BY SUSPENSION.

198. BESIDES the *Essential Discords* hitherto considered, there are two other large classes of Discords: viz. *Unessential Discords*—treated of in chap. xxiii.—and *Discords by Suspension.*

199. A DISCORD BY SUSPENSION, or by *Prolongation,* is produced by prolonging a note of one chord, during part of a second chord, of which it does not form an integral part; *delaying,* thereby, the appearance of a note of the second chord.

Thus, at Fig. 155, instead of the two chords as at (*a*), the highest

Fig. 155. (a) (b)

note of the first chord is, at (*b*), prolonged during part of the chord of F, subsequently proceeding to the A. The B, so prolonged, is a *Discord by Suspension: suspending* the appearance of A.

200. A Discord by Suspension is always *one degree* only from the note which it delays: generally one degree *above* it, but sometimes one degree *below* it, producing a *rising* suspension.

201. Thus, for a Suspension, three processes are requisite: (*a*) *Preparation:* the appearance of the note in the first chord, as an essential note: (*b*) *Percussion* (or *Retention*, as by a *tie*): the appearance of the note, as a discord, in the second chord: (*c*) *Resolution:* its progression, by one degree, to the proper note of the second chord.

The *Preparation* should generally be *at least equal* in length to the Suspension; except in slow time, when it is sometimes shorter, in which case the note should be repeated, not tied (§ 287).

202. A Discord by Suspension always appears at the *accented* part of a measure or beat; with occasional exceptions in *Triple time*, when it sometimes appears at the *second beat* of the measure.

203. The note deferred by a Suspension should not appear, in another part, *during the Suspension;* nor its 8ve (Fig. 156), with the exception of the cases in which the 8ve

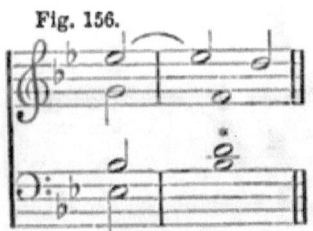

Fig. 156.

to the *Bass* is delayed, either by the suspension of the 9th (Fig. 159, *b*), or by that of the Major 7th (Fig. 159, *c*). Occasional exceptions occur, when the *Root* of a chord, though not in the Bass, is delayed by a Suspension; in which case the 8ve to that Root may appear in a lower part to that in which the Suspension occurs.

It follows, from this rule, that the Suspension of the 2nd, resolving into a unison, is inadmissible.

204. A Suspension should never be used to disguise a bad progression: in other words, it is not good, unless that which it delays is good,—the passage being pure without the Suspension.

Therefore, such progressions as those in Fig. 157 (*a*, *b*) are ob-

jectionable, because of the implied consecutives, only broken by the Suspensions: and that at (*c*) is faulty, because the progression of the Leading-note in the Alto is hindered by the Suspension.

Exceptions to this rule are to be found in good writers; but the student should be cautious in departing from it.

205. No part should proceed, by skip of a 3rd, to the note (or its 8ve) on which a Suspension is resolved, on account of the strong effect of implied, or covered consecutives, as indicated in Fig. 158 by the small note. (Compare with § 167.)

206. Two, three, or more notes may be suspended simultaneously, producing Double or Triple Suspensions, &c.

With these general explanations, the student will be prepared to consider the particular Suspensions introduced on the different chords.

Suspensions on the Triad.

207. These, with the appropriate figuring, are exhibited in Fig. 159, which must be carefully studied.

In all these examples the suspended note is *joined* (by a tie) to that which prepares it. This is most usual, but not invariable: the

Suspensions on the Triad.

Fig. 159.

note may be *repeated* instead of *prolonged*. In all cases, however, the preparation *must* be in the *same part* as the Suspension.

The figuring 4 3 at (a) must be distinguished from $\frac{4}{3}$, the second inversion of a chord of the 7th (§ 174); the accompanying, or complementary intervals being quite different. $\frac{4}{3}$ is accompanied by a 6th: 4 3, by a 5th and 8ve. Similarly, the 9, at (*b*, *d*, *h*), must not be confounded with $\frac{9}{7}$; none of these carry a 7th. And the $\overset{6}{\underset{2}{4}}$ at (*i*) is a *Triple Suspension*, not a third inversion of the Chord of the 7th.

The *single* rising suspension at (*c*) is less frequent than when *combined*, as at (*e*, *f*, *g*, *i*, *k*, *l*, *m*).

The *preparation* of a suspension *must* be an *essential*, but *need not* be a *consonant*, note. It is a *dissonance* at (*d*, *f*), in the Soprano: at (*h*), in the Tenor: at (*i*, *l*), in the Alto: at (*g*, *k*, *m*), in the Soprano and Tenor; the Suspension, in all these cases, delaying, and thereby agreeably varying, the resolution of the essential discord.

In none of these Examples, be it particularly observed, does the note deferred by the Suspension appear, simultaneously with the Suspension, in any other part (§ 203), except where that note is the *Root* of the chord, as at (*b*, *c*), &c.

The validity of all these (as of all other) Suspensions may be tested by eliminating the Suspension (which, in all these Examples, occurs at the beginning of the second bar), and examining whether the progression is good *without* the Suspension.

208. Sometimes the 6th is suspended, as at Fig. 160

Fig. 160. (*a*)   (*b*)   (*c*)

(*a*); but it hardly can be called a *discord* by suspension, being, rather, a *foreign concord*, giving the harmony, in this case, of E minor, interpolated. This is sometimes combined with the 4th, as at (*b*); but this has nothing distinct from an ordinary 2nd inversion of a Triad. As at (*c*), however, there is much more the effect of a double-suspension; as the *Dominant* harmony awakens expectation of *Tonic* harmony, which the prolonged notes delay, and to which they are dissonant. (Compare Fig. 254, *a*, *b*.)

209. The *Bass-note* of a Triad may be deferred by suspension, as at Fig. 161, in which case the Root must

Fig. 161.

not be doubled, at least in vocal music. The figuring may be either of the two ways indicated. An oblique mark / in a Figured-bass signifies that the Bass-note is to be accompanied with the chord **proper** to the succeeding note. This is the preferable figuring in this case, as the $^6_2$ might be mistaken for a $^6_2$.

Suspensions on *Inversions* of *the Triad*.

210. These are exhibited in Figs. 162 and 163: the

first, exhibiting those on the Chord of the 6th : the second, those on the $^6_4$.

Fig. 162. The figuring at (*a*) must not be thought to indicate a *Chord of the* 7*th,* followed by a 6th : no 5th must be added. The

100 *Suspensions on Inversions of the Triad.*

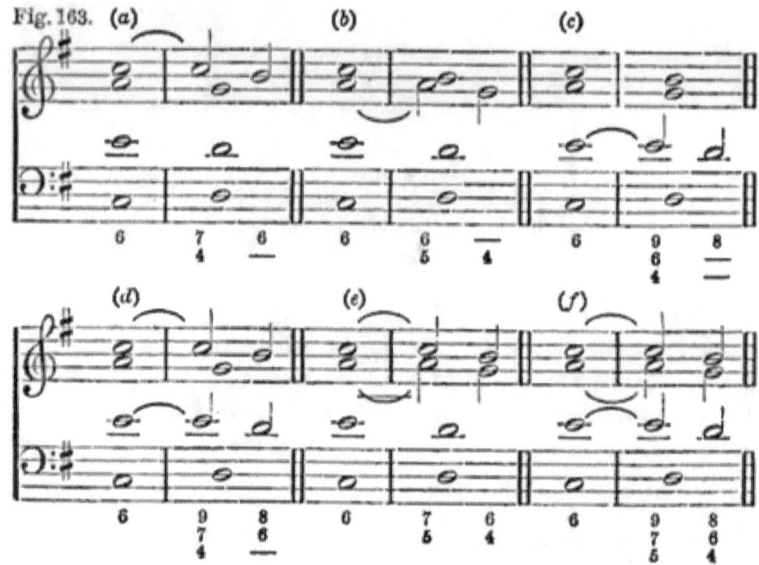

context alone can determine all these cases. It must be remembered that a Chord of the 7th would not resolve on an unchanged Bass-note, unless that Bass-note bore a $^6_4$ (§ 167).

Similarly, the $^9_7$ at (*c*), and the $^9_7_4$ at (*d*), must not be confused with a *Chord of the* $^9_7$, and must contain no 5th. (Compare (*d*) with Fig. 169, *a*.)

Either figuring may be taken at (*e*), as in Fig. 161; the Suspension being in the Bass. This is an inversion of Fig. 159 (*a*).

Fig. 163. Compare (*a*) with Fig. 159 (*f*). In Fig. 159 both 7th and 4th are Suspensions, and (being on a Triad) the 5th is added. In Fig. 163 the 7th only is a Suspension, and, the chord being a $^6_4$, no 5th must be added.

Similarly, the $^6_5\ ^-_4$ at (*b*) is not a first inversion of a Chord of the 7th.

Compare, in like manner, Fig. 162 (*d*) with Fig. 163 (*d*). The

Suspensions on the Chord of the Seventh. 101

$^7_6$ at (e) is not a Chord of the 7th; and the $^9_7$ at (f) is not a Dominant $^9_7$: in neither case must a 3rd be added.

The Double Suspensions at Fig. 164 are inadmissible, on account of the two 4ths without accompanying 6ths, which are very harsh in effect.

Suspensions on the Chord of the Seventh.

211. These are exhibited in Fig. 165.

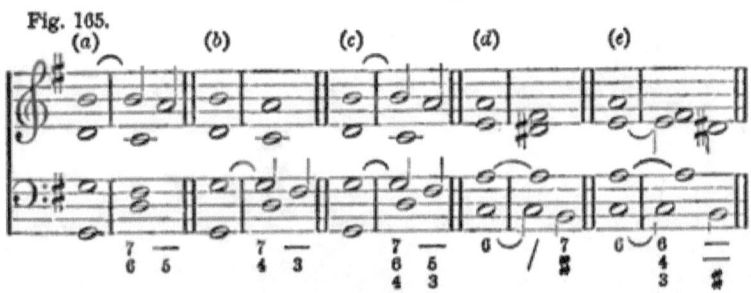

Fig. 165.

Compare and distinguish $^7_6$ (a), in this Fig. and Fig. 159 (g), as in similar cases above. The succeeding context must determine the difference.

Similarly, very carefully compare Fig. 165 (b) with Fig. 159 (f) and Fig. 163 (a), and observe the remarks on those Examples, in §§ 207, 210.

Also, compare (c) with Fig. 159 (k).

The Suspension in the Bass (d) is more frequent in the *Minor* key, as here, than in the Major.

Suspensions on Inversions of the Chord of the Seventh.

212. These are exhibited in Figs. 166, 167, 168.

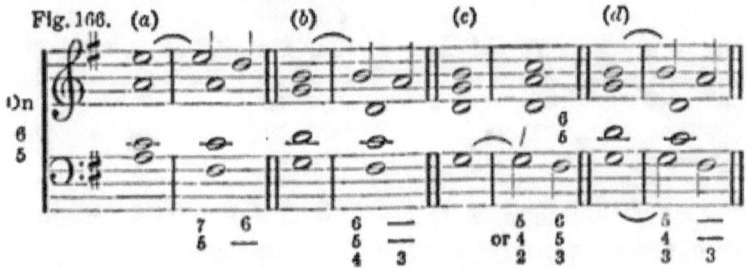

Fig. 166.

Fig. 166 (a) is, in fact, a *Leading* 7th, followed by a $^6_5$. (Fig. 144.) The Suspensions in Fig. 167 (c, d) are rare.

102 *Suspensions on the Chord of the Dominant $\frac{v}{7}$.*

Suspensions on the Chord of the Dominant $\frac{9}{7}$.

213. These are exhibited in Fig. 169.

See §§ 196, 197; and compare Fig. 169 (*a*), 1st chord of 2nd measure, with Fig. 153 (*a*): also Fig. 169 (*b*) with Fig. 153 (*b*). The 6th in all the Examples, Fig. 169, might be figured 13, in its compound position, as there given; and the 4th, if so taken, might be figured 11.

---

214. Double and Triple Suspensions are sometimes resolved *successively*, instead of *simultaneously*.

Thus, Fig. 159 (*d*) may be varied as at Fig. 170 (*a*): Fig. 159 (*f*) as at Fig. 170 (*b*): Fig. 159 (*h*) as at Fig. 170 (*c*). Similarly,

Suspensions on the Chord of the Dominant ⁷⁄₇. 103

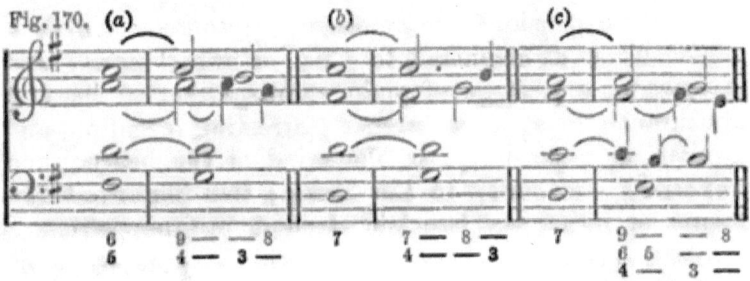

at Fig. 169 (c) the 6th resolves to the 5th prior to the resolution of the 4th to the 3rd.

When a note is common to two successive chords, it may be delayed by a suspension in the first, and appear by the resolution in the second chord.

Thus, the progression at Fig. 171 (a) is better,—*broader*,—as at

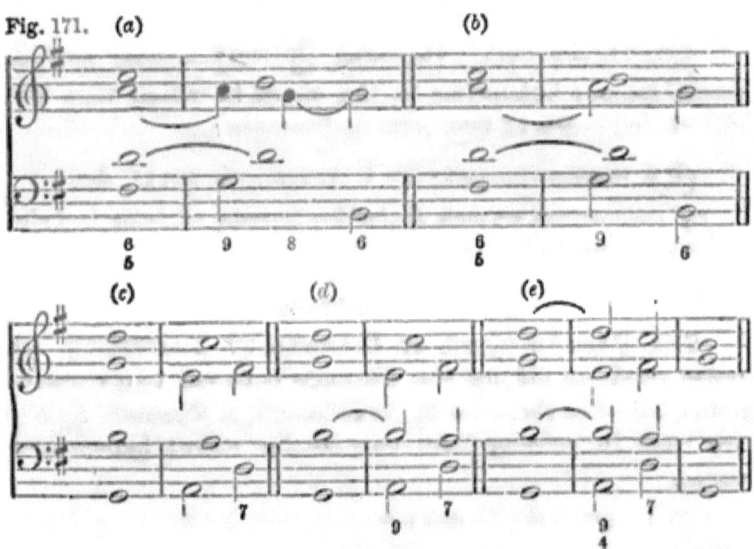

(b). And the A, common to both chords in the second measure at (c), may be delayed by the Suspension in the first chord, and appear in the second chord, as at (d, e). The varieties of procedure of this kind, and, consequently, of figuring, cannot be specified, but must be learned by practice and observation. (See § 312.)

215. Discords by Suspension, like Essential Discords, may be resolved ornamentally. (See §§ 168, 288.)

216. Suspensions are among the resources which a musician has at command to vary, or impart power and interest to, a passage of plain chords, either at its first appearance, or at its recurrence; arresting attention, and awakening expectancy, in the mind of the hearer, and imparting continuity to the Music; two important elements, or rather one two-fold element, in Composition.

Chapters xxviii., xxix., xxx., fourth division, may advantageously be read in connection with this chapter.

CHAPTER XXIII.

UNESSENTIAL DISCORDS.

217. UNESSENTIAL DISCORDS (§ 198)—notes not *essential* to, nor belonging to, the chord in which they are introduced—are of two principal classes:

(1.) PASSING-NOTES; (2.) AUXILIARY NOTES, &c.

By some writers no such distinction is made, all being included under the head of *Passing-notes*.

Passing-notes.

218. PASSING-NOTES, or DISCORDS BY TRANSITION, are notes used to fill up the distance between two *essential* notes, whether these latter be *consonant* or *dissonant*: they are used in *passing* from one to the other: hence their name.

Fig. 172 presents a phrase consisting entirely of essential notes

Fig. 172.

Fig. 173 presents the same phrase, varied by *Passing-notes*, which are marked ×.

Fig. 173.

The judicious use of such transient notes is another resource (besides Suspensions—see § 216) for embellishing, varying, and imparting continuity of movement, and, often, graceful smoothness to a passage: also, when at the accent, boldness of effect.

219. Passing-notes at the *unaccented* part of a measure or beat are termed *Regular:* those at the *accented* part, *Irregular:* a distinction of no importance, however. Discords of *regular* transition are the more common: those of *irregular* transition are, generally, the more bold.

220. Passing-notes may be used in two or more parts, simultaneously; either proceeding together, or by contrary motion (Fig. 174).

Fig. 174.

The last beat of the third measure, Fig. 173, has Passing-notes in Bass and Soprano.

221. Passing-notes, being used in *proceeding from one note to another*, are, properly, *progressional.* Therefore such a note as that marked × in Fig. 175, though *unes*

Fig. 175.

sential, is not, strictly, a *Passing-note*, as it *fills up no distance;* but is generally classed among Passing-notes.

222. When two successive Passing-notes occur, as at Fig. 176, the *second* should proceed in the same direction,

as at (*a*); not return to the first, as at (*b*); on the same principle as that explained in the last paragraph.

223. Passing-notes, like Suspensions (§ 204), are not admissible when the passage in which they are introduced is not correct without them.

Therefore, such progressions as those at Fig. 177 are objection-

able, because of the Consecutives which the Passing-notes only ineffectually disguise. (Compare § 267.)

224. In *Figured-basses*, Passing-notes are often not indicated by figures, unless somewhat slow and important. When occurring in the Bass, the mark of continuation is useful (Fig. 178 *a*). When proceeding in 3rds with the Bass, they may be indicated as at (*b*). At (*c*) is another example.

Much, however, was left, in former times, to the intelligence of the performer from a Figured-bass. It is the less necessary to dwell on this matter, on account of the little use now made of the system of figures, except in works like the present. It is impossible to specify the various complications of figuring that may arise from an endeavour to indicate Passing-notes. Should a competent musician be called upon to accompany from an old Figured-bass, he will generally find the figuring sufficiently indicative of the accompaniment required; especially if, as is usual, the *Score*, or *Solo-part*, is before him.

In connection with this division, chapters xxviii., xxix., xxx., second and third divisions, may advantageously be read.

Auxiliary Notes.

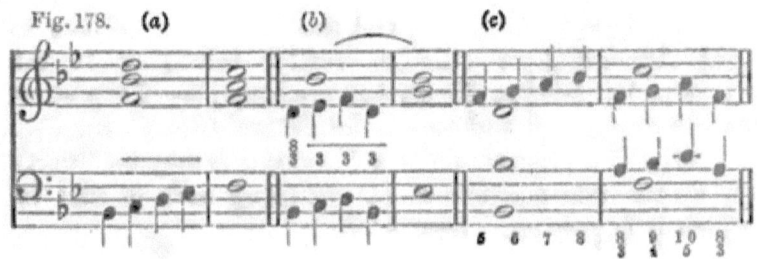

Fig. 178. (a) (b) (c)

Auxiliary Notes, &c.

225. AUXILIARY NOTES are notes one degree above or below *essential* or *unessential notes*, preceding such notes, either with or before the accompanying harmony.

Thus, though an *Auxiliary note* may be *approached* by skip, unprepared, it is not *quitted* by skip, but is immediately followed by the principal note, to which it is a prefix.

226. The *Appoggiatura, Acciaccatura,* &c., are examples of such notes. The Appoggiatura is an auxiliary note to an *essential* note, and is not always written as a small note, but also as at Fig. 179, it being a *leaning-*

Fig. 179.   BENNETT.

note to the essential note. See remarks, p. 19. The *Acciaccatura* may precede an *essential* note, as at Fig. 180; or an Appoggiatura, as at Fig. 181, in which the

Fig. 180.   MOZART.

Fig. 181.

D is an *Appoggiatura* to C, and the E an *Acciaccatura* to that Appoggiatura (though really belonging to the harmony). *Shakes, Turns,* &c., are examples of the alternation of *essential* and *unessential* notes. (See § 38).

227. The progression of a *Passing-note* may be diverted by the interposition of an *Auxiliary* note to that to which it is passing. (See § 275.)

Thus, Fig. 182 (*a*) may be altered as at (*b*) the C being an *Appoggiatura* to the B.

Fig. 182. (*a*) (*b*)

Similarly, the passage at Fig. 183 (*a*) may be changed by the

Fig. 183. (*a*) (*b*) &c.
(*c*) &c. (*d*)

unessential notes (×) at (*b*): or as at (*c*): or by these combined, as at (*d*): an example from Chopin's *Studies*. Thus, an Unessential note, *succeeding* an Essential note, may be quitted by skip, for an Unessential note *preceding* another Essential note. In both cases the Unessential note is distant *one degree* from an Essential note. In no case must it be approached *and* quitted by skip.

228. *Anticipations.* — Sometimes a note, *un-essential* (Fig. 184, *a*, ×) or *essential* (*b*, ×) is *anticipated* during the previous harmony.

Fig. 184. (*a*) (*b*)

229. *Retardations*.—On the other hand, the appearance of a note in a chord may be *retarded*, by the prolongation of a note in the previous chord; such retardation differing from an ordinary *Suspension*, in that the prolonged note may proceed by *skip*, instead of resolving by proceeding one degree (Fig. 185). Such retardations are sometimes termed *Driving-notes*.

Fig. 185.

These various procedures are here mentioned to explain notes and progressions to be found in the works of good composers, but respecting which no rules can be given to the student. Experience, judgment, and taste can alone determine the propriety of their use.

CHAPTER XXIV.

CHROMATIC CHORDS, AND CHROMATIC ALTERATIONS OF CHORDS.

230. STRICTLY speaking, a CHROMATIC CHORD is one that contains a *Chromatic Interval*, e. g. a *Dominant* $^9_7$ in the *Minor key*, which has a Diminished 7th. This, however, is not the sense in which the term is customarily used by musicians. By a *Chromatic Chord* is meant a chord in which one or more of the notes of a Diatonic Chord is chromatically altered (§§ 50, 64). Thus, as will be seen, a chord which contains only *Diatonic Intervals* may be termed *Chromatic;* which is anomalous, but, nevertheless, customary.

231. The *Major Triad* may be chromatically altered by the Augmentation of its 5th. This is termed the AUGMENTED, or EXTREME TRIAD. Its *Inversions* are subject to similar alteration. The progression of a *Chro-*

matically *raised* note is to *ascend*, forming part of the ascending *Chromatic Scale*. Therefore, these chords are usually followed as at Fig. **186.**

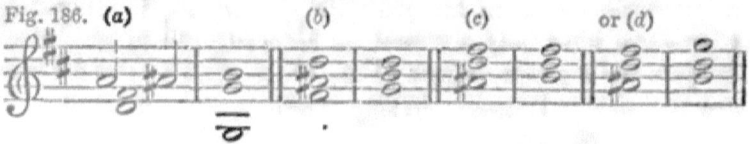
Fig. 186. (a)   (b)   (c)   or (d)

The Root, likewise, of a *Major Triad* may be chromatically raised, producing an *Imperfect*, or DIMINISHED TRIAD ; not occurring on the Leading-note, and not having the Dominant for its root.

Thus, in Fig. 187 (*a*), the D♯ is simply a chromatic alteration of

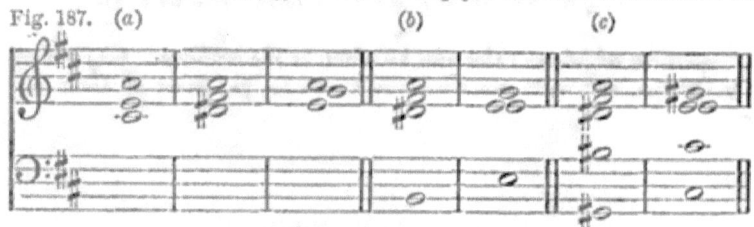
Fig. 187. (a)   (b)   (c)

the Root, and is followed as the Diatonic note might be. If either of the Roots at (*b, c*) be applied, the chord will become an *Essential chord*, the D♯ will be an *Essential note*, the key at (*b*) will be E minor; and, at (*c*), C♯ minor, and the chords must be followed accordingly. Thus, then, the chord on D♯, at (*a*), has a *Chromatically altered note*, but not a *Chromatic Interval*. The same alterations may be made in the Inversions of the Chord (Fig. 188).

Fig. 188.

The Chromatic chord is often preceded by the Diatonic form (as in Fig. 186, *a*), but not always.

232. The chord of the *Augmented* 6th may be taken on the Minor 6th of the scale: this 6th of the scale being Minor by *Chromatic lowering*, in the *Major* key, but Minor according to the signature in the *Minor* key (Fig. 189, *a*). The progression of a chromatically *lowered* note is to *descend*, being part of the *descending* Chromatic scale.

Chromatic Alterations of Chords. 111

Fig. 189.

Therefore, this Chord (sometimes termed the *Italian* 6th) is usually followed as at (*a*) or (*b*). In four parts, the 3rd should be doubled. A chromatically altered note must *not* be doubled.

The 4th may be added to this Chord of the 6th, which then becomes a Chromatically altered $^6_{4\,3}$ (*c*). This is sometimes termed the *French* 6th.

Or the 5th may be added, the chord then being a Chromatically altered $^6_5$ (*d*). This is sometimes termed the *German* 6th.

The *Root* of the Chromatic Chords at (*b, c, d*) is E: the 5th to that Root being flattened, chromatically.

233. The Chord of the 6th on the *Sub-dominant* of the *Minor Scale* sometimes has its 6th lowered, for a certain softness of effect (Fig. 190). This is called the *Neapolitan*

Fig. 190.

6th. These names were given on account of the nations alleged to have first used the chords so designated. (See § 128.)

234. The Dominant 7th, like the Major Triad, may have its 5th augmented; and its 1st Inversion correspondingly (Fig. 191); not often its 2nd or 3rd Inversion.

235. The *Sub-dominant* of the *Major Scale* is sometimes chromatically raised, and a Chord of the 7th taken

Fig. 191.

on it, with the 7th chromatically lowered. This will give a chord of the *Diminished* 7th; not, however, derived from the Dominant $^9_7$, but occurring only accidentally (Fig. 192). Some musicians prefer a different Notation, as at Fig. 194. Fig. 193 is in the *Minor* key.

Fig. 192. (a)   or (b)

Fig. 193. (a)   (b)

Fig. 194.

At (b), Fig. 192, the chromatically lowered 7th is restored to its *Diatonic* form prior to its resolution. (See § 350.)

236. The above specified are the principal Chromatic Chords and alterations in use. But it is quite possible to alter, chromatically, other intervals of chords besides these. Only let the general principle be borne in mind, that a chromatically *raised* note should *ascend*: a chromatically *lowered* note should *descend*. (See Appendix I.)

CHAPTER XXV.

PEDAL-NOTES.

237. THE *Tonic*, or the *Dominant*, is sometimes retained in the Bass, during various changes of harmony,

to some of which harmonies, that retained note does not belong; constituting what is termed a PEDAL-BASS: the term originating in Organ Music, wherein the device is frequent; the *Pedals* sustaining the Tonic or Dominant, the changes of harmony being taken on the *Manuals*.

Such passages frequently occur in the course, and towards the end of *Fugues*, &c.; and are termed *Pedal-points* (also *Organ-points*). Sometimes both Tonic and Dominant are retained, constituting a *Double-Pedal*.

Beethoven's *Sonata Pastorale*, Op. 28, commences with a subject on a *Tonic Pedal*. Bach's *Fugue* in C, No. 1 of the 48, terminates with four measures on a *Tonic Pedal*. Towards the close of the *Prelude* in F minor, No. 12, is a passage on a *Dominant Pedal*. See, also, *Prelude*, No. 22, in B♭ minor. Beethoven's *Sinfonia Pastorale* begins with a *Double-Pedal*.

Occasionally the *Sub-dominant* is used as a Pedal-note; but usually, by modulation, becomes a *Tonic* (Fig. 195).

Fig. 195.

238. In *Pedal-points*, the lowest part above the Pedal-note is considered and treated as the real Bass; and the parts proceed quite independently of the Pedal-note.

239. A *Pedal-point* may *begin*, but never *ends*, with a harmony of which the Pedal-note does not form an essential part.

240. Modulations (chap. xxxiii.) are not usual in the course of a Pedal-point, except, on a *Tonic Pedal*, a Modulation to the Sub-dominant, in which case the Pedal-note becomes the *Dominant* of the new key; and, on a *Dominant Pedal*, a Modulation to the Dominant, in which case the Pedal-note becomes the *Tonic* of the new key. In any other modulation the Pedal-note would not be

either *Tonic* or *Dominant* (see also § 237, on *Sub-dominant Pedal*).

241. In Pedal-passages of any considerable length and elaboration, the *real* Bass-part is sometimes written, in a *Figured-bass*, in addition to the **Pedal-note**; and the figuring written above that real Bass. Often, however, in an organ-part, the words Tasto Solo are written, signifying that the *Pedal-Bass* is to be retained, but no harmonies played; these being performed by other instruments, or voices. In short and simple passages the Pedal-Bass is frequently figured according to the actual intervals of the chords, reckoned from that Bass.

242. Of *Single Chords* on a *Pedal-Bass*,—sometimes termed *Pedal Chords*,—the following may be specified:—

(*a.*) The *Dominant* 7th (or either of its inversions) on a *Tonic Pedal*: figured $\smash{\substack{7\\5\\4\\2}}$; or, if the Fundamental note be omitted, $\smash{\substack{7\\4\\2}}$ (Fig. 196).

Fig. 196.

(*b.*) The *Leading* 7th, or *Diminished* 7th (or inversions), on a *Tonic Pedal*: figured $\smash{\substack{7\\5\\2}}$ (Fig. 197); or, if incomplete, $\smash{\substack{7\\6\\4}}$ (Fig. 198).

Fig. 197.   Fig. 198.

The *Root* of the $\begin{smallmatrix}7\\5\\4\\2\end{smallmatrix}$ and $\begin{smallmatrix}7\\4\\2\end{smallmatrix}$, Fig. 196, and of the $\begin{smallmatrix}7\\6\\4\\2\end{smallmatrix}$ and $\begin{smallmatrix}7\\6\\4\end{smallmatrix}$, Figs. 197 and 198, is F : of those in Fig. 195, C.

243. The *Pedal-note* is sometimes taken in an upper part, and is then termed an INVERTED PEDAL.

In Fig. 199 the repeated D is an *Inverted Pedal-note*.

Fig. 199.

CHAPTER XXVI.

ARPEGGIOS. GROUND BASS.

244. THE notes of a chord may be played *successively*, instead of *simultaneously*. This is termed an ARPEGGIO (*Arpeggiare*, to play the harp: chords being frequently played in this manner on that instrument).

Thus, the series of chords at Fig. 200 (*a*) may be played as at (*b*, *c*, *d*), &c.

245. *Arpeggios* are not good, unless the chords which they represent are good.

Fig. 200. (*a*)   (*b*)

Thus, the passage at Fig. 201 (a) is objectionable, because the passage of chords at (b), *represented* by the *Arpeggios*, is bad, on account of the consecutive 8ves and 5ths.

246. *Auxiliary notes* may be intermixed with the essential notes of an *Arpeggio*, as at Fig. 202: another form of the passage at Fig. 200.

247. The various devices of Harmony which have been treated of, open up considerable resources to a musician for presenting the same passage, in Melody, Bass, or Harmony, in different aspects. The same Bass, for example, may be repeated with different positions of the same harmony, with different harmonies, with suspensions, unessential notes, &c. A Bass thus repeated, with varied accompaniments, is termed a GROUND BASS.

CHAPTER XXVII.

GENERAL OBSERVATIONS ON COUNTERPOINT.

248. THE signification of the term COUNTERPOINT, distinction from, and in connection with, *Harmony*, has been explained (§§ 79, 81). In case, however, a fuller answer be desired to the natural question often asked,—What is the difference between Harmony and Counterpoint?—the following observations are offered.

Whereas, in studying *Harmony*, the nature and treatment of chords are considered; and the student learns how to fill up a *Figured Bass*, or to harmonize a *Melody*,—such melody being predominant, and the other parts more or less subordinate: in studying *Counterpoint*, he learns how to add one or more parts to a given musical phrase, or *Subject*, as it is termed, either *above* or *below* it, or both; such parts not being subordinate, but of equal individuality with the subject itself. He thus learns to treat the same subject either as a lower, upper, or middle part; and to enhance its interest by developing its resources, and illustrating its suggestiveness.

Still further, the capability in a subject of different *forms* of accompaniment is shown: not merely different *harmonies* (see § 247), but different *manners* of treatment, termed the FIVE SPECIES of COUNTERPOINT. The student is thus trained to the consideration of the susceptibilities, in a musical idea, of being presented in a variety of aspects;—one of the first essentials of interesting musical composition. A *contrapuntal passage* is understood by musicians to be not merely a well-ordered *succession of chords*, but a *combination of melodies*, more or less equally interesting and contrasted. One great cause of the unflagging interest excited and sustained by the larger number of Handel's Choruses (for example) is that, by marvellous contrapuntal skill, the same idea is presented in such various forms; and, moreover, such interest and individuality are imparted to each voice-part, that, more or less consciously and intelligently, the listener is compelled to follow four or more simultaneous *careers*, bearing relation to one another.

A course of contrapuntal study, therefore, is indispensable to a composer, who would acquire the **power of developing** musical ideas; while to the non-composing performer or listener, it is calculated to add to the intelligence, and, therefore, to the interest, with which he will perform or hear the highest productions of musical genius and art.

Undoubtedly, **much that is** learned in studying *Harmony*, is presented, in somewhat different form, in the rules of *Counterpoint;* especially all that relates to the progression of individual parts, and **to the relation of part to part.** In fact, **every law of Part-writing is applicable to Counterpoint. And a** knowledge of **the principles of** Harmony **is very helpful in the** study of Counterpoint. **In this respect we have greatly** the advantage **over the earlier musicians,** who wrote *Counterpoint*— combined parts—before the principles of *Harmony*,— the classification and treatment of Chords,—as we now understand them, had been enunciated. Herein lies some explanation of the comparative crudity of some of the harmonic progressions in the compositions of the earlier contrapuntal composers, of, for instance, the Madrigalian period. This crudity, to modern ears, however, arises also **from the fact of many of those** early works being in the old *Modes* (§ 62).

249. It is considered advisable, as a mental discipline, **for a musical student to pursue,** in **the first instance, a course of** Simple or Plain Counterpoint, **in the** Strict Style. *Simple Counterpoint*[1] **is** *non-invertible*, as distinguished from *Double Counterpoint, &c.*, hereafter explained (chap. xxxii.). The *Strict* (or *Ancient*) *Style* of Counterpoint or **composition** admits only of *Diatonic*

---

[1] The term is, by some writers, applied *only* to the 1st species; the other four being all termed *Florid*, or *Figurate* (§ 250).

progressions and combinations; and does not recognize *Essential Discords*, admitting Dissonances only **as** *Suspensions* (chap. xxii.) or *Passing-notes* (§ 218), the **exception** being the Chord of the 6th from the Imperfect **Triad**, on the Super-tonic of **the** Scale, which has a dissonant combination, **the** Tritone 4th. In the *Free* (or Modern) Style, Chromatic progressions and combinations, as well as Essential Discords, **are** used.

This distinction of *Strict* and *Free* Styles is interesting as illustrating the **growth of the art: showing how** gradually musicians felt their way, **using very cautiously that which was** at all questionable,—(a caution which it is so desirable for the student to observe;) how they seem to have written under such restraint **as we** may think needless, and with so few available or permitted **resources;** and yet wrote such noble works: a lesson well worth pondering by **the student.** The use of Essential Discords—the Dominant 7th [1]—was, at first, considered a daring innovation.

The study and practice of *Strict Counterpoint* is adapted **to** cultivate a pure and solid manner of writing. *Free Counterpoint* **is** soon learned after the student has subjected himself to the discipline of a course of *Strict Counterpoint;* from the restrictions of which he will then easily emancipate himself, with greatly increased power, from having worked under them; albeit that they may have seemed to him somewhat arbitrary and irksome.

250. The course of study in Simple Counterpoint consists in **the** consideration and practice of five different manners **of** accompanying **a given** *Subject*, or musical phrase: these being termed **the FIVE SPECIES** of Counterpoint.

It is customary to take a subject consisting of notes of **equal** length, which is termed the CANTO FERMO, or PLAIN-SONG; **the** term applied, originally, to Ecclesiastical Chants, because of **their** grave, plain character. The term TENOR was afterwards applied to it, because it *sustained—continued—*the chant, while Counterpoint (extempore or otherwise) **was** added to it. This *Tenor* being **sung by men with** medium voice, and, moreover, often being the *middle* part, **the term** was, probably, on that account applied to that *voice*, **as is now** customary.

The *Five Species* of Counterpoint are as follows:—

---

[1] **By Claude** Monteverde, *cir.* 1580, though he was not absolutely the first to introduce them.

1st. Note against note: *i. e.* one note of the Counterpoint to each note of the Canto Fermo: *Concords* only being used.

2nd. Two—or, in Triple time, three—notes of the Counterpoint against each note of the Canto Fermo: the first note Consonant, the second, either Consonant, or a Passing-note.

3rd. Four, six, or eight notes to each note of the Canto Fermo: an extension of the 2nd species.

4th. Syncopations and Suspensions.

5th. FLORID, or FIGURATE Counterpoint, also called *Mixed* Counterpoint; being a combination of the preceding four species with some additional features of an ornamental character.

CHAPTER XXVIII.

SIMPLE COUNTERPOINT IN TWO PARTS.

251. IF the *Principles* illustrated in the chapters on *Harmony* have been understood, and if the *Laws of Part-writing* (chap. xii.) have been mastered, the *Rules* which follow will be readily understood and applied. They are, therefore, here given in very brief form.

252. In all Two-part writing, the *two* notes in combination must be considered as representing, in incomplete form, a complete and defined harmony. And the harmonies so represented must succeed one another according to the various principles which have been explained in connection with the different Chords. There should be no ambiguity as to the harmony intended; but it should be understood how it should be filled up, were the complementary parts added. And there should be no *False Relation* between successive combinations. (§ 263). The only Chords used are the Triad and the 6th.

253. In all Five Species, the *Canto Fermo* is to be taken, firstly, as the *lower* part, and afterwards as the *upper* part: a counterpoint being written, in the one case *above*, in the other *below* it.

First Species: note against note.

254. *Concords* only are used in this species, and the

First Species: Note against Note.

Perfect 4th is excluded, having a bare, harsh effect, as a *Concord*, in two parts, requiring the complementary notes of the harmony to satisfy the ear. A due admixture of Perfect and Imperfect Concords is desirable. (§§ 101, 107.)

255. The *first bar* must contain a *Perfect* Concord. When the Canto Fermo is in the *lower* part, the Perfect 5th, 8ve, or Unison may be written above it. When the Canto Fermo is in the *upper* part, the Counterpoint must have the 8ve or unison.

256. The *final bar* must have the 8ve or Unison. When, as is generally the case, the Canto Fermo *descends*, in the last two bars, from the Supertonic to the Tonic, the Counterpoint *above* it will take the Major 6th (the *Leading-note*), followed by the 8ve (the *Tonic*). The Counterpoint *below* it will take the Minor 3rd (or 10th), followed by the Unison (or 8ve). These terminations give the most satisfactory impression of the key (see Examples). They should not occur in the *course* of the Counterpoint: nor should a Perfect Cadence. (§ 128.)

257. The avoidance, not only of *Consecutive Perfect Concords* (§ 103), but also of Hidden Consecutives (§ 104), is most strictly to be observed in *Two-part* Counterpoint, in *all* the species. Therefore, a Perfect Concord can only be approached by *contrary*, or by *oblique* motion. (§ 105.)

Two Perfect Concords of different kind—an 8ve and a 5th—may occur in succession by *oblique* or *contrary* motion. (Fig. 203.)

Fig. 203. (a)   (b)

258. The 8ve should not be approached, even by contrary motion, when the upper part proceeds by skip, and the lower part moves; an effect termed, by the Italians, *Ottava Battuta* (Fig. 204, *a*). The same prohibition applies to the Unison (*b*).

259. The 8ve and the Unison—especially the latter—

First Species: Note against Note.

Fig. 204. (a) (b) (c)

should not be used much, except in the first and last bars, **on account** of their comparative poverty of effect.

260. More than three 3rds or 6ths should **not occur in** succession, on account of their puerility : the parts ceasing to have an individuality.

261. Contrary and oblique motion are preferable to similar. The latter is generally to be avoided, if practicable, when both parts skip. Especially avoid proceeding, by similar motion, to a higher note, in the lower part, than the upper part had in the previous combination ; or, *vice versâ*, to a lower note, in the upper part, than the under part had (**Fig. 205,** *a*, *b*). This is occasionally inevitable, however.

Fig. 205. (a) (b)

262. All the progressions, in **individual** parts, prohibited in § 108, are rigidly forbidden in Strict Counterpoint. **By the older** theoretical writers, the skip of a *Major* 6th was **forbidden,** on account of its *alleged* difficulty to sing.

The skip of an Imperfect 5th and that of a Minor 7th are generally followed **as** at Fig. **206 (compare** § 108, Fig. 78) ; it being a

Fig. 206. (a) (b) (c) (d)

general principle in melody, that **of two notes** in *succession*, embracing a *dissonant interval*, the *latter* one, at least, should take the progression that it would have taken had those notes appeared in combination (compare Fig. 78 with **Fig.** 206). These **two** skips were forbidden, in **the** strictest Counterpoint, however. Generally, after **a** wide skip, **in** either direction, even by a *consonant* interval, there had better be a *return :* not a further progression in **the same** direction, which disturbs the compactness of the melody, **or indi-**

vidual part (§ 107). To this, however, **there are inevitable exceptions.**

The skip of a Major 7th is forbidden because difficult to sing; and this difficulty is not evaded by the interpolation of one note, approached and quitted by skip (Fig. 207); unless, sometimes, in

Fig. 207.

ascending, by **the 5th to** the lower note, or the 2nd or 6th to that note; in which latter cases, however, the formerly forbidden Major 6th (see above) occurs (Fig. 208, *a*, *b*, *c*).

Fig 208. (*a*)   (*b*)   (*c*)

263. **It is** forbidden to have, between **a note of the Canto Fermo in one** bar, and a note **of the Counterpoint** in the next measure (or *vice versâ*), **the Interval of the** *Tritone*, when both parts proceed **a** 2nd (Fig. 209, *a*, *b*,

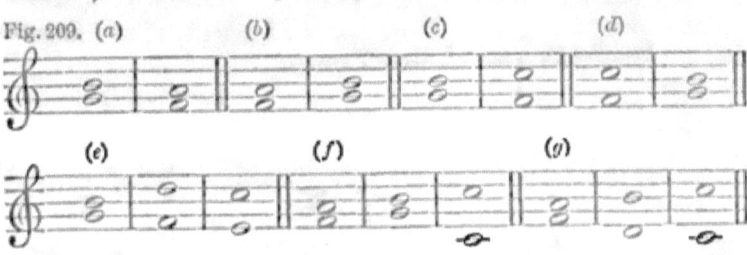

Fig. 209. (*a*)   (*b*)   (*c*)   (*d*)

(*e*)   (*f*)   (*g*)

c, *d*). When one part skips, it is permitted (*e*, *g*). The breach of this rule occasions that which is termed the *False Relation of the Tritone:* or, in old form of expression, *Mi contra Fa.*

This requires further explanation. The abhorrence with which the Ancients regarded the Tritone arose partly from their system of music being founded on the *Tetrachord*, in which the Tritone had no place. The juxtaposition, then, of two notes a Tritone apart, gave the impression of two *Modes*, not related to one another; or, in our modern language, of two unrelated *Keys*. Subsequently, when the system of *Hexachords* was introduced (§ 62), the Tritone, similarly, had no place; except by bringing into close connection the *Mi* (3rd note) of the *Hard Hexachord* with the *Fa* (4th note) of the

Natural Hexachord: which was considered a confusion, or *False Relation* of keys. For the 7th note (*Si* or B) was not added to the *Natural Hexachord* as yet. The hard effect of the Tritone was often avoided by *flattening* the Si (B *mollis*: from which *bémol*, originally applied to B flat *only*, but subsequently to *all* flats). Ultimately the Germans retained the name B for B♭; and called B♮, H (§ 5), on account of the resemblance of ♮ to ♭. In our modern phraseology, it would be more correct to describe the *False Relation of the Tritone* as *Fa contra Si*, than, according to the old nomenclature, *Mi contra Fa*.

The *Sol* and *Si*, Fig. 209 (*a*), if regarded as *Dominant* harmony in C, suggest *Tonic* harmony, or that of the 6th of the Scale, to follow. If, however, followed as at (*e*), the progression is simply *deferred*. The progression at (*d*) is less unpleasant than that at (*c*), but still to be avoided, in Two-part Counterpoint.

Some writers permit an exception to this rule, in approaching a cadence, as at (*f*). This is preferable, however, in three or more parts. The progression at (*g*) is better.

264. *Crossing of the parts*, though not absolutely forbidden, is rarely needful or advisable, at least in the *first species*, and should be avoided in Two-part Counterpoint.

Fig. 210 is an example of this species of Counterpoint *above* the Canto Fermo; and Fig. 211, of a Counterpoint *below* the same Canto Fermo.

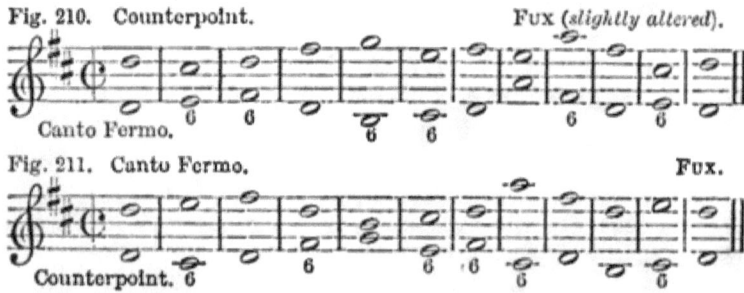

Fig. 210. Counterpoint.   Fux (*slightly altered*).

Canto Fermo.

Fig. 211. Canto Fermo.   Fux.

Counterpoint.

The Leading-note in the second bar of Fig. 210 proceeds to the Tonic in the *next bar but one*, in the original by Fux. But, as has been remarked (§ 109), the old writers did not observe the progression of that degree of the Scale.

Second Species: two (or three) notes against one.

Chapter xxiii. *may be studied with this section, and that which follows.*

265. The *first* note in each bar is to be *Consonant:*

Second Species: Two Notes against One. 125

the *second* note either a *Passing* (or intermediate) note (see § 221), approached and quitted by conjunct degrees, or a *Consonance*. Passing-notes are preferred, giving zest to the Counterpoint; but are not always practicable. The *Unison* is permitted at the second (or unaccented) beat. Crossing of the parts, likewise, *may* take place at the unaccented beat: rarely at the accented beat.

Occasionally, in the prosecution of a design (§ 139), or to preserve a melodious progression, **a** discord of irregular transition—*i. e.* at the *accented* beat (§ 219)—is permitted (Fig. 212).

Fig. 212.

266. It is considered more pointed to *begin* the Counterpoint after a half-bar's rest; and then the first note must, of course, be consonant (see Examples).

267. Consecutive 8ves, 5ths, and, of course, unisons, are forbidden between the *accented* notes of successive bars: the intermediate note not destroying the ill-effect (Fig. 213. See also § 223).

Fig. 213.

Some writers permit these consecutives when a wide skip—a 4th, 5th, or 6th—intervenes (Fig. 214); but, except in very slow passages,

Fig. 214. (a)   (b)   (c)

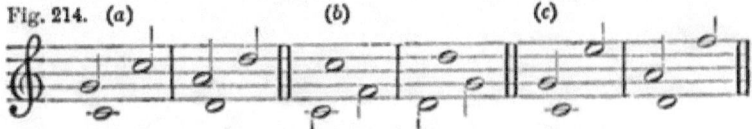

such progressions are of very questionable effect, in two parts; and, even in more than two, between the *extreme* parts. The progression at (*c*) is not so objectionable as those at (*a*, *b*).

126 *Second Species: Three Notes against One.*

These consecutives are permitted between the *unaccented* notes of successive bars; especially 5ths, when they are Passing-notes, **Fig. 215** (*a*), **or when** skips by contrary motion intervene (*b*). The progressions at (*c*, *d*) **are** hardly **so good, except in** slow **passages**; suggesting the effects at (*e*).

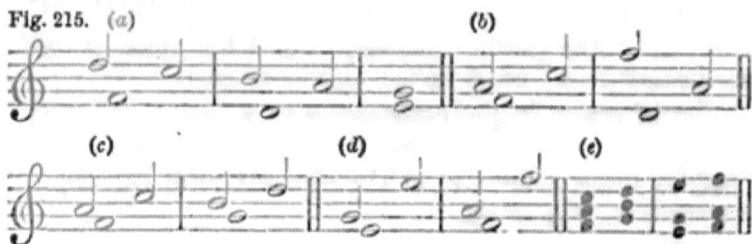

Fig. 215. (*a*)   (*b*)   (*c*)   (*d*)   (*e*)

268. Monotony should be avoided, and melodious variety aimed at. Therefore, the same passage should not occur twice **in the** Counterpoint, **even when the Canto Fermo** changes, as in Fig. 216.

Fig. 216.

269. The terminations available in this species are shown in Fig. 217.

270. When three notes are **written** against one, the second **and** third may be either concords or passing discords: **the** first is least desirable.

Fig. 217.

EXAMPLES.

Fig. 217. (*b*)   Fux.

Third Species of Counterpoint. 127

Fig. 218.

Third Species: four, six, or eight notes against one.

271. The first **note** must be consonant: the others may be either **consonant** or Passing-notes.

272. After **rising** or **descending** by seconds **three** or **four** notes, it is bad to skip in **the same** direction **to** the accented note. The progressions at (*a, c*), Fig. **219**, are

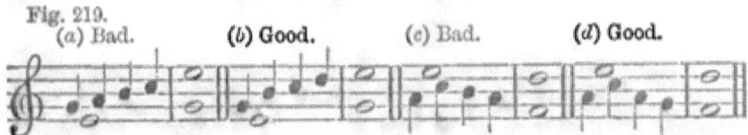

Fig. 219.
(*a*) Bad.   (*b*) Good.   (*c*) Bad.   (*d*) Good.

corrected at (*b, d*), the skip being at the *beginning* instead of the *end* of the ascent and descent.

273. Consecutive 8ves, 5ths, and unisons between successive or even alternate accented notes should be avoided (Fig. 220, *a, b*). Sometimes, however, contrary

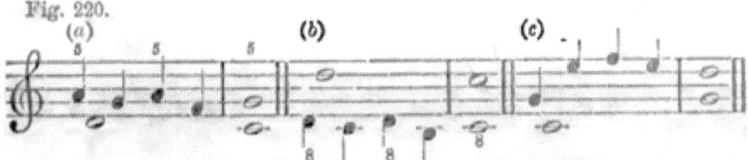

Fig. 220.
(*a*)   (*b*)   (*c*)

motion, and the intervention of three notes, will mitigate the ill effect, as at (*c*).

Moreover, two notes intervening will not generally excuse consecutives between accented and unaccented **notes** (Fig. 221, *a, b*); **nor will even three** intervening **notes** excuse them between unaccented notes, when those **notes** form the *extremes* of the passage (*c, d*), unless in **slow passages.**

274. The ill effect of the *Tritone*, as an interval of

melody, is not destroyed by the intervention of one or two notes (Fig. 222, *a, b*); except when the two notes

forming the Tritone are not at the *extremes* of the melody, but occur in a continuous passage (*c, d*), or even as at (*e*).

275. It is allowed, when the second note is a dissonance, to take a skip of a 3rd, *ultimately* taking the note to which the dissonance would have passed, as at Fig. 223 (*a, b*), the passage being viewed as at (*c*), with

the intermediate note omitted. The note so skipped from is termed strangely, a *Changing-note* (*wechsel-noten: nota cambiata*), or a *Discord by Supposition*. (See § 227.)

Some writers object to this licence, and prefer the passage as at (*d*).

276. It is recommended to *commence* with a crotchet rest in the Counterpoint, the first note then being consonant. The usual terminations are shown in Fig. 224.

277. To write six or eight notes against one is merely

Third Species of Counterpoint. 129

Fig 224.   &c.

an extension of this species, and requires no special directions.

EXAMPLES.

Fig. 225.

Fig. 226.   Fux (altered).

Fourth Species: Syncopation.

Chapter xxii. *may, with advantage, be studied in connection with this section.*

278. In this species, two notes of the Counterpoint are written to each note of the Canto Fermo; and syncopation (§ 27) takes place from bar to bar. The first note *may* be a Concord; but, as often as practicable, should be a Discord by Suspension, resolved on the second note, which must be a Concord, and will prepare the succeeding suspension.

279. The suspensions permitted in the Counterpoint *above* the Canto Fermo are the 7th resolving to the 6th; the 5th to the 6th on the Mediant; the 4th resolving to the 3rd; and the 9th resolving to the 8ve (Fig. 227).[1]

Fig. 227.

Those permitted in the Counterpoint *below* the Canto Fermo are the 2nd resolving to the 3rd (the best of all); the compound form of the same: the 5th to the 6th: sometimes the 4th resolving to the 5th (occasionally, even the *Imperfect* 5th, if it afterwards rises); and, though sparingly, the 7th resolving to the 8ve (Fig. 228).

Fig. 228. Compare with Figs. 161, 162 (*c*), and 258 (*b*, *c*).

The 4th resolving to the 5th is better in *Three-part* Counterpoint.
When the first note is a Concord, although syncopated, it may, of course, be quitted by skip.

280. The rule that suspensions must not be used to disguise forbidden consecutives (§ 204) is of stringent application in Two-part Counterpoint. The progressions in Fig. 229 are very objectionable, on account of the consecutives, broken only by the suspensions.

Fig. 229.

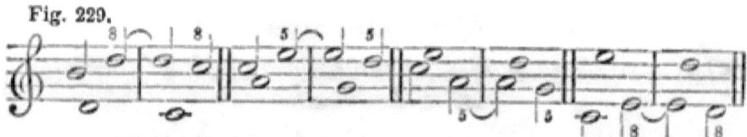

281. The Syncopation may, in case of exigency, be interrupted; but not (if avoidable) in *two successive* bars (Fig. 230). A bar of the second species is thus interpolated.

---

[1] Fux sanctions the 2nd resolving to the Unison; but the effect is bad.

Fourth Species: Syncopation.

Fig. 230.

282. As in the second species, it is considered more pointed to commence with **a rest of a half-bar in the Counterpoint.** The terminations are shown in **Fig. 231.**

Fig. 231.

283. In Triple time, if three notes are written against one, the second note may be either a **Passing-note** or a **Concord** (Fig. 232, *a, b*); or the ornamental resolution may be introduced (*c*).

Fig. 232. (*a*)   (*b*)   (*c*)

EXAMPLES.

Fig. 233.

Fig. 234.   Fux (*slightly altered*).

The third and fourth bars in Fig. 234 have consecutive 5ths between the second notes. This is not recommended, except in very slow time; but thus Fux has it.

Fifth Species: Florid, or Mixed Counterpoint.

284. This Species combines the preceding four, the Counterpoint being varied, and quavers being permitted, by *conjunct* degrees: rarely by skip.

285. Point and variety being the objects aimed at, there should not be *more* than two successive bars of the second or third species.

286. Not more than two successive quavers should be introduced, and those at the second or fourth divisions: their introduction at the first or third division, followed by a crotchet, has the effect of arresting the flow, or continuity, of the Counterpoint. And care must be taken lest, by the too frequent use of quavers, the dignity of the Counterpoint be destroyed. Two quavers are generally sufficient in one measure.

287. A *minim* at the end of the bar should generally (and, if preceded by crotchets or quavers, *always*), except in the last bar but one, be tied to the first note of the following bar, to prevent a halting effect, and preserve the continuity. The first of such tied notes must not be of less length than the second. (§ 201.)

A *crotchet* at the end of the bar should *not* be tied to the next bar, as its progress would thereby be arrested; such crotchet belonging, properly, to the *third* species.

288. The ornamental resolutions of Suspensions, explained in § 215 and Fig. 125, are very available in this species of Counterpoint; especially in a series of Suspensions, to obtain variety. (Fig. 235.)

Fig. 235.

Simple Counterpoint in Three Parts. 133

289. The terminations should be as in the fourth species; or the same varied, as in Fig. 235.

EXAMPLES.

By some theoretical writers, the *Fifth Species of Counterpoint* is to be regarded, rather as a development of the fourth species, than as a mixture of all the other four species.

CHAPTER XXIX.

SIMPLE COUNTERPOINT IN THREE PARTS.

290. In THREE-PART COUNTERPOINT, the Canto Fermo is taken, successively, in all the parts, becoming, in turn, the *highest*, the *lowest*, and the *middle* part. All the rules for Two-part Counterpoint remain in force, unless in the nature of the case inapplicable, or expressly relaxed. As a general rule, the laws are less strict as the number of parts, and, therefore, the difficulties increase.

First Species: *note against note.*

291. The *Triad* and the *Chord of the* 6th are the only

Chords used. The old masters preferred the Triad; but the Chord of the 6th is generally best on the 3rd and the Leading-note of the Scale (§ 149), and often elsewhere.

292. *Complete harmony* should be aimed at as much as possible; but, to secure a melodious progression, or to avoid errors, incomplete harmony may be taken. The *doubling* should then be according to the principles explained in §§ 115, 145, 146; though some writers recommend the doubling of the Bass-note as *always* preferable, even in the Chord of the 6th, and *forbid* the doubling of the 6th. Doubling should, generally, be approached by contrary motion. Similar motion to the 8ve is permitted, however, even between the extreme parts, when the highest part moves a 2nd, and the lowest skips a 4th or 5th (§ 104). In the like cases, the 5th, likewise, may be approached by similar motion. In all such progressions, the other part should take contrary motion: all the parts should not move in the same direction. This last remark applies, generally, throughout this Counterpoint. Similar motion to the 5th or 8ve is still more allowable between the *middle* part and one of the extremes, though forbidden by some very strict writers.

293. Conjunct movement is desirable in *one* at least of the parts, unless one remain stationary, producing oblique motion. (See § 102.)

294. In the terminations, the last bar but one should have a complete chord. The old writers always terminated with a *Major* Chord, even when the composition was in the *Minor* key; unless, which was frequently the case, they omitted the 3rd altogether. The terminations generally prescribed are shown in Fig. 238. The Perfect Cadence (§ 128) may be used, however.

EXAMPLES.

At the 8th and 9th bars of Fig. 240 the upper parts cross, almost inevitably, on account of the structure of the Canto Fermo.

Second Species: two notes against one.

295. One part is to have notes of equal length with those of the Canto Fermo, while the other has two notes, according to the rules for this species in Two-part Counterpoint. Every variety of superposition should be practised: the Canto Fermo and the Counterpoints being placed, successively, in highest, middle, and lowest parts. This applies to all the remaining species: likewise, in four (and more) parts.

296. Some writers permit Consecutive 5ths and 8ves

between the accented notes of successive bars, when one of the parts is the *inner* part, if a skip of a 3rd intervene, as at Fig. 242 (*a, c*); but the effect is generally question-

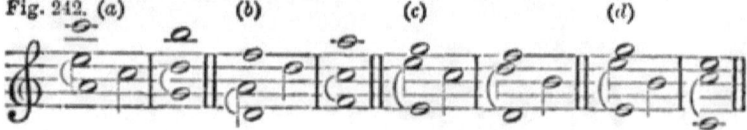
Fig. 242. (*a*) (*b*) (*c*) (*d*)

able. A skip of a 4th, however, greatly mitigates the ill-effect, as at (*b, d*). Such consecutives must not occur between the *extreme* parts.

297. The 3rd to the root should not be doubled at the *accented* beat, except by contrary motion; nor should the Unison be used at the *accent*. Both are permitted at the *unaccented* beat.

298. It is good to *borrow* from the *Fourth Species* for the termination, as shown in Fig. 243; in which other

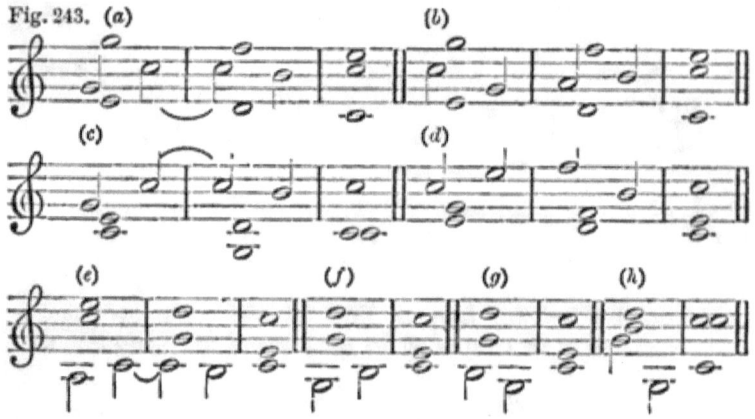
Fig. 243. (*a*) (*b*) (*c*) (*d*) (*e*) (*f*) (*g*) (*h*)

forms of cadence are also exhibited. The upper two parts in all these examples can be inverted.

EXAMPLES.

Fig. 244. O. F. Fux.

Two Notes against One: Examples. 137

Fig. 245.   Fux (*slightly altered*).

Fig. 246.   Fux.

Fig. 247.   C. F., *only, by* Fux.

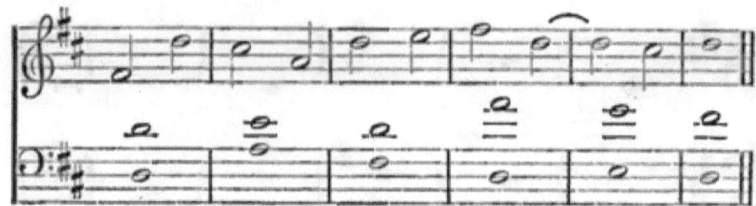

Third Species: *four notes against one.*

299. Nothing has to be added to the directions given for this species in two parts, except that when *complete* harmony does not occur at the *beginning* of the bar, it should, if practicable, be obtained at the *second crotchet* (Fig. 248, *a*). It *may* be delayed by a Passing-note,

however, as at (*b*). Some terminations are shown in Fig. 249.

300. Of course, six or eight notes in a bar may be written in the Counterpoint, as in two parts. Moreover, the second and third species may be *combined*, as in Fig. 253; a useful and interesting exercise, to which the student should accustom himself, as well as to similar combinations, in the succeeding species.

EXAMPLES.

Fig. 250.

Fig. 251.

Fig. 252.

140   *Fourth Species: Syncopation.*

Fig. 253.

Fourth Species: Syncopation.

301. The *Complementary part*, note against note with the Canto Fermo, must be consonant with it, and with the note which resolves the suspension.

302. The *Suspensions* available when the Syncopation is in an *upper* part are the 4 3 on the Triad, accompanied by the 5th: the 4 3 on the Chord of the 6th (see § 208), when, as on the Leading-note in the Minor key, it is a *Diminished* 4th (Fig. 254, *a*): the 7 6 on the Chord of the

6th, accompanied by the 3rd, or *occasionally* by the 8ve: the 9 8 on the Triad, accompanied by the 3rd: rarely, the 9 8 on the Chord of the 6th; the 6 5 on the Triad, as at Fig. 254 (*b*): the *rising* suspension, 5 6, as at (*c*): and, lastly, the suspensions on a $^6_4$, when the bass is stationary, as at Fig. 255; the only case in which the Chord is used, in strict Counterpoint: forbidden by some writers.

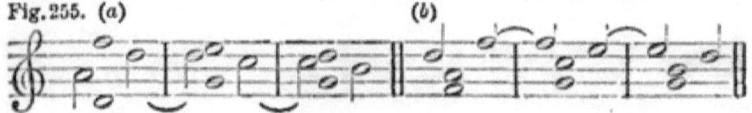

Fourth Species: Syncopation.   141

The syncopations at Fig. 254, if the G were ♮, though quite allowable, would not have the power of *Discords by Suspension* (see § 208). That at (c) is rather *modern*.

The suspensions available in the *lowest* part are 2 3, accompanied by the 4th, being a suspension of a Triad; or by the 5th, being a suspension on a Chord of the 6th; and, according to some authorities, as was said, § 279, the 7th descending to the 8ve, accompanied by the 2nd.

303. Prior to the Cadence, a Dominant Pedal may be introduced (§ 237); and, in a passage proceeding by conjunct degrees, a dissonance to that Pedal-note may occur, at the first beat, even in the Canto Fermo (Fig. 256). The laws respecting Pedal Basses (chap. xxv.) must be observed.

Fig. 256.

The third note in the Canto Fermo (middle part), Fig. 256, is dissonant to the Pedal Bass.

304. The old masters permitted consecutive 5ths, broken by suspensions, in Three-part Counterpoint, as in Fig. 257 (a). The student is advised to be very sparing

Fig. 257. (a)   (b)

in the use of such a progression, especially in the *extreme* parts. With the middle part in syncopation (b), such a progression may be tolerated in *slow* passages.

305. Some terminations are shown in Fig. 258, in addition to that at Fig. 256.

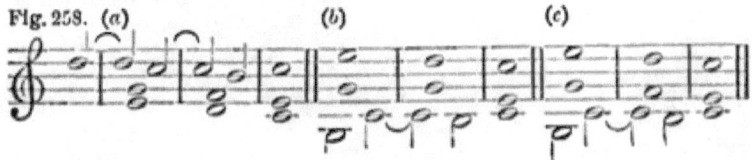
Fig. 258. (a)   (b)   (c)

142   Fourth Species: Syncopation.

306. This species may be *combined* either with the second or the third species (Fig. 262).

EXAMPLES.

Fifth Species: Florid Counterpoint.

Fig. 262. (a)

(b) C.F.

Fifth Species: Florid Counterpoint.

307. Nothing need be added on this species in addition to that which was said on it in two parts, except that the $^6_4$ may occur at the second, third, or fourth crotchets, when the bass moves in Arpeggio (Fig. 263).

Fig. 263. (a)   (b)   (c)

This species may be combined with the second or third species; or *both* the contrapuntal parts may be Florid, as in Fig. 265.

EXAMPLES.

Fig. 264.

C. F.

Fig. 265.

C. F.

In Fig. 264, bars 7 and 8 of the inner part take the second species, to obtain fuller harmony. This is quite allowable.

CHAPTER XXX.

SIMPLE COUNTERPOINT IN FOUR PARTS.

308. THE rigour of certain rules is still more relaxed in Four-part Counterpoint, than in three parts.

Simple Counterpoint in Four Parts. 145

Thus, consecutive 5ths, by *contrary motion*, are allowed between two upper parts; but not with the Bass.

Similar motion to the 5th is allowed, even between the extreme parts, when the highest moves a second. Some authors permit it, even when the highest part skips; but the effect is questionable.

Similar motion to the 8ve should be avoided in the extreme parts, except in the cadence, when the highest part must move one degree.

309. The principles explained in § 101, respecting the distribution of parts, will be highly serviceable in Counterpoint in four, or a greater number of parts.

310. Many successive 3rds should be avoided between the Bass and Tenor.

311. Commence, when practicable, with *complete* harmony.

312. In the fourth species, when the Counterpoint is in an upper part, the Bass, or the other parts, may, occasionally, take a *second* note in the bar, thus giving a change of harmony, on which the suspension will resolve (Fig. 266). (Compare with § 214.)

Fig. 266.

Moreover, in either of the species, it is permitted, occasionally, for any part that has the Counterpoint of the first species, to take two notes in one bar, to avoid consecutives or an awkward progression (see Fig. 269, bar 7 : Fig. 271, bar 7).

313. The species may be combined, in various ways, in Four-part Counterpoint.

Thus, in Fig. 272, the 2nd, 3rd, and 4th species are combined. In Fig. 273, all the counterpoints are florid. In this last example *dotted notes* are used; but, as the other parts are moving, the flow of the parts is not arrested, there being notes struck *at the beat*, which is compulsory. The same explanation applies to the syncopation in the Tenor, last bar but one.

Simple Counterpoint in Four Parts.

EXAMPLES.

Fig. 267. Fux.

Fig. 268.

Fig. 269.

Simple Counterpoint in Four Parts. 147

Fig. 273.

CHAPTER XXXI.

COUNTERPOINT IN MORE THAN FOUR PARTS.
FREE COUNTERPOINT.

314. MERE doubling of the notes in a chord to obtain increased fulness, as in Pianoforte or Orchestral music, may take place without increasing the number of *real parts*. Counterpoint, as has been seen, consists in combining melodious parts, each having an individual *walk* or *progression*. This becomes very difficult in many parts; and, of necessity, therefore, the rules are very much relaxed as the number of parts increases.

Thus, consecutive perfect 5ths are permitted, by *contrary* motion, even between the extreme parts; and a Perfect 5th, followed by an Imperfect, even by *similar* motion.

315. In Counterpoint for many parts, one part may take, as a *transient* note, the 8ve below a note on which a suspension would resolve during the retaining of that suspension (Fig. 274).

Fig. 274.

316. Eight-part writing may assume the form either of an *Otet*—the parts being superposed according to the compass of the voices:
{ 2 Sopranos.
  2 Altos.
  2 Tenors.
  2 Basses. } and all moving together *en masse*—or of a *Double Quartet*, or *Double Chorus*. In this latter case each choir should have *complete* harmony, and its own (combined) walk.

This latter is the form adapted for *Antiphonal* (responsive) effects, and is adopted in cathedral music. The Double Choruses in Handel's '*Israel in Egypt*,' and Bach's Motet '*I wrestle and pray*,' may be likewise instanced as examples.

Counterpoint in the Free Style.

317. Having exercised himself well in all the species of *Strict* Counterpoint, the student will easily pass to that in the *Free* or Modern Style; in which chromatic progressions are permitted, and essential discords used, subject to the principles laid down and illustrated in the chapters on those subjects in the present work. And he may write Counterpoint, not only, as hitherto, to a Canto Fermo, but, likewise, to subjects consisting of notes of unequal length, such as the Fugue Subjects, p. 297.

CHAPTER XXXII.

DOUBLE, TRIPLE, AND QUADRUPLE COUNTERPOINT.

318. DOUBLE COUNTERPOINT is a counterpoint that may be *inverted: i. e.* placed either **above** or below the Subject.

> The word *Inversion* is sometimes used in the sense of *inverse*, or contrary *movement* (§ 367).
> It is here used with reference to the *position*, not the *progression* of the parts.

319. There are three principal kinds of *Double Counterpoint:* viz. Double Counterpoint in the 8ve, that in the 10th, and that in the 12th : the terms indicating the distance from its original position at which the Counterpoint can be taken, above or below. Double Counterpoint may be written in the 9th, 11th, 13th, or 14th; but these kinds are very little used. They may, however, be soon learnt, when the other kinds, which are most in use, have been mastered.

Double Counterpoint in the Octave.

320. Double Counterpoint in the 8ve or 15th—the latter being effected by taking the Counterpoint two octaves higher or lower, or, which comes to the same thing, the Subject an 8ve higher, and the Counterpoint an 8ve lower, or *vice versâ,*—is constructed in the following manner :—

The student should, at first, have before him the following table, which shows what the Intervals of the Counterpoint will become by inversion (§ 77, and Fig. 60).

$$\begin{matrix} 1 & 2 & 3 & 4 & 5 & 6 & 7 & 8 \\ 8 & 7 & 6 & 5 & 4 & 3 & 2 & 1 \end{matrix}$$

In Double Counterpoint in the 8ve the Counterpoint should not, generally, exceed the distance of an 8ve from the Subject, as a 9th would become a 2nd, &c., ceasing to

Double Counterpoint in the Octave. 151

be an *inversion*. For a like reason, the parts should **not** cross, except momentarily **at the** unaccented beat. In Double Counterpoint in the 15th the parts may **exceed** the distance of an 8ve from one another.

321. The **8ve** should not be approached **by skip**, especially by similar motion, as, when inverted, it **would** become a unison, **which** should never be taken by skip, or by similar **motion**. In Double Counterpoint **in the** 15th, the **8ve** may **be taken** by **skip**, by contrary motion.

The 8ve and Unison should, in fact, be *avoided* in Two-part Double Counterpoint at the *accented* beat, except at the beginning **and end**; and, **even at the** unaccented **beat, it is best syncopated, as at Fig.** 275.

322. As the Perfect 5th becomes **a** Perfect 4th, by inversion, it can only be taken (*a*.) prepared and resolved: (*b*.) as a Passing-note: (*c*.) as a Changing-note (see § 275, Fig. 223). Fig. 276 (*a*, *b*, *c*).

Obviously, likewise, even in Double Counterpoint with additional, complementary parts, consecutive 4ths between **the** parts to be inverted are inadmissible, as their inversion would produce consecutive 5ths.

323. The Tritone 4th **or** Imperfect 5th may be taken, **in combination, even** in **Two-part Double** Counterpoint, **especially** by conjunct degrees. Fig. **277.**

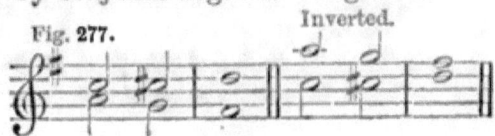

324. The Counterpoint should not commence *with* the Subject, but its entry should be preceded by a rest, as giving more point to the effect. Moreover, throughout, the Counterpoint and Subject should differ in their character and movement as much as possible: the parts preserving their individuality. Fig. 278 is an example from Bach (Fugue 17, Vol. II. of the 48).

325. Two-part Double Counterpoint may be extended to three or four parts, by adding 3rds above or 6ths below the Counterpoint, or the Subject, on the following conditions:—

(*a.*) 3rds, 6ths, and 8ves, only may be used at the *accented* beats; and these, not consecutively (*i. e.* at consecutive accented beats), but *alternately;* and the intermediate notes must be Passing-notes.

(*b.*) Contrary and oblique motion only may be used.

When the parts are thus added, they are susceptible of every variety of inversion or superposition (Fig. 279).

Each part of added 3rds becomes, in fact, a Double Counterpoint in the 10th; and, by the addition to one or both parts, Triple or Quadruple Counterpoint is produced.

The student should complete the examples (*d, e, f, g*); and, likewise, invert the parts in all other ways. He may also analyze the example, Fig. 280, from Bach (Fugue 16, Vol. II. of the 48), in which 3rds are added to Subject and Counterpoint; and superpose (invert) them in like manner.

Although a 5th occurs at the beginning of bars 2 and 3 of this example, which is contrary to the condition (*a.*) above, yet this 5th is really a suspension of the F and E, in the two bars, and, in each case, resolves, ornamentally, at the 3rd beat, as indicated by the dotted line. So that the *letter* only, not the *spirit* of the condition, is broken. The reason of the 5th not being included among the per-

Double Counterpoint in the Octave. 153

mitted intervals is, obviously, that when the 3rd is added, a 7th is obtained, as in the Fig. (*b*). When properly prepared and resolved, however, as in the example, it is quite admissible.

Double Counterpoint in the 8ve is the kind most used, and is almost indispensable in Fugue writing.

Double Counterpoint in the Tenth.

Fig 280. (a)

(b)

Double Counterpoint in the Tenth or Third.

326. This is a Counterpoint in which the lower part may be taken a 10th above its original position, or the upper part a 10th below; or, the lower part an 8ve higher, and the upper part a 3rd lower; or, the lower part a 3rd higher, and the upper part an 8ve lower. Sometimes one form may be more agreeable than the other. The introduction of accidentals is often necessary in this and other Double Counterpoints (except that in the 8ve), rendering intervals Minor for Major, &c.; likewise, the addition of one or more *free parts* may be desirable, to complete the harmony.

The following table shows what the Intervals will become, by inversion.

1	2	3	4	5	6	7	8	9	10
10	9	8	7	6	5	4	3	2	1

The parts should not, except transiently, exceed the distance of a 10th from one another.

327. Consecutive 3rds, 6ths, and 10ths are forbidden by similar motion; as, by inversion, they become, respectively, 8ves, 5ths, and unisons. When there are accompanying parts, however, these consecutives may be taken by contrary motion. Similar motion to these intervals should likewise be avoided, in two parts, with the exceptions heretofore pointed out with regard to hidden 5ths, 8ves, and unisons

Obviously, all other consecutives are forbidden: so that, in fact, from this Counterpoint, *all* consecutive intervals are excluded, with the above exceptions. Therefore, **contrary and** oblique motion are almost exclusively used.

328. The 2nd cannot be prepared by the 3rd, as, when resolved, its inversion would cause a 9th prepared by an 8ve (Fig. 281, *a, b*). It may be prepared as at (*c*) or (*e*).

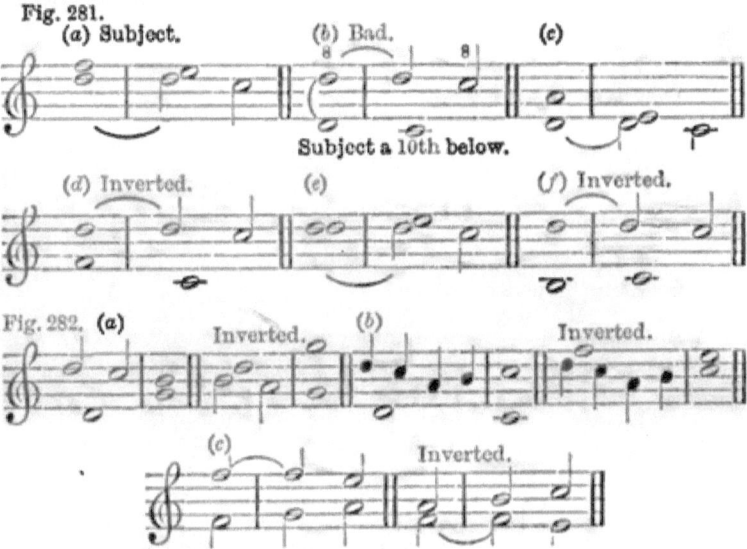

Fig. 281.

329. The 4th and the 7th can only be used, (*a.*) as Passing-notes: (*b.*) as prepared discords: (*c.*) as Changing-notes, in **Two-part** Counterpoint of this kind. As a prepared discord, the 7th is preferred in the *upper* part, in Two-part Counterpoint (Fig. 282).

330. Two-part Double Counterpoint of this kind may be so constructed as to admit of 3rds or 10ths to either or both of the parts, thus giving a form of *Triple* or of *Quadruple* Counterpoint (Fig. 283, *e, f, g*). See § 325, with the help of which the student can work out this elaboration by himself. The general rules are the avoidance of all discords, and of the 5th, except as Passing-notes; and the use, exclusively, of Contrary and Oblique motion. Cases may occur, however, in which these conditions may be disregarded.

Double Counterpoint in the Tenth.

EXAMPLE.

Double Counterpoint in the Twelfth or Fifth.

331. In Double Counterpoint in the 12th, the intervals, by inversion, are as follows:—

1	2	3	4	5	6	7	8	9	10	11	12
12	11	10	9	8	7	6	5	4	3	2	1

The parts should not be at a greater distance than a 12th.

332. The only consecutive intervals allowable are the 3rd and the 10th. These, also, are the only intervals that should be approached by similar motion, in two parts, except in quite free writing.

333. As the 6th becomes a 7th, by this inversion, it must be used either as a Passing-note or as a prepared discord, resolved generally in the lower part, which, by inversion, gives a 7th resolved in the upper part. (Fig 284.)

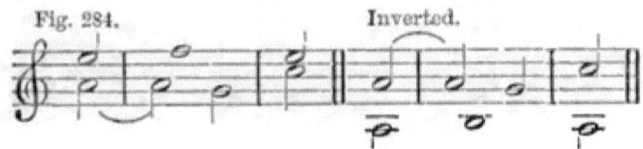

Fig. 284.   Inverted.

334. The 7th in the upper part must not be prepared by the 6th, as that 6th would be a 7th in the inversion (Fig. 285, *a*, *b*). But the 6th may occur as a Passing-

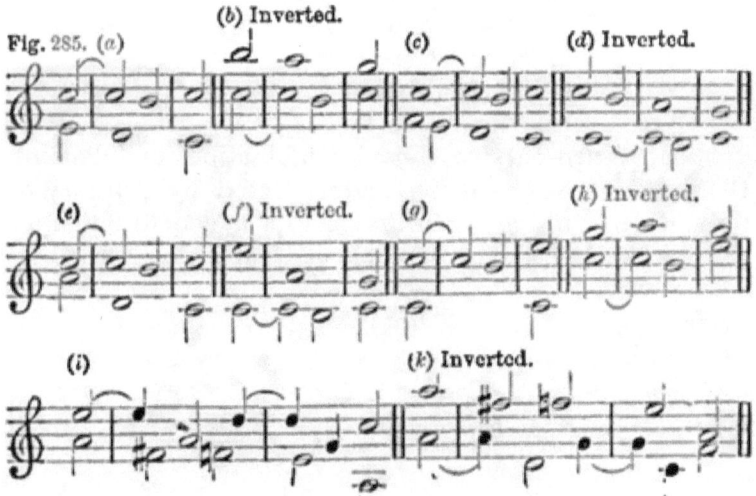

Fig. 285. (*a*)   (*b*) Inverted.   (*c*)   (*d*) Inverted.

(*e*)   (*f*) Inverted.   (*g*)   (*h*) Inverted.

(*i*)   (*k*) Inverted.

158   *Double Counterpoint in the Twelfth.*

note, preceding the 7th, as at (*c, d*). The 7th may be prepared by the 3rd or 8ve, as at (*e, f, g, h*). In all these cases, the 6th, on which the 7th resolves, must rise, either a 2nd (*e*), or a 4th (*g*); or else the resolution must be ornamental, as at (*i, k*).

The terminations, in this Counterpoint, frequently require some modification or addition, as is the case in Fig. 287 (*f*).

EXAMPLES.

By the inversion at (*c*), a Modulation to the Dominant is effected (§ 351).

335. When only consonant combinations and Passing Discords are used, and the parts proceed by Contrary or Oblique Motion, 3rds or 10ths can be added to either or both parts, as in the other kinds of Double Counterpoint.

EXAMPLES.

Triple and Quadruple Counterpoint.   159

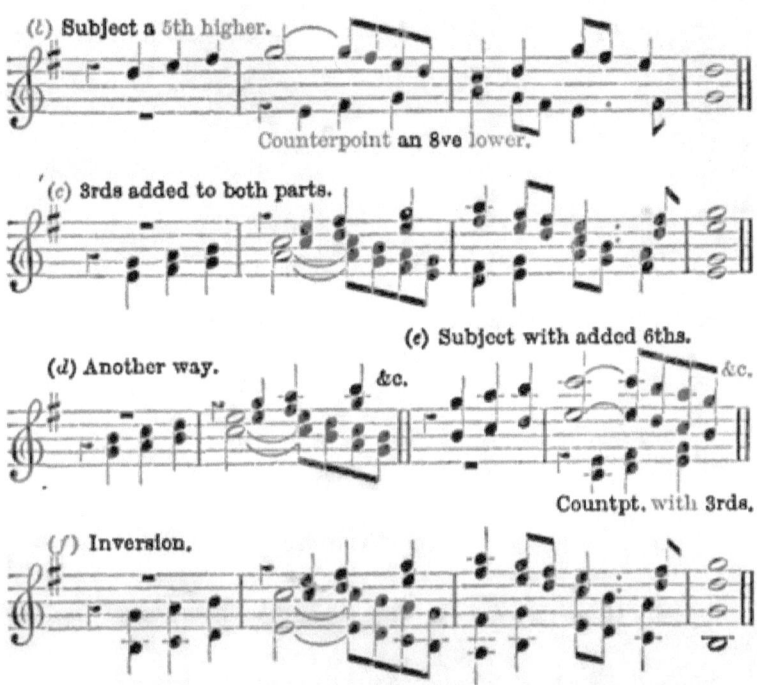

Triple, Quadruple, and Quintuple Counterpoint.

336. These kinds of Counterpoint consist of three, four, or five parts, susceptible of every variety of inversion (in the 8ve) or superposition, either one of the parts making a good Bass to the others. In such Counterpoints the Perfect 5th is seldom used, but an additional free part may often be desirable to render the harmony complete. The parts may cross in such intricate Counterpoint. Beyond these remarks little need be said, as the student who has acquired facility in Double Counterpoint can work out these advanced and elaborate forms for himself. In fact, the added 3rds or 10ths, already spoken of, furnish, as has been said, examples of Triple and Quadruple Counterpoint (§ 325).

PART III.

ELEMENTS OF COMPOSITION.

CHAPTER XXXIII.

MODULATION.

337. MODULATION is the passing from one key to another.

Formerly, the term signified simply a change of *sound* (in Melody or Harmony), without involving a change of *key*.

The term TRANSITION is also used, though principally to designate very brief modulations, to keys not dwelt in.

Most compositions *begin* and *end* in the same key;—sometimes with a change of *Mode*,—*Minor* to *Major*, or *vice versâ;* but few compositions except very short ones continue throughout in one key, which would be very tiresome in effect. Most compositions have at least one modulation; and compositions of considerable length, especially for *instruments*, have several.

338. Modulations into the *Attendant* or *Relative* keys— also called *Auxiliary* keys (§§ 53, 54, 56, 61),— to the principal key of the composition, are the most frequent. These are, to a *Major* key, its Dominant and Sub-dominant Major, their Relative Minors, and the Relative Minor to the original key. To a *Minor* key, the Attendants are its Dominant and Sub-dominant Minor, their Relative Majors, and the Relative *Major* to the original key. Modulation to these Attendants is termed NATURAL Modulation: to other keys, EXTRANEOUS Modulation.

Natural Modulation. 161

Some writers apply the term *Transition* (§ 337) specially to *Extraneous* Modulation.

Thus, the five Attendant keys to G Major are D and C Major, B, A, and E Minor. The Attendants to G Minor are D and C Minor, F, E♭, and B♭ Major.

Notwithstanding that which is stated in §§ 53 and 61, Modulation to the key with the same Tonic, but of different Mode, is generally considered *Extraneous;* as, also, is Modulation from a Minor key to its Dominant Major, although all musicians agree that the true *Dominant harmony* is always Major. At least these keys are not reckoned *Attendants* to the original key by most writers.

Natural Modulation.

339. Modulation is effected by means of one or more chords *characteristic* of the key to which it is desired to modulate. As has been seen, the *Dominant* harmony is that which determines the key (§§ 113, 162, 166, &c.), especially the Dominant 7th, though, often, the Dominant Triad is sufficiently indicative of the Tonic. The Dominant 7th, then, and its inversions, are the Chords most frequently used for Modulation.

340. A Modulation *may* be effected by proceeding at once from the Triad of the original key to the Dominant 7th of the new key, followed immediately by its Triad. Sometimes, however, the immediate succession of the first two chords is not agreeable; and then an *intermediate* chord is interposed,—sometimes more than one,—prior to the *modulating (Dominant)* Chord, to gradnate the progression. Such intermediate chord should be *ambiguous:* *i. e.* common to the two keys, and, therefore, not *characteristic* of either.

This is exemplified in Fig. 288, in which are modulations from G

Fig. 288. (a)   (b)   (c)   (d)
    G to D;   or thus.   G to E Minor: better thus;

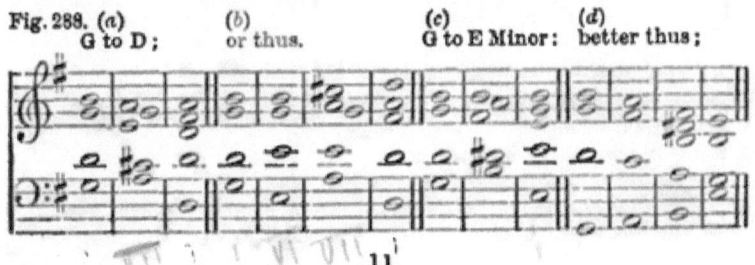

Major to each of its Relative keys, **by means of the Dominant 7th;** and in Fig. 289 similar modulations from G *Minor.* The Dominant *Triad* might have been used instead (§ 339).

In Fig. 288 the Modulation at (*a*) is good: that **at** (*b*) is more gradual, and avoids two proximate fundamentals: the intermediate Chord of E Minor prepares the way for the Modulating Chord, having **two notes in** common with it.

Similarly, the second chord at (*d*), belonging to *both* keys, graduates, agreeably, the somewhat abrupt effect at (*c*). At (*e*), the progression of the Bass is more agreeable than that at (*c*); but the inversion

Natural Modulation.

($^4_3$) of the Dominant 7th is hardly **powerful enough** to determine the Modulation, which is *confirmed*, therefore, by additional chords.

At (*h*), the third chord is foreign to the key that is being quitted, but is not *characteristic* of a key, therefore cannot serve as a Modulating Chord. It follows the Chord **of C** well, however; and serves to graduate the Modulation, which is somewhat abrupt at (*g*).

The first two chords at (*i*) have nothing in common; and, though that progression is possible, that at (*k*) is more agreeable.

In Fig. 289, at (*c*) **and** (*e*), **the** Modulation is effected **by the second** chord; **in both** cases, an *inversion* of the Dominant 7th in **the new key**; **but is** *confirmed* by the few following chords; a Modulation being scarcely decisive till a Perfect Cadence is introduced.

In these, and similar examples, it must be understood **that the representation** is given, **in brief** form, **by a** few chords, of that **which**, in a composition of any elaborateness, would **be** extended over **a number** of bars. Except where the special effect of sudden modulation is desired, one great art in composing is so to effect the Modulation **as to lead almost** imperceptibly from **one** key to **another, by delays, and** ingenious contrivances in the harmonies introduced. These may be studied in the works of the great composers: only *outlines* **can here** be given.

341. Obviously, the Dominant $^9_7$ can be used **as a** Modulating Chord, wherever the Dominant 7th can **be used.** More frequently, however, its derivatives, the **Leading 7th,** or the Diminished 7th, **are used.** See Fig. **290, in which** Modulations are **effected by** these chords.

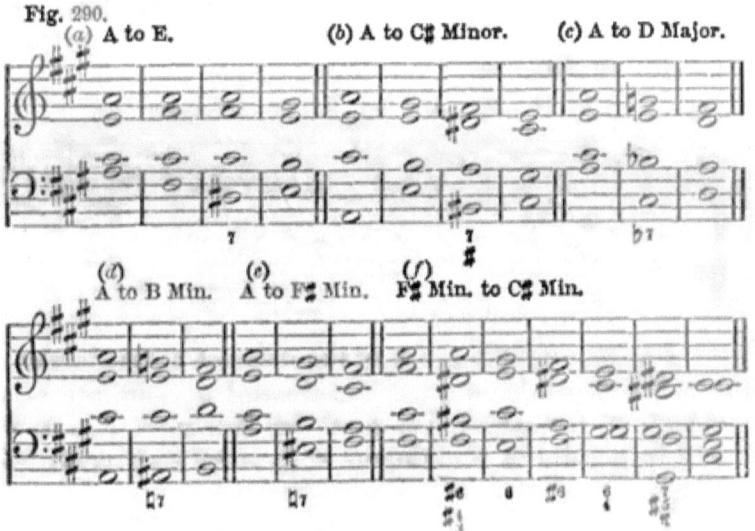

Fig. 290.
(*a*) A to E.   (*b*) A to C♯ Minor.   (*c*) A to D Major.

(*d*) A to B Min.   (*e*) A to F♯ Min.   (*f*) F♯ Min. to C♯ Min.

The Diminished 7th is more frequently used than the Leading 7th, even in modulating to a *Major* key.

The Modulations at (*a, k*) are by the *Leading* 7th: those at (*b, c, d, e, i*), by the *Diminished* 7th: those at (*f, g, h*), by the 2nd *inversion* of the *Diminished* 7th, with confirmatory chords added.

Extraneous Modulation.

342. Modulation to other than *Relative* keys may be effected, (1.) by proceeding *through keys related to one another*, by Dominant chords, Fig. 291. This is termed *Compound Modulation*.

Or, (2.) by taking one of the notes of a Triad belonging to the key to be quitted, and treating it as an interval either in the Tonic Triad or the Dominant 7th, in the key to which the Modulation is to be effected (Fig. 292, *a, b*).

Extraneous Modulation.   165

Fig. 292. (a) G to E♭.

(b) G to F Minor.

Or, (3.) by resolving the Dominant Chord of a Relative *Major* key to a *Minor* chord, instead of a *Major*, or *vice versâ*.

Thus, C *Minor* is Relative to G Minor; but, in Fig. 293, the ⁴⁄₃

Fig. 293.   G Minor to C Major.

on F (2nd inversion of Diminished 7th in C Minor), is resolved to the 1st inversion of the Triad of C *Major*. Thence, it would be possible and good to proceed to any of the attendants of C Major.

Or, (4.) by changing the Tonic Triad of the key to be quitted, from *Major* to *Minor*, or *vice versâ*, and then proceeding to any of the attendants. This is very similar to the last method.

These are among the most frequent methods of Extraneous Modulation, besides *Enharmonic Modulation*, to be immediately explained. The *possible* ways of modulating are, however, so numerous as to preclude enumeration, and must be learnt by the study of the works of the best composers.

343. Extraneous **Modulation is most** frequently made into keys, the Tonic Triads of **which** contain one of the notes—generally the fundamental note—of the Tonic Triad of the original **key.**

This is exemplified in Fig. 292 (*a*): **the Triad of E♭** containing G, the Tonic of the key quitted. Modulations could also very well be effected to B♭, the Triad of which would contain the 5th, or to B or E Major, **the** Triads of **which would contain** the 3rd **of the Triad of G: but these two would** be remote.

344. Extraneous Modulation is also frequently made into keys whose *Leading-note* forms part of the Tonic Triad of the original key, thus rendering it easy and natural to take the Dominant 7th to the new key (Fig. 294).

Fig. 294. G Major to A♭.

345. Modulation to **the** *Double Dominant, i. e.* the Dominant to the **Dominant, is to be** deprecated: *e. g.* C to D, the Dominant to G.

Enharmonic Modulation.

346. ENHARMONIC MODULATION is effected by **a change** of notation: *i. e.* **by changing** the name of one or more notes in a chord.

The Greeks are said to have had **three** *Genera :* the *Diatonic,* the *Chromatic,* **and the** *Enharmonic;* the latter containing intervals smaller than a semitone, termed *Dieses.* In our modern notation we should represent such distances by C♯ and D♭, E♯ and F natural, &c. Practically, however, on all *keyed* instruments, no such difference is recognized: one key representing both notes. But, by this arrangement, the real difference between such notes has to be adjusted or *equalized.* This **process** is termed TEMPERAMENT; and when the adjustment of these and similar discrepancies (if they may be so called) **is effected equally** throughout all the keys, the instrument is said to be tuned by *Equal Temperament.* At one time this method was not adopted, certain keys being left very much out of tune; this manner of tuning by *Unequal Temperament* having, until quite recently, prevailed with regard to the Organ, and being still contended for by some. The Pianoforte, however, has, for long, been tuned by Equal Temperament. This gave rise to the title of Bach's 48 Preludes and Fugues *in all the keys:* '*Das Wohltemperirte Klavier.*' For further information respecting Temperament, the student may consult *Woolhouse*, &c.

347. This *Enharmonic change* may be effected with one of the notes of a Triad, and the Tonic at once changed, without any Dominant Chord; such Dominant Chord, however, being ultimately introduced, to *confirm* the Modulation.

Thus, in Fig. 295, the A♭ is Enharmonically changed to G♯, and

Fig. 295.

treated as the 3rd in the harmony of E♮, with the 1st inversion of which the 3rd bar begins.

After all, however, the *Enharmonic Notation* is simply a matter of convenience in this and some other cases. It is adopted, in this Example, merely to avoid writing in F♭ *Major*—a key not in use. If the original Tonic had been A♮ instead of A♭, that A would not have changed notation in order to become the 3rd in the harmony of F♮, which would have been precisely the same Modulation. So, in many cases, the *Enharmonic change of notation is* adopted simply to avoid using, as Tonics, notes whose scales would require double sharps or double flats. It has nothing to do with the musical relation of the two keys: does not affect the *principles* of Modulation; and is only an *apparently* distinctive method of conducting (generally) an *Extraneous Modulation*.

348. It is otherwise, however, with some Enharmonic Modulations, in which a change is effected in the nature and *Root* of a chord, by means of a change of notation. One of the most important of these is that of the change of notation in the Chord of the Diminished 7th and its in-

versions (§ 195), by means of which different Roots are obtained; and, by various Resolutions, different keys are reached.

Thus, the first Chord in Fig. 296 (a) is a Diminished 7th in the

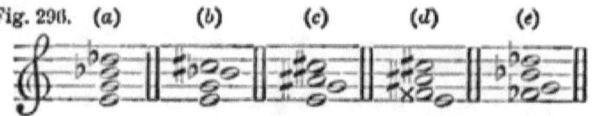

Fig. 296. (a) (b) (c) (d) (e)

key of F Minor: that at (b) is the first inversion of a Diminished 7th on C♯, in D Minor: that at (c) is the second inversion of the Diminished 7th on A♯, in B Minor: that at (d) is the third inversion of the Diminished 7th on F double sharp, in G♯ Minor: that at (e) is only another way of expressing the same as the previous one, being in A♭ Minor. The Root of the first Chord is C: of the second, A: of the third, F♯: of the fourth, D♯: of the fifth, E♭. Their respective resolutions are shown in Fig. 297. And, as each one might resolve

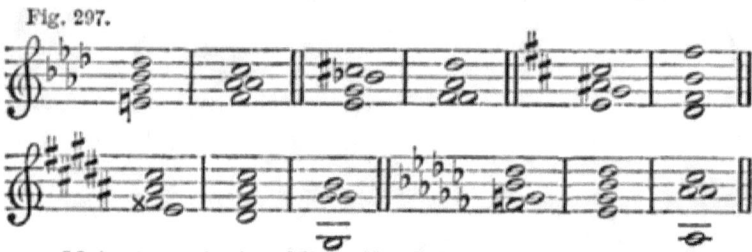

Fig. 297.

to a *Major* instead of a *Minor* Chord, it is obvious what facilities this Enharmonic change affords for Modulation. And as, in addition, each of these Diminished 7ths may be considered as occurring, not on a Leading-note, but on an accidentally raised Sub-dominant (§ 235), still further Resolutions and Modulations are available. This is illustrated in Fig. 298.

Fig. 298. (a) (b)
(c) (d)

Thus, the Chord at (a) is treated as a Diminished 7th on the accidentally raised Sub-dominant in B♭; the 7th being chromatically raised (or, rather, *restored* to its diatonic position) prior to Resolution. Those at (*b*, *c*, *d*) are treated, similarly, as *inversions* of Diminished 7ths on the accidentally raised Sub-dominants of G, E, and C♯, respectively, and resolved accordingly. All these might resolve to *Minor* Chords instead of *Major*. So that, a Diminished 7th, by these Enharmonic changes of notation, and different treatments, may resolve on eight different Roots (irrespective of the different names to the same Root, as at (*d*, *e*, Fig. 296); each of which may bear either a *Major* or a *Minor* Chord: in all, sixteen keys. The very facility of these Modulations, however, may prove a snare to young composers, for whom they seem to possess a peculiar fascination. Undoubtedly the effect of them is often beautiful, and unexpected; but the composer may often exhibit greater power by other methods of modulation than this,—a short and easy method. See, however, § 195, Fig. 152.

349. The Chord of the *Dominant* 7th, likewise, may be Enharmonically changed, and become a $\smash{\substack{6\\5\\3}}$ with an Augmented 6th, and, by its changed Resolution, effect a Modulation (Fig. 299). Such Modulations are generally

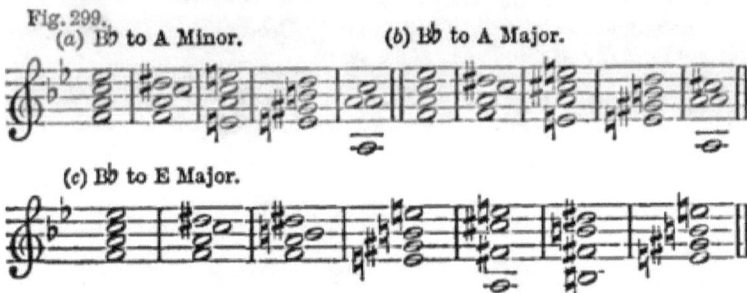

Fig. 299.
(*a*) B♭ to A Minor.   (*b*) B♭ to A Major.

(*c*) B♭ to E Major.

better somewhat *prolonged*,—dallied with, in ways which the ingenuity of the composer must suggest.

350. The *Augmented Triad* may be Enharmonically changed, and effect a Modulation.

Thus, the Augmented Triad on the Dominant of G (Fig. 300, *a*),

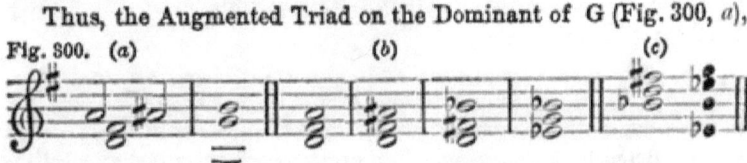

Fig. 300. (*a*)   (*b*)   (*c*)

may be Enharmonically changed to a 6th as at (*b*), being the first inversion of the Augmented Triad on the Dominant of E♭ (*c*), and proceed accordingly.

351. Modulation may be effected in conjunction with Double Counterpoint in the 10th or 12th (see Figs. 283, *d*, and 286, *c*).

352. The first Modulation in a composition in a *Major* key is, usually, to the Dominant Major. The first in a composition in a *Minor* key is, usually, to the *Relative Major:* sometimes, to the *Dominant Minor*. In a *short* composition, such as a Psalm-tune or a simple vocal work, these are often the *only* Modulations. In a composition of greater length, other Modulations, into the various Related keys, or into Extraneous keys, are introduced at the fancy of the composer.

Young composers are advised to be sparing in the use of *Extraneous* Modulation: not to be misled by the modern cry against what has been termed '*the tyranny of the Tonalities.*'

353. Modulation should not be made to the same key *twice* in the course of a composition.

The student is recommended to study Beethoven's *Two Preludes through all the Major keys*. Op. 39.

CHAPTER XXXIV.

RHYTHM.

354. RHYTHM (ῥυθμος, measure, time) or metre has to do with the symmetrical arrangement of music, with regard to *time* and *accent;* music being *rhythmical* when the accents recur *periodically*. (See Chap. III.; especially § 19 to § 27.)

This rhythmical regularity is an important element in the agreeableness of music, apart from the elements of *tune* and *harmony;* as is illustrated by the pleasure with which those with little or no culture listen to *Marches* and *Dances*, in which the rhythmical divisions are strongly marked. Marches are usually written in Quadruple or in Duple time because of the regular alternation, in those times, of accented and unaccented beats.

Rhythm: Periods, Sections, Phrases. 171

355. A musical idea or passage, more or less complete in itself, and terminating, most frequently, with a *Perfect Cadence* (§ 128), constitutes a Rhythmical PERIOD, or STRAIN.

356. A *Period* is generally divisible into two or more *Sections;* a SECTION being a less complete idea than a *Period,* and terminating, generally, with an *Imperfect* or an *Inverted Cadence* (§§ 130, 132); though sometimes with a *Perfect, Interrupted,* or other cadence (§§ 128, 131).

Fig. 301, from Mendelssohn's '*Elijah,*' includes two sections

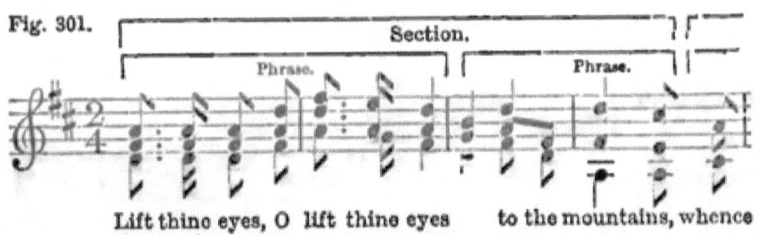

In such a Period, the first Section gives what is termed the THESIS, or *Proposition:* the second Section is termed the ANTITHESIS, or *Counter-proposition,* forming a sort of corollary, or confirmation of the *Thesis.*

357. A *Section* generally includes two or more *Phrases;* a PHRASE being a short portion of a *Section,* its termination having no sense of finality or repose, but being analogous to the division of a sentence into parts, by commas.

A *Phrase* may consist of two, three, or more bars; sometimes of only one. The first Strain or Period of the English National Anthem consists of three Phrases of two bars each.

The terms *Section* and *Phrase* are somewhat loosely and interchangeably used; as, indeed, is the term *Period,* which is sometimes used for *Section,* and *vice versâ.*

358. A *Phrase* includes two or more *Feet;* a FOOT including one *accented,* and one or two *unaccented* beats.

There are different kinds of *Foot,* to which the terms applied to classic verse are sometimes given, though not in frequent use.

(1.) The IAMBIC: the accented beat being *preceded* by an unaccented (Fig. 302, *a*).

(2.) The TROCHAIC: the accented beat being *followed* by an unaccented (*b*).

(3.) The DACTYLIC: the accented beat being *followed* by *two* unaccented beats (*c*).

(4.) The ANAPÆSTIC: the accent being *preceded* by *two* unaccented beats (*d*).

(5.) The AMPHIBRACHIC: the accent being *between* two unaccented beats (*e*).

Properly, therefore, the *Iambus* and the *Trochee,* being dissyllabic, belong to *Duple* or *Quadruple* Time (§ 20); and the *Dactyle,*

the *Anapæst*, and the *Amphibrach*, being trisyllabic, to Triple Time (§ 21). But in the setting of music to words this is not observed; as an Iambic *poetical* foot is often set, in Triple Time, to an Amphibrachic *musical* foot; and a Trochaic *poetical* foot, to a Dactylic *musical* foot (Figs. 303, 304); increased *quantity—length*—being thus given to the accented syllable.

In the above examples the foot is of the same *length* as the bar, though, in the Iambic, Anapæst, and Amphibrach, consisting of portions of two bars. A bar, however, may be of twice the length of a foot. A bar of Compound Duple time (§ 23), $\frac{6}{8}$ or $\frac{6}{4}$, may be of the length of a foot (Fig. 305); or a *Compound* of two Dactyles, when in *slow* time (Fig. 306).

It must be observed that the length or nature of a musical foot has nothing to do with the *number* or *length* of the notes which it includes: simply upon the *accents*. In this, it differs from a poetical foot, in which the number of syllables is limited, and in which the nature of the foot depends, in classic metres, upon the *quantity* of the syllables. Thus, in Fig. 307 (*a*), the commencement of a Theme

by Mozart, there are two feet; each, in the Melody, consisting of four notes. At (*b*) is the commencement of a Variation on the same Theme, the *feet* remaining the same, the number of *notes* doubled.

Moreover, the *kind of foot* may be changed, in a musical passage, the *accent* being preserved;—thus affording variety (Fig. 308).

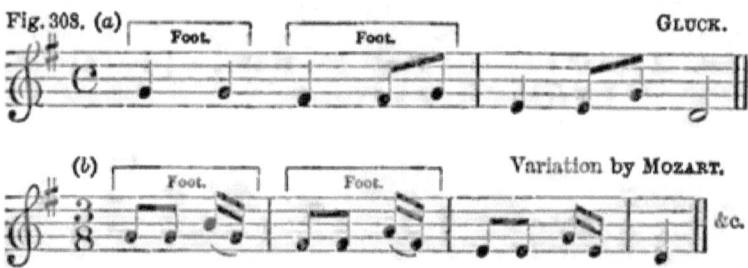

359. In compositions of simple structure, such as Ballads, Marches, Minuets, Waltzes, &c., there is usually a well-defined rhythmical *proportion* observed, as regards the number of Feet in the Phrases, of Phrases in the Sections, &c.; subject to the same kind of variety in form as the different metres in verse. Departures from this symmetry, however, frequently occur, to break monotony, in the following ways.

(1.) By *Prolongation:* as, by lengthening a Section of four bars to five or six bars. (See the Episode in E Major, of the last movement of Mozart's Sonata in E minor, for Pianoforte and Violin.)

(2.) By *Contraction*: as, by reducing a four-bar Section to three bars.

(3.) By *Addition* of a *Codetta* (short appended termination) of one or two bars to a Section or Period; often a repetition or *Echo* of the last Phrase. (See the terminations of the Periods, preceding the Double Bars, in the *Trio* to the *Minuet* of Mozart's Symphony in G Minor.)

(4.) By interspersing Phrases of one, two, or three bars, with Phrases of different length, thus producing BROKEN or *Irregular* Rhythm. Such devices serve to avert *squareness*, or *tameness*, especially in the *development* of musical ideas,—in the *second part*,—(that which intervenes between the first Double Bar and the return of the *Subject*,) in Instrumental movements of *continuity* (§ 401). The works of Haydn abound with admirable examples of these various contrivances; both his Minuets and his longer movements. The Minuet of Mozart's Symphony in G Minor, referred to above, is also a fine study of varied Rhythm.

(5.) By *interweaving* the Phrases and Sections,—one beginning before another has terminated; or the terminating bar, for instance, of one section serving as the commencement of another. The interweaving is especially observable in Fugues, Canons, and elaborate compositions in several parts.

(6.) By Syncopation, changing the position of the accent, and producing *Cross Rhythm*: the effect, sometimes, for instance, of a passage of *Duple* Time in a *Triple* Time movement, &c. (See the *Scherzo* of Beethoven's *Eroica* Symphony: the last movement, 2nd Subject, of Schumann's Concerto in A Minor, &c.) This device, like the last two, occurs principally in compositions of some elaborateness.

360. The principles thus far explained may guide the young composer, both in *timing* and in *barring* his compositions, and in setting music to words. Compositions must be written in Quadruple, Duple, or Triple Time, according to the alternation of accented and unaccented beats; and must be *barred* so as to bring the notes which are to have the strongest accents at the beginning of the bar. (See also § 26, and Fig. 24.) And, in setting music to words, the accented syllables should be given to notes which occur at the accented parts of the bar or beat; and the most emphatic, or prominent words, at the beginning of the bar.

From lack of attention to, or knowledge of, the principles of Rhythm, young composers have sometimes written *Triple Time* subjects in Duple Time, and *vice versâ*. And, frequently, *unaccented* syllables, or words, are given to *accented* notes, and *vice versâ*. Some have termed the whole arrangement of bars *arbitrary;* but, when once it is agreed, as it is, among musicians, that the division into bars or measures shall be regulated by the principles of Rhythm, —the proportions of accented and unaccented beats,—it is a most wilful arbitrariness to bar compositions in defiance of that understood arrangement.

361. The due indication of Rhythmical divisions, in *performance*, is termed Phrasing, and is of great importance, though much neglected. The giving the proper *stress* to the accented notes, without any *jerking*, or clocklike monotony, is one element in such indication. And the dividing of the Phrases is indicated, partly, by the *raising of the hand*, in Pianoforte playing ; by the *bowing*, in stringed-instrument playing ; and should regulate the *breath-taking*, in singing.

362. The accents which occur at the beats, as already explained, are termed *Grammatical* accents. Those which are introduced elsewhere, for expression, or to give prominence to particular words, are termed *Rhetorical, Oratorical*, or *Æsthetic* accents. Some term such an accent *Emphasis*, by way of distinction. (See § 36.)

CHAPTER XXXV.

IMITATION AND CANON.

363. One important application of Counterpoint to the treatment of musical ideas consists in the Imitation or *repetition* by one part of that which another part has announced, while that original part continues with a contrapuntal passage ; such passage often being the inversion of the Counterpoint which has accompanied the subject in the first instance : *Imitation* being thus closely connected with *Double Counterpoint*.

364. *Imitation* may be only of the *general form* of a

passage, as in Fig. 309. Or the *intervals* may be *exactly*

imitated, which is termed STRICT Imitation. It may commence either with the *same note* as the imitated passage,—Imitation in the *Unison*,—or at any interval above or below it. When it is at any other interval than the Unison, the 8ve, the 4th below, or the 5th above,—the most frequent imitations,—some alteration of the intervals, as from *Major* to *Minor*, &c., will be found necessary, to prevent too wide a departure from the original key. Some other modifications will be explained in treating of *Fugue* (chap. xxxvi.).

In Fig. 310, the lower part imitates the upper at a 9th below it:

the intervals are changed, in some cases, from Major to Minor, &c. But this lower part, in its turn, is imitated *exactly*, in the 8ve above, by the upper part. In Fig. 311, the Imitation is in the 4th below; and is *strict*, as long as it continues.

Fig. 311.

365. *Strict Imitation* of one part by another, throughout an entire passage, is termed CANONICAL Imitation; and a composition in which such imitation is maintained throughout is termed a CANON. (§ 370.)

366. A Subject announced for imitation is termed the PROPOSITION, GUIDE, or ANTECEDENT. The imitation of it is termed the ANSWER, or the CONSEQUENT. The *Answer* may commence at any point in the *Proposition*.

Fig. 312 contains three examples from a Sonata by Mozart. At (*a*), the imitation is in the 8ve below, at the distance of only one quaver. At (*b*), it is in the 8ve below, at the distance of a whole bar.

Fig. 312. (*a*)   MOZART.

Examples.

At (*c*), it is in the 8ve above, at the distance of half a bar. Fig. 313

Fig. 313.

gives an example in four parts: the highest part imitates the *Guide* in the interval of a 2nd above: the Tenor imitates it in the 8ve below, and the Bass a 7th below the Tenor (corresponding with the highest part). The imitative *style* is continued in the remaining bars.

367. Imitation may take place by *Contrary motion:* the Consequent *rising* where the Antecedent *descended*, and *vice versâ*. (Fig. 314.) Such imitation may commence with the same note as the Antecedent, with its 8ve, with its 4th below, or 5th above, &c., and is termed *al rovescio*.

The term *Per arsin et thesin* is applied by some writers to this kind of Imitation (from ἄρσις, elevation; θέσις, placing, laying down). This term is more usually applied now, however, to that kind of Imitation in which the Answer has that at the *unaccented* (or *up*) beat which the Proposition had at the *accented* (or *down*) beat. (Fig. 315: see also Fig. 312, *c*.)

Fig. 314.

Fig. 315.

368. There is also a kind of Imitation termed RETRO-GRADE, or reversed: the Consequent answering the Proposition from *end* to *beginning*. However ingenious, this is of little value, and not much used now. It is also termed Imitation *Per rectè et retrò:* also *Cancrizans* (crab-like).

369. Imitation by AUGMENTATION and that by DIMI-NUTION are frequent. In the first kind, the Answer is in notes of *greater* value than in the Proposition: twice, or even four times the length.

Fig. 316 gives an example, in which, besides the Imitations indicated, there are short imitations between the upper parts, in the third and fourth bars.

In Imitation by *Diminution*, the Answer is in *shorter* notes than in the Proposition: generally half the length. Both these kinds may be by Contrary or by Similar motion, and the different kinds may be combined. (Fig. 317.)

In Fig. 318 (*a*), the lower part has the Diminution of the upper Subject, as its Counterpoint. At (*b*), these are inverted in the 12th, with an inner part added to complete the harmony. Compositions in which Contrapuntal devices, such as those above explained, are

Fig. 316. From *Fugue* by MOZART.

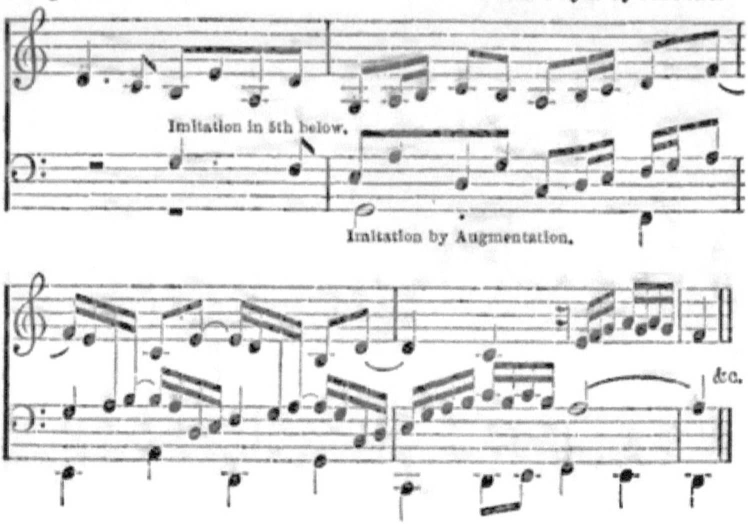

Fig. 317. Imitation by Diminution and Contrary Motion. BACH.

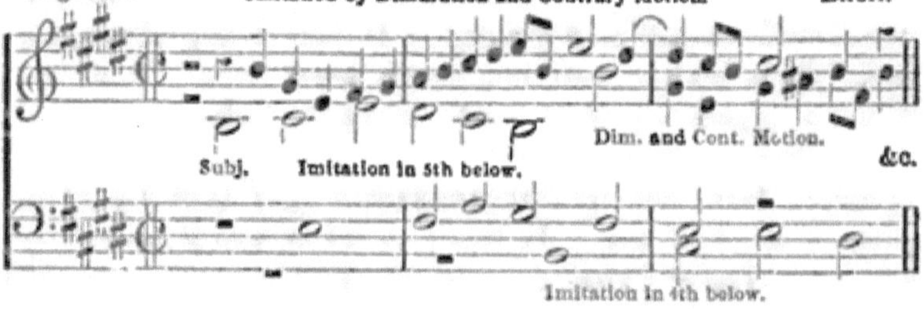

Fig. 318. (*a*) HANDEL.

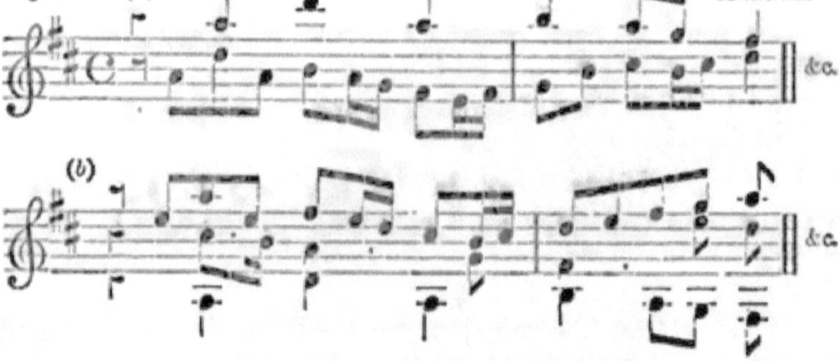

combined, are sometimes termed RICERCATI or RICERCARI (*sought out*, exhibiting *research*).

As will be seen from the above examples, Imitation may occur either between two, or between more parts; and, in a composition in several parts, some of the parts may imitate, while one or more other parts proceed independently, filling up the harmony. Moreover, the Imitation may continue for only a few notes, or for several bars, or still longer. The proper management and introduction of Imitations is one of the most important elements in elaborated Composition; serving to develope the ideas, to connect the parts, and to give unity of design to the whole. Bach, Handel, Mozart, Haydn, &c., are among the composers whose works furnish the finest examples of this device; and the study of those works is the best method of learning how to employ it with advantage. A good exercise is to form Imitative Counterpoints, in the Florid Species, on a Canto Fermo. Short Imitations occur in some of the Examples of Counterpoint in this work. (See Figs. 174, 273, 287: also Fig. 25.)

370. A CANON (§ 365)—is so termed either because the Proposition serves as a *rule* (κανών, rule) to the Answer,[1] or because of certain marks,—*canoni, rules* of performance,[2]—formerly used in Canons, to indicate the entry of the parts, &c. A Canon was formerly termed a *Perpetual Fugue* (*Fuga Legata : Fuga Obbligata*).

371. A Canon in which, at the completion of the imitated part, that part, instead of terminating, recommences, or returns to a 𝄋, the other part or parts continuing the imitation, and recommencing in like manner, is termed a PERPETUAL or INFINITE Canon. It can be continued *ad infinitum ;* some place of termination being usually indicated by a *Pause*, or the word ***Fine***. When no such recommencement occurs, but the termination is effected by a short *Coda*, or the parts leave off one by one, the Canon is termed FINITE.

372. A Canon may be in any number of parts. When one part gives the pattern, which is imitated by one other part only, the Canon is said to be *Two in One* (Fig. 319). If in three or more parts, the imitation still being of *one Guide* only, the Canon is said to be *Three in One, Four in One* (Fig. 320), &c. When, however, two parts give

---

[1] Martini.   [2] Borardi.

patterns for imitation,—a *Subject* and a *Counter-Subject*,— which are imitated, respectively, in two other parts, the Canon is termed *Four in Two: i. e.* four parts, with two imitated subjects (Figs. 321, 322). Similarly, a Canon

Fig. 321. FINITE CANON, 4 in 2.   From MARTINI's "*Esemplare.*"

may be *Six in Two, Eight in Two, Six in Three, Eight in Four*, &c.

Fig. 322.   FINITE CANON, 4 in 2, *in the 8ve.*   H. PURCELL, 1658—1695.

373. Canons, like other imitations, may be at any interval,—may be by Contrary motion, by Augmentation, by Diminution, &c. Obviously, however, a Canon by Diminution cannot long be continued, as the imitation part will soon overtake the Guide. Similarly, in a Canon by Augmentation, the Guide will soon so far outstrip the Consequent, that imitation will be lost.

Some Subjects are capable of being treated, canonically, in a variety of ways: at different intervals, in various numbers of parts, by Direct movement, by Contrary movement, by Augmentation, by Diminution, by the Imitation commencing at various points of the Proposition, &c. Such Canons are termed POLYMORPHOUS (many formed).

The older composers exercised themselves very much with Canons of all kinds, and manifested considerable ingenuity in their construction. Moreover, they would leave much to the ingenuity and knowledge of the performers; often writing only the *Theme* which was to be treated canonically, without indicating how it was to be treated,—at what intervals, &c. Canons so written were termed

ENIGMATICAL Canons, or CLOSE Canons (*Canons Fermés, Canoni chiusi*); this last term, however, being also applied to Canons in which, though only one part was written, certain signs (§ 370) were used, to indicate the points at which the parts were successively to enter (Fig. 323, in which the §§ shew the entries of the Voices).

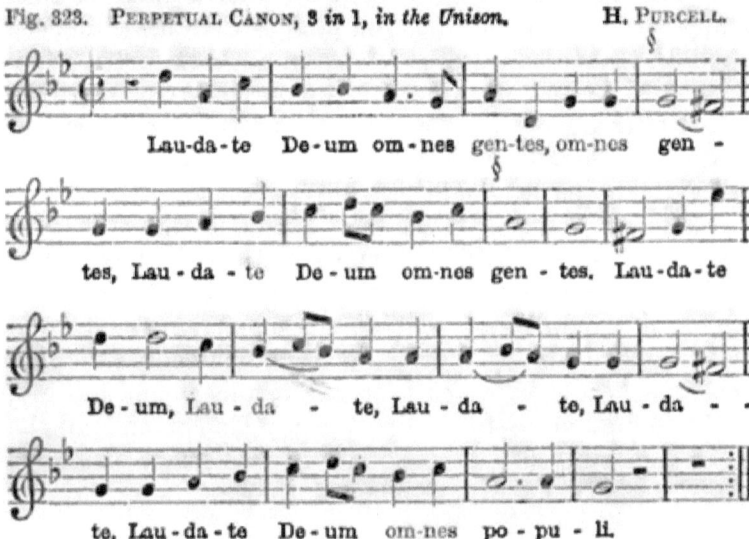

Fig. 323. PERPETUAL CANON, 3 in 1, *in the Unison*. H. PURCELL.

Lau-da-te De-um om-nes gen-tes, om-nes gen - tes, Lau - da - te De - um om-nes gen - tes. Lau-da-te De - um, Lau - da - te, Lau - da - te, Lau - da - - te, Lau-da-te De - um om-nes po - pu - li.

When such Canons were written out in full,—their RESOLUTION, as it was termed, being shewn,—they were termed OPEN Canons. Sometimes, Canons were so contrived that, at each recurrence of the Theme, it commenced a note higher than the previous time, and so the circuit was made of the twelve major or minor keys: these were termed CIRCULAR Canons,—a term also applied, however, to other *Perpetual* Canons (§ 371). Sometimes, the Theme only of an Enigmatical Canon being given, no other indication was given of the manner of its performance than a Latin or Italian *motto*,—almost as enigmatical as the Canon itself,—but supposed to furnish some clue to the solution of the Canon. We smile at these pedantries; but it is hardly wonderful that, as the resources afforded by the almost boundless possibilities of combination and contrivance were first discovered, a sort of learned childishness should thus exhibit itself: that skill in construction should take precedence of imagination. Be this as it may, the utility of the practice of Canon writing to a student who desires to attain mastery of the art of treating musical ideas, and the power of continuity in writing, is undeniable. Only he must regard it as a *mean* to an *end*.

188 *The Round.*

For matchless Examples of Canon, the student is referred to the four Canons in J. S. Bach's *Art of Fugue :* also, to his 30 *Variations in G*, which include Canons in all the intervals, from the Unison to the 9th ; some being by inverse movement.

374. The general principles of Florid Counterpoint apply in Canon, as in other imitational writing. Cadences should be avoided: one part should not *rest* except when the other (or one of the others) is moving : Syncopation between the bars frequently used: and the parts should not proceed much by thirds and sixths. Indeed, variety between the parts should be aimed at.

375. A ROUND is a species of Canon, for three or more equal voices, in which one voice sings a short complete melody, which is then sung by a second voice, the first voice proceeding to another accompanying melody : when both have concluded, the third commences the first melody, the second voice proceeds to the second melody, and the first voice to a third melody, and so on ; all the voices singing all the melodies in succession, *round and round*, for an indefinite number of times.

Fig. 324 is an Example: the figures at the *end* of each part indicate which of the lines each voice is to proceed to.

Fig. 324. ROUND *for 3 Voices.* H. C. B.

Such compositions were, at one time, frequently set to words capable of some jocose second meaning, by a *play upon words ;* and were then called CATCHES.

CHAPTER XXXVI.

FUGUE.

376. A FUGUE is a Composition in which a *Subject*, announced by one part, is *imitated*, or *answered*, by the other parts, successively; not *canonically* (§ 365), but with interruptions, possible modifications, &c.: *Subject* and *Answer* appearing in all the parts, at intervals, throughout the movement. The term is from *Fuga* (a flight), because the parts seem (it is alleged) to *fly* from, or chase one another.

In former times the term was applied to imitative Counterpoints, generally.

377. The principal constituents of a Fugue are the SUBJECT, the ANSWER, the COUNTER-SUBJECT, the STRETTOS, and the EPISODES.

378. The SUBJECT, or *Guide* (*Dux*, Leader), should be of moderate length,—rarely *more* than eight bars, and, in slow time, *less*. It should present a *complete* idea, of an interesting and marked character, worth working; so that it may be recognized readily whenever it enters, and be welcome. It should, moreover, be susceptible of good fugal working; containing in it the germs of good *Strettos* and *Episodes*. In order to this, it should, generally, include two, three, or even more different *figures*, in proportion to its length. It rarely exceeds, except briefly, the compass of an octave. No modulation should occur in it, except to the Dominant. Examples: (Fig. 325, *a*, *b*.)

Fig. 325. (*a*) &c.

Fugue: Subject and Answer.

379. The ANSWER (*Comes,* companion) is a reproduction of the Subject in another part, at a different pitch: generally a 5th above or a 4th below. Sometimes it is made in the 8ve, or even at other intervals; but that in the 5th or 4th is much the most frequent, and will be treated of here. Examples: (Fig. 326, *a, b.*)

In both these examples, the Answers are exact transpositions of the Subject into the Dominant of the original key, and are harmonized accordingly. This exact Answer to the Subject, unaltered, is only practicable when the Subject continues in the original key, throughout, without modulation, as in these two Examples. When the Answer is so made, the Fugue is termed a REAL FUGUE.

380. Often, however, some alteration in the intervals of the Subject is made in the Answer.

The older musicians divided the 8ve of notes in two ways. The 8ve from Tonic to Tonic they divided by the Dominant (Fig. 327, *a*):

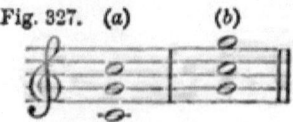

that from the Dominant to its 8ve, they divided by the Tonic (*b*). A Subject lying between the Tonic and its 8ve was termed *Authentic :* while one lying between the Dominant and its 8ve was termed *Plagal* (see § 62). A *Plagal* Subject had an *Authentic* Answer, and *vice versâ*. And, moreover, a Subject, or portion of a Subject, included by either *division*, was answered in the corresponding division: Tonic to Dominant, by Dominant to Tonic, and *vice versâ*. Although we are in no sense bound by the old division, yet there is no doubt that this manner of answering the Subject tends to preserve a sense of the original key; and it is generally observed, with some modifications. When the Answer is subjected to some alterations in compliance with this principle, the Fugue is termed a TONAL FUGUE.

(1.) When the *Subject* begins or ends with the *Tonic*, the *Answer* should begin or end with the *Dominant*, and *vice versâ*.

(2.) When, in the *Subject*, the *Tonic* skips to the *Dominant*, the *Answer* will, generally, skip from the *Dominant* to the *Tonic*, and *vice versâ;* especially when the skip occurs at the *beginning* of the Subject: but this is not invariable. The same is often observed when the skips are filled up; the Tonic and Dominant answering one another, when practicable, without too much alteration of the Subject.

(3.) When the *Subject modulates* to the Dominant, the *Answer*, commencing in the Dominant, will modulate to the Tonic; and if the *Subject returns* to the original key, after such modulation, the *Answer* will return to the Dominant.

The observance of these rules, however, will often necessitate some alteration of the Intervals: frequently a 5th in the Subject will be answered by a 4th, and *vice versâ;* and as a result of this, a 2nd by a 3rd, a 2nd by a unison, and *vice versâ:* the alteration seldom, if ever, exceeding a 2nd. The Diminished 7th is never altered.

Thus, Fig. 328 (*a*) will be answered as at (*b*); and, therefore, (*c*) generally as at (*d*). Similarly, (*e*) as at (*f*); and, therefore, (*g*) as at (*h*). So, the skip of a 4th and rise of a 2nd, at (*i*), are answered by a 5th and 3rd (*k*).

The absolute necessity of such alterations, in some cases, may be illustrated from Fig. 325, p. 189. If the Subject at (*a*), which begins on the *Dominant*, be answered literally, beginning on the

192   *Fugue: Subject and Answer.*

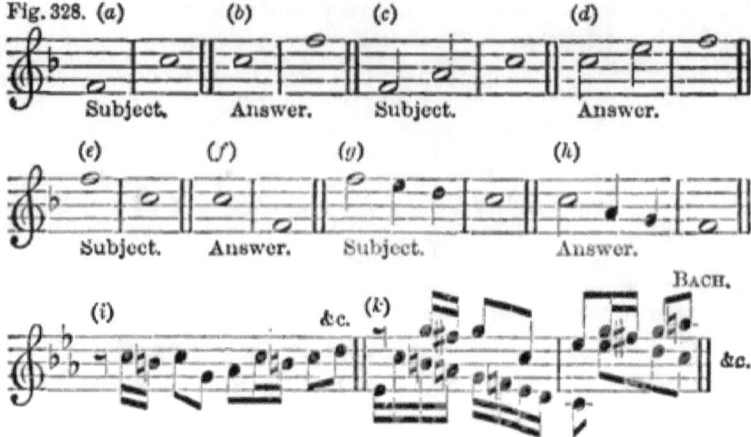

Fig. 328. (a) Subject. (b) Answer. (c) Subject. (d) Answer. (e) Subject. (f) Answer. (g) Subject. (h) Answer. (i) &c. (k) &c.   BACH.

Tonic, the Answer will be in F, the *Sub-dominant*, instead of in the Dominant (Fig. 329, *a*), contrary to the rule (see § 381). This

Fig. 329. (a) Wrong Answer to Fig. 325 (a). &c.
(b) Answer.   BACH.

is not nearly so desirable, early in a composition, as Modulation to the *Dominant*. Therefore it is answered as at (*b*), being in the Dominant, as the Counterpoint shows. Between the first and second notes, the Subject has a tone, the Answer a *Semitone :* between the third and fourth notes the Subject skips a 5th, the Answer a 4th. These are the only alterations, there being none (and there never should be any) of the general *figure*.

Similarly, the Subject at Fig. 325 (*b*), if answered exactly, would give a Modulation to the Sub-dominant in the first part (Fig. 330, *a*) ; therefore, it is answered as at (*b*).

Fig. 330. (a) Wrong Answer to Fig. 325 (b). (b) &c.   BACH. &c.
Answer.

Fugue: Subject and Answer. 193

The Answer at Fig. 331 *repeats* a note at the commencement, instead of descending a 2nd, to avoid a Modulation to the Subdominant.

Fig. 331.   MOZART.

Rule (2.) is not invariable, even at the beginning of the Subject and Answer. Thus, while Bach answers the Subject at Fig. 332 (*a*),

Fig. 332. (*a*)   (*b*)   (*c*)   BACH.

as at (*b*); that at (*c*), he answers as at (*d*): the Answer being exact—*real*—instead of *tonal*, which would have required G, the Tonic, for the Answer, to the Dominant, D (*e*). See also (*f*, *g*). And even in a *tonal* Answer, similar exceptions are frequent (*h*), to avoid too great a dissimilarity between Answer and Subject, or to avoid Modulations.

Fig. 333 illustrates Rule (3). Were the Answer to be *real*, a Modulation to D Major—far too remote—would be the result.

Fig. 333. Mod. to Domt. BACH.
Return to Tonic.

381. Many Subjects, however, present some difficulty as to the necessary alterations in the Answer, being answerable in more than one way. The following directions may assist the student in this matter.

(1.) All alterations must be made in *quitting* or *approaching* the *Tonic* or the *Dominant*. This may be verified by examining all the Answers in Bach's "*Das Wohltemperirte Klavier*."

(2.) With the exception of taking *Tonic* for *Dominant*, or *vice versâ*, make no alterations but such as result therefrom; or such as, on account of modulation in the Subject, are necessary to preserve the tonality. This has been partly illustrated already: see Figs. 328 to 333, with the remarks thereon. And make such resultant alteration *at once*: *i. e.* as soon as possible after the change from Tonic to Dominant, or *vice versâ*, has rendered it desirable; so that the *succeeding* portion of the Answer may accurately imitate the Subject.

Thus, starting with the principle that the Answer is to be a 5th above, or a 4th below, the Subject (§ 379): if the *Dominant* which commences the Subject, Fig. 334, be answered by the *Tonic*, a 5th

Fig. 334. HANDEL.

below it (§ 380, 1.), that *extension* of the distance necessitates an *abridgement* of an interval in the Answer. This is effected *at once*, by the *repetition* of the note, instead of the descent of a 2nd; and the remainder of the Answer is in exact imitation, a 4th below the Subject. It would be unreasonable to defer the alteration by repetition till the *end* of the descent, long after its cause, as at Fig. 335: more-

Fig. 335.

over, the intervals in the descent would not be in exact imitation. Fig. 331 is a similar instance.

Again, at (*h*), Fig. 332, the *Dominant* which begins the Subject is answered by the *Tonic*, a 4th (only) *above* it. This *contraction* of the prescribed distance necessitates rectification, which is effected *at once*, by descending a 2nd instead of a 3rd; the remainder of the Answer being in exact imitation, a 5th above the Subject.

Similarly, in Fig. 336, the Answer rising only a 4th, from Do-

Fig. 336.   BACH.

minant to Tonic (§ 381, 2.), instead of a 5th, like the Subject, this contraction is at once rectified by the *repetition* instead of the descent of a 2nd. (See also Fig. 332, *a*, *b*.)

If, then, a skip from Tonic to Dominant, in the *Subject*, followed by some notes *beyond* that Dominant, be answered by a skip from Dominant to Tonic, an extension, by one degree, of the interval following that skip will be requisite; as in Fig. 337. The reverse will

Fig. 337.   EBERLIN.

hold good in a similar *descent* (Fig. 338, *a*). The Answer might be *real*, however, as at (*b*).

Fig. 338. (a)

(b) &c.

In some cases, the place of alteration will be optional. Thus, the Subject at Fig. 339 may be answered either as at (*a*), or as at (*b*).

Fig. 339. (a)

(b) &c.

382. When the Subject commences with any other note than the Tonic or Dominant, and does not modulate, the Answer may be exact, a 5th above or a 4th below; as in Figs. 340 and 341.

Fig. 340. Commencing with Mediant. MOZART.

&c.

Fugue: Subject and Answer. 197

An alteration, similar to those already explained, may be made in the Answer, as in Fig. 342, in which the C A

in the first bar of the Subject are treated as ornamental; and, the *outline* being a descent from Tonic to Dominant, the Answer (*b*) gives a descent from Dominant to Tonic, immediately compensated for by a smaller interval than in the Subject. The Answer *might* have been as at (*c*), however, which would have been *real*, instead of *tonal*.

Sometimes, however, when the Subject begins or ends with the 2nd, 3rd, 6th, or 7th notes of the scale, the Answer may begin with the 4th above, or the 5th below, —an alteration, as in other cases, of one degree, in order to preserve the figure of the Subject, in the Answer. See Figs. 343 and 344.

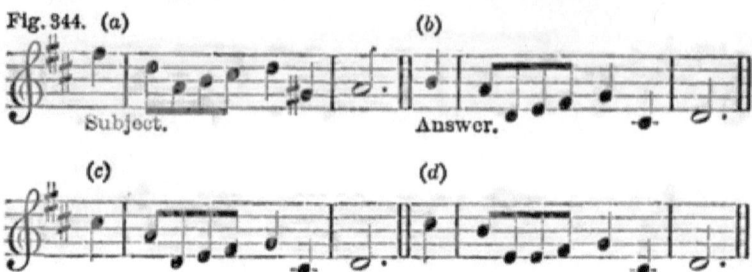

Fig. 344. (a) Subject. (b) Answer.

(c) (d)

The Answer at (b), Fig. 343, involves less alteration than that at (c); and the latter, if continued a 5th above (instead of the note being repeated), would modulate to A. The Answer at (b), Fig. 344, though beginning a 5th below the Subject, is preferable to those at (c, d). That at (c) is ugly, on account of the Major 7th with only one intervening note. That at (d) involves a repeated note, deranging the ascending figure of the Subject; but is better than the Answer at (c). Examples might be multiplied.

383. The Answers to *Chromatic* Subjects are best ascertained by reducing the Subject to the Diatonic form.

Thus, the Subject at Fig. 345 (a) is a variation of the Diatonic

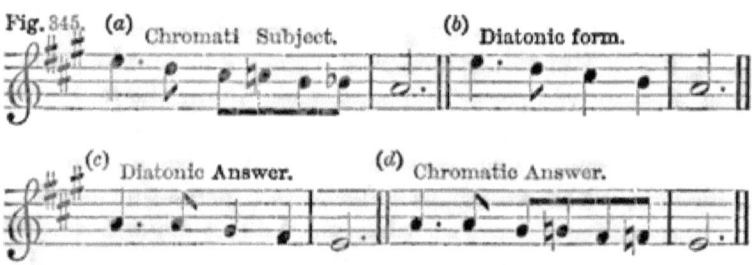

Fig. 345. (a) Chromatic Subject. (b) Diatonic form.

(c) Diatonic Answer. (d) Chromatic Answer.

outline at (b), which would be answered as at (c); and this Answer, with the Chromatic additions, is as at (d).

384. The value of the notes and rests in the Subject must not be changed in the Answer, except that the *first* note may be of less value,—e. g. a *crotchet* for a *minim*,—which sometimes gives more point to the entry. Moreover, the *last* note of the Subject may be *prolonged* in the Answer, as when tied to a note in the succeeding Counterpoint.

Still further, the *whole Answer* may be by *Augmentation*, or by *Diminution* (§ 369). This is one of the devices occurring in the development of a Fugue, more frequently than at the commencement.

385. Similarly, an answer by *Inverse Movement* (§ 367) is more frequently found in the *course* of a Fugue, than at the commencement, though sometimes occurring in the opening. (Fig. 346. See also Bach's *Art of Fugue*, and Fig. 317.)

Fig. 346.   BACH.
Answer by Inv. movement.   &c.

Moreover, sometimes an ascent is made instead of a descent, to accommodate the voice, or for some such reason. (Fig. 347.)

Fig. 347.   BENNETT.

386. The COUNTER-SUBJECT is the Counterpoint with which the part that has announced the Subject accompanies the Answer: see the examples already given. This should be a Double Counterpoint, in the 8ve at all events, if not invertible at other intervals; as it will have to appear, during the Fugue, above and below the Subject and Answer. When the Answer does not strictly resemble the Subject, the Counter-Subject will probably be liable to some slight alteration, according to which of the two it accompanies. It does not always accompany the Subject or Answer in the course of the Fugue, however.

200 *Fugue: the Counter-Subject.*

Sometimes the *Counter-Subject* is announced *conjointly* with the Subject, and appears throughout the Fugue in that conjunction. It is then more truly a *Counter-Subject* than when not so appearing; and the Fugue is then termed a *Fugue with two Subjects*, or, more briefly, a DOUBLE FUGUE. It is more imperative in this case, than otherwise, that the two Subjects be in Double Counterpoint. Fig. 348 gives an example of the opening of a

Double Fugue. Even in a Double Fugue, however, one Subject may be worked separately without the other.

There are also Fugues with more than two Subjects; but these are seldom announced together. (See § 395.)

387. The STRETTO (from *Strignere*, to pull close) con-

sists of the entry of the Answer, in the course of the Fugue, before the close of the Subject, or *vice versâ;* and, therefore, at an earlier point than at the commencement of the Fugue; the Answer and the Subject being brought partially together.

Thus, at (*a*), Fig. 349, are shown the Subject and Answer as

originally **announced**. At (*b, c, d, e, f*) are shown *Strettos* which occur in the course of the Fugue, the entries being indicated by V.

The obtaining of good Strettos is a very important point in the construction of a Fugue; the entry of the Subject at unexpected places adding **greatly** to the interest. Some Subjects furnish better or more Strettos than others : some are scarcely susceptible of such treatment at all. The Strettos may be made at various intervals; and sometimes are made by Inverse movement, by Augmentation, by Diminution, &c. Fig. 350 is an example from the Fugue of which

the opening is given **in** Fig. 332 (*h*). Fig. 317 also furnished an example.

388. **The constant alternation of Subject and Answer in a Fugue might become wearisome**; and is therefore, in many Fugues, broken by EPISODES : short passages,—

of one, two, or more bars,—generally formed of short imitations, or prolongations of some fragment of the Subject or Counter-Subject, or of both combined.

Thus, the Subject at Fig. 325 (*a*), p. 189, being answered as at Fig. 329 (*b*),—the **Counterpoint being** formed of **part of** the second figure of the Subject,—the Bass then takes **the Subject (Fig. 351)**;

and then follows an *Episode* of several bars, consisting of short imitations of the first figure of the Subject, in the upper two parts, the Bass having a Counterpoint, founded, as before, on the second figure.

389. A Fugue may be in any number of parts: sometimes only two, but generally more ; it being difficult to obtain much variety of device in a two-part Fugue. See, however, No. 10 of Bach's 48, and his *single* two-part Fugue (*pour les commençans*) in C Minor.

390. Assuming that the Fugue is in four parts, the entry of the parts may be in any *order* that the nature of

the Subject and the judgment of the composer dictate. In writing a *Choral* Fugue, however, it is well to remember that the voices *pair :* the *Soprano* and *Tenor*, and the *Alto* and *Bass*, respectively, having similar compass, an 8ve apart. It will, then, be advisable, generally, that, whichever voice announces the *Subject*, one of the other pair shall take the *Answer :* then, the fellow voice to that which took the Subject, will take the *Subject* an 8ve higher or lower; and, finally, the remaining voice will take the *Answer*, at the distance of an 8ve. Thus, frequent orders of entry will be

1. Bass.	S.	1. Soprano.	S.	1. Tenor.	S.	1. Alto.	S.
2. Tenor.	A.	2. Alto.	A.	2. Alto.	A.	2. Tenor.	A.
3. Alto.	S.	3. Tenor.	S.	3. Soprano.	S.	3. Bass.	S.
4. Soprano.	A.	4. Bass.	A.	4. Bass.	A.	4. Soprano.	A.

Sometimes, however, the *Answer*—*i. e.* the Subject transposed—is responded to by its own repetition, an 8ve distant, prior to the recurrence of the Subject in its original key. Thus, No. 1 of Bach's 48 opens as follows: 1. Alto, S. 2. Soprano, A. 3. Tenor, A. 4. Bass, S. It is generally best for the *final* entry to be in an *extreme* part. The Answer sometimes commences simultaneously with the last note of the Subject: sometimes immediately after its termination: sometimes a few notes are added, as a Codetta to the Subject, before the Answer commences. The Answer does not always commence at the same part of the bar as the Subject; but, generally, accented notes are answered by accented, except in the Strettos; though not always by the *same* accent: *e. g.* the *first* beat, in quadruple time, may be answered at the *third* beat, &c. (See Figs. 337, 338, 340, &c.)

391. During the successive entries of the Subject and Answer, the other parts continue with counterpoints, invertible or not; and this entry of all the parts constitutes the EXPOSITION (or *Repercussion*), exhibiting the material of which the Fugue is to be formed. No notes of shorter length than those which are contained in the *Exposition* should appear in the Fugue, except when the Subject is

treated by *Diminution*, or when a new Subject is announced in the course of the Fugue (§ 395).

392. A short *Episode* or *Codetta*, generally, though not always, follows the Exposition; one or more of the parts being silent, while the others work, imitatively, leading to the COUNTER-EXPOSITION,—(Ital. *Rivolto*),— sometimes termed the *Inversion* of the Fugue, or of the Exposition. This consists of the successive announcement of the Answer and Subject, in different order from that of the *Exposition;* the parts which, in that, took the Subject, taking, in this, the Answer, and *vice versâ :* the Answer, in fact, being treated as Subject, and being responded to by the Subject.

This is an interesting feature in the Fugue; but it does not enter into all Fugues, though, generally, in whole or in part, into those of considerable development. Frequently, *Strettos* are here introduced, abbreviating the length of the *Counter-exposition*, in comparison with that of the *Exposition*.

393. After the *Counter-exposition* frequently follows an imitational Episode, often of a *sequential* form, effecting a *Modulation*. The Modulations, in a Fugue, should generally be into attendant keys: remote Modulations are unsuited to the dignified character of the composition. A grand exception, however, may be noted in Handel's Fugue in E Minor, *Suite* IV., vol. 1.

If the Fugue be in the Major mode, the first Modulation will generally be to the Dominant: after that, to one or more of the attendant Minor keys: then, probably, back to the original key, with, possibly, a brief modulation to the Sub-dominant, towards the close. If the Fugue be in the Minor mode, the first Modulation is generally into the Relative Major: then into the Dominant Minor, and, through other Relative keys, back to the original key. But no invariable *rule* can be given (though some treatises offer very precise ones): the study of good models must guide the student. All these Modulations should be conducted in connection with imitations, and workings of the Subject. Thus, for instance, if the Subject, or Answer, be imitated in some other interval than the 4th or 5th, a Modulation can be effectively introduced.

For, in the course of the Fugue, it is not always necessary to answer the Subject in the 5th or 4th. Moreover, the Answer may be treated as Subject, **and** imitated in **the 5th or 4th,** thus effecting a Modulation.

394. The Subject need not, as has already been seen, be always given in its entirety: a short portion of it may be taken and worked by imitation in various intervals: such short portion being termed an *Attacco;* frequently worked by free imitation. Fugues consisting principally of such workings are termed *Fugues by Imitation,* as distinguished from *Strict Fugues.*

Thus, by means of these various imitational devices,—Augmentation, Diminution, Inverse movement, Strettos, workings of portions of the Subject, or Counter-subject, &c.,—the interest is to be sustained. Short Canons are frequently introduced in the course of the Fugue. (See **Handel's Fugues in D** Minor and F♯ Minor, *Suites* III. and VI., vol. 1.) Few Fugues include all of these devices: all Fugues contain some. Some Subjects lend themselves better to one kind of contrivance than to another.

395. In the course of a long Fugue a *Second Subject* is often introduced, which is worked independently, on the same principles as though it were a first Subject. It should be contrasted in character and form to the first Subject; but it is most desirable that it should be so constructed as to be susceptible of being afterwards combined with the first Subject, furnishing a new Counterpoint to that Subject. Sometimes more than one new Subject is thus introduced. One of the finest examples is furnished by Bach's Fugue in C♯ Minor, No. 4 of the 48: altogether one of the noblest of all musical compositions. In it the three Subjects in Fig. 352 (*a, b, c*) are successively announced and separately worked; and afterwards combined, as at (*d*).

396. Towards the end of a Fugue, a *Pedal-point* (§ 237) is often introduced: frequently two such points, one on the *Dominant,* the other on the *Tonic.* The *Dominant Pedal* in that case must always *precede,* not *follow,* the Tonic Pedal; its effect being to awaken expectancy of the close, by its delay of the Tonic harmony. The effect and purpose of the *Tonic Pedal* being to confirm and deepen the impression of the close in the key:

Rules for Construction of a Fugue. 207

Fig. 352. (a) 1st Subject.
(b) 2nd Subject.
(c) 3rd Subject.
(d) 1.

this being still further effected, frequently, by a *Plagal Cadence*, towards the close of, or sometimes introducing, a *Tonic Pedal-point.* On these Pedal-notes, Strettos and other imitations should be introduced, to intensify the interest as much as possible.

397. In the construction of a Fugue, the following general rules should be observed.

(1.) No passage or point should be repeated in the same form and key.

Thus, if the Subject and Answer occur successively, they must appear in different parts, on recurrence, with different superposition of the counterpoints, &c. Should the same Stretto occur twice, it must be with inversion of the parts, or with different accompanying counterpoint, &c. A complete command of contrapuntal resources is therefore necessary.

(2.) No two Episodes should be formed from the same section of the Subject or Counter-subject, unless with different contrapuntal treatment. There are good examples to the contrary, however.

(3.) After any part has rested for a bar or more, its

re-entry must be by the announcement of the Subject or Counter-subject, or with some imitational artifice. Moreover, every entry of the Subject is more effective, preceded by a rest : but this is not invariable.

(4.) The interest should increase as the Fugue advances. Therefore, the most elaborate workings, and the most ingenious contrapuntal artifices, must be introduced latest in the composition. And, if a variety of Strettos be practicable, they should be closer and closer,—the closest occurring towards the end.

(5.) The Subject and Answer should appear as much in the *inner* as in the *extreme* parts. In genuine contrapuntal, and especially in fugal writing, there are no *subordinate* parts.

(6.) Perfect Cadences should be avoided in the course of a Fugue, except at the close of important sections, and in keys to which a Modulation has been made, but which are about to be quitted; and this quittance should be marked by an entry of the Subject.

The student will derive great advantage from the use of Wesley and Horn's edition of J. S. Bach's *Das Wohltemperirte Klavier;* as certain marks (fully explained in the Preface) are therein used, to indicate the entries of the Subject and Answer in various ways, which will much assist in the analysis of the Fugues: the best of all ways of studying when intelligently pursued.

In Bach's *Art of Fugue*, abundant illustration is given of the various methods of construction, and of the ways in which one Subject may be treated and combined with other Subjects.

CHAPTER XXXVII.

FORM IN COMPOSITION.

398. A NUMBER of musical ideas properly following one another, and linked together so as to form a connected whole, constitute a MOVEMENT.

Thus, a SONATA, in the modern sense of the term, is a

work for one or for two instruments, in several *movements;* —usually three or four. Many old Sonatas had only two, and, in some cases, only one. When the work is for more than two instruments, it usually is named accordingly,—a *Trio, Quartet,* &c.; the Sonata *form,* however, being retained. When it is for an *Orchestra,* it is termed a SYMPHONY (*Sinfonia*): a Symphony, therefore, being, in fact, a *Sonata* for a *band.* Such works were formerly termed CONCERTOS: a term now applied only to works for one principal instrument,—(or, sometimes two, three, or even four,)—with orchestral accompaniment. In these, the Sonata form is *extended.* When a Concerto is for more than one principal instrument, it is sometimes termed a *Concertante.*[1]

Suite de pièces, and *Partita,* were terms applied to the Sonata in its earlier forms. In those, the movements were generally all in the same key: in the *modern* Sonata, they are generally in different, but more or less related keys; or, at least, *one* movement is in a different key from the others. The *first* and *last* movements invariably have the same *Tonic;* though the one may be in the *Minor* and the other in the *Major* mode. This Tonic gives the *key-name* to the Sonata, as *Sonata in C,* &c.

399. Besides the *Canonic* and the *Fugal,* there are two principal *forms* of instrumental *Movement:* the Movement of CONTINUITY, or *Development;* and the Movement of EPISODE. An *Episodical* Movement may include some *development;* and *both* forms of movement may include passages of *Canonic* or *Fugal* structure.

400. The *First Movement* of a Sonata is generally a *Movement* of *Development:* sometimes preceded by an *Introduction,* the form of which is not fixed.

The first movements of some Sonatas are not in this form: *e. g.* Beethoven's Op. 26, Op. 27, Nos. 1 and 2, &c. But it is the most usual form of first movement.

401. This form of movement opens with a clearly de-

---

[1] By *concerted* music is meant music in *parts* which are of equal importance: *contrapuntal,* as distinguished from accompanied melody. See § 397, p. 242 (5.): also under "*Madrigal*" in Glossary.

fined SUBJECT, in the principal key. Supposing it to be in a *Major* key, after the *Subject* some passages, either derived in the way of short development from the Subject, or quite new, lead, by a Modulation, to the *Dominant Major;* in which a SECOND SUBJECT, clearly defined, contrasted, but in keeping with the *First Subject,* is announced. After this, passages of a free kind, short subjects or phrases, &c., lead to a close in the Dominant at the first *Double-bar.* The whole of this, the *First Part* of the Movement, is generally repeated; as it contains the material afterwards to be *worked* or *developed,* and it is supposed that the listener should have the principal ideas impressed on his mind, before hearing them developed.

Up to this point there will only be two principal keys dwelt in: the Tonic and the Dominant. Other keys may be briefly touched, however. And, in this first part, there is little *development* of the ideas; that being reserved for the *Second Part* of the Movement, which commences after the *Double-bar.*

In this *Second Part,* occasionally some *entirely new* matter is introduced,—perhaps episodically; but, generally, this division of the Movement consists entirely, or nearly so, of the development of the ideas contained in the First Part. The Movement being (as has been assumed) in the *Major* key, the Second Part will generally be principally in one or more of the attendant *Minor* keys, or in keys nearly connected with them. Sometimes Extraneous Modulation is introduced. The *development* or *working* of the ideas may be of various kinds, according to the nature of the different Subjects, &c. It may be *contrapuntal,*—which includes the *imitational,* of all kinds: or *ornamental,*—the *embellishment* or *varying* of the Subjects (§ 369). The Subjects may be *brought together,* which were announced separately in the First Part: or presented with *different harmonies:* or *inverted,*— *i. e.* treated by Double Counterpoint: or worked in *fragments,* or by *prolongation,* &c. &c. In short, all the learning, skill, and fancy, of the composer may here be brought into requisition. The *weakest device* in a second part is the mere presentation of the Subjects in a different key from the first part, without any such new *treatment* as presents them in any different *aspect*, or develops their resources (see §§ 247, 248). The assiduous study of the best models is the only way of learning how to construct this important part of the Movement.

The Second Part should ultimately lead back to the original key, in order to the *Recapitulation*, marked by the return to the First Subject. This *third* division of the movement is mainly, as its name implies, a repetition, with varying changes, of the First Part; but, instead of a Modulation to the Dominant, the passages are so contrived that the Second Subject appears in the Tonic, in which key the Movement will continue with little exception to the end. Frequently,—especially in an extended movement, a CODA will be added,—*summing up*, as it were, in some cases, the material of the Movement, with, perhaps, *abridged* workings, after the manner of a *Stretto* (§ 387).

If the Movement be in a *Minor* key, the *Second Subject* is generally in the *Relative Major*, in which key the First Part will end: sometimes in the *Dominant Minor*. In no case must any portion of the *Second Part* (except its commencement) be in the key which has been Modulated to in the *First Part*. (See § 353.)

This brief sketch of the outline of a Movement of Continuity will serve the student's purpose in attempting to analyze the concise movements of Haydn, Mozart, &c. In later times, as the length of movements has been increased, more than two principal subjects are often introduced, as in Beethoven's Symphonies, and many of his Sonatas: *e. g.* the Sonata Pastorale, Op. 28, &c. But the general construction of the Movement remains the same.

402. As a specimen of this form of Movement, the Sonata by Mozart, of which the opening is given in Fig. 353, may be taken. The student is advised to obtain it, and examine it in connection with the following remarks.

The first section of the Subject consists of four bars, ending on the Dominant. Then the first phrase (given above) is inverted, and a Perfect Cadence made in the Tonic. A passage succeeds, formed

Fig. 353.

from the first five notes of the Subject; extending for eight bars and a half. The first phrase of the Subject is then taken for the commencement of a passage of Modulation, of some extent, leading to the Second Subject, in F, the Dominant, commencing as in Fig. 354,—resembling

the first Subject more than is usual. The first section of four bars includes two phrases: the second section, by a prolongation of its second phrase, consists of *three* bars (besides its commencing fraction); this prolonged rhythm (see § 359) breaking the *formality*. Then follows a florid passage of eleven bars, ending with a shake, and succeeded by a *Codetta* of five bars formed from the same opening notes as had previously done service, quite differently used, however. Thus the First Part closes.

After the Double-bar the final chords of the First Part are echoed, so to speak; but on the Dominant to G Minor,—the *relative* to the original key. The first phrase of the first Subject is then taken in the bass, in the new key, with a new florid accompaniment above it,—extended to form a phrase of *three bars*, varying the rhythm. This is *inverted* in C Minor, with slight alteration; and then worked, for some time, passing rapidly through various keys, leading to D Minor,—(the relative to the Dominant). The opening few notes are again used, on a Dominant Pedal (Fig. 355); and, by

an enharmonic change of the notation of the Diminished 7th in D Minor, to one on the accidentally raised Sub-dominant of the original key (§§ 195, 348), the return to that key, and the first Subject, is easily effected (Fig. 356). The substance of the First Part is then

Fig. 356.

recapitulated with little alteration, but such as is necessary to keep in the key.

The *Second Part,* in this Movement, is mainly built upon the first Subject, treated in Double Counterpoint, and with Modulation. Other manners of working may be discovered in other works, by the student's own analysis.

403. An EPISODICAL Movement may be of the simplest form, containing only *one* Episode : a Movement *within* a Movement, with little or no development.

Many *slow Movements* of Sonatas, &c., are of this form. Many, however, are *Movements of Continuity:* e. g. those of Beethoven's Sonatas, Op. 10, No. 3; Op. 22 (a very fine example), &c. Sometimes the form of a *Movement of Continuity* is adopted, but without the *development,*—the Second Part,—as in the Slow Movements of Beethoven's Sonatas, Op. 2, No. 1; Op. 10, No. 1, &c.

Of the *Simple Episodical Movement,* the slow movements of Beethoven's *Sonata Patetica,* Op. 13; *Sonata Pastorale,* Op. 28, and *Sonata,* Op. 79, may be cited as examples. That of Op. 28, for instance, has a complete division, with its own second part, in *D Minor;* then a complete division,—the *Episode,*—in *D Major,* likewise with its own second part : then the recapitulation of the Minor division, with embellishments ; and then a Coda, with reminiscences of both divisions.

404. The more extended *Movement of Episode,* however, contains more than one Episode, and is termed a RONDO : coming *round* to the Subject after each Episode.

This is a frequent form for the *last* Movement of a Sonata, &c. : e. g. Beethoven's Sonatas, Op. 2, Nos. 2 & 3 ; Op. 7, Op. 10, No. 3, &c. Sometimes, however, the *Finale* of a Sonata is in the form of a

Movement of Development: *e. g.* Beethoven's Sonatas, Op. 10, No. 1; Op. 27, No. 2 (commonly called the "*Moonlight*"), &c.

The Rondo of the Sonata Op. 22 may be taken as an example of an Episodical Movement. It commences with a complete Subject, in B♭, of eighteen bars extent; Fig. 357. Then follows episodical

Fig. 357.   BEETHOVEN.

matter of a diversified character; at first very marked (Fig. 358);—

Fig. 358.

a *Motivo* (or short Subject), which is worked later in the Movement; then a florid passage; followed by a passage of imitation, formed from the Subject, to which it leads back. After this, the *Motivo* above noticed is taken in B♭ *Minor*, leading to a contrasted Episode in F Minor. To this, the *Motivo* is made to serve as *second part*, or short Episode, with imitational working (Fig. 359); followed by the

Fig. 359.

original figure of the Episode, in B♭ Minor, for eight bars (Fig. 360).

Fig. 360.

Then, by a short passage,—*Conduit*,—built on the opening of the Subject, it is again returned to: this time, however, in an inner part, accompanied in 6ths and 3rds below, and lightly above; afterwards varied, in the upper part. **Then** recurs the first episodical matter, so varied as to lead, charmingly, **to** the first Subject in the *Sub-dominant*,—E♭ Major,—soon to be quitted, however, for the original Tonic, with the Subject again varied, in triplets. **The** Movement closes with a *Coda*, suggested by the above-noted Motivo (Fig. 361); terminating with a *Codetta*, built, imitationally, **on the** opening of the first Subject.

Fig. 361.

Sometimes one of the Episodes in a Rondo **is** of the character of *development: working* the Subject or Subjects. In this case, **several** keys may be passed through.

The different Episodes in a Rondo should not **be in the same key**, either as one another, or as the first Subject. If **the Subject be in a** *Major* key, one, at least, of **the** Episodes should be **in a Minor key**, and *vice versâ*.

405. The MINUET and TRIO, included in many Sonatas, Symphonies, &c., furnish an example of the union of the *concisely developed* movement with the *Episodical* form. The Minuet, an old, rather slow, dance movement, **is of** very concise structure,—a Movement of Continuity in miniature,—the second part being **of the nature of brief** development. The TRIO, or *Second Minuet*, as it was formerly called, **is** of similar structure, **but** contrasted with the first; and is followed by the recapitulation of that first; serving thus as an **Episode in the** Movement. Beautiful examples occur in Haydn's and Mozart's Symphonies; and in Beethoven's Sonatas: *e. g.* Op. 2, No. 1; Op. 10, No. 3; Op. 22; Op. 31, No. 3, &c.

The term *Trio* was probably applied to the Second Minuet on account of its having been originally in **three** *parts:* for three instruments of the band.

The old *Minuet* has given place, **in** modern compositions, to the SCHERZO: a term meaning simply a playful movement, and applied either **to** a movement **in** Triple time, of quicker pace **than** a *Minuet*, or to a playful movement in any other time: frequently in $\frac{2}{4}$.

406. In some Sonatas, &c., **one** of the Movements is

a THEME with VARIATIONS. A *Variation* may consist simply of an *embellishment* of the Theme: its dispersion into Arpeggios, &c.—Or it may be the presentation of the Theme under different aspects: differently harmonized, or taken as an inner, or as the lowest part; or with contrapuntal treatment. Or it may consist of quite different melodic forms, constructed upon the same harmonic progressions as the Theme.

The first style of Variation is the easiest to construct; and is that principally adopted in the Variations of Herz, and similar writers. The comparative facility with which Variations of this kind may be written has caused a large number of inferior writers to adopt this style: and this, with the flimsiness so often characteristic of such Variations, has brought Variations into some disrepute. But, written in the other styles, they afford abundant opportunity for manifesting the skill of a composer; and, more than skill, his feeling for harmony or melody, and the extent to which it is *suggestive* to him of different forms of presentation. Fine examples of Variations are found in the works of Mozart, Hummel, Beethoven, Mendelssohn. Bach's inimitable 30 Variations have been before alluded to (§ 373).

407. There are various free kinds of Instrumental Movement, such as the FANTASIA, the CAPRICCIO, &c., which do not necessarily range themselves under either of the forms which have been described. The names are arbitrary, and are given to compositions in which the composer has given free play to his fancy, not holding himself strictly amenable to the laws of form; or, rather, not binding himself to conform to these models. But, except in *Fantasia*, a well-trained composer generally does, as a matter of fact, construct even his fugitive and lighter effusions on one or other of the plans that have been sketched. And, even in the *Fantasia*, a good composer does not *rhapsodize*. To write a fine *Fantasia* is not to give way to the *vagaries* of a disordered imagination. A true composer always keeps his fancy under control, regulating it by his knowledge; and, when most unfettered, and least formal, still exhibits *design*,—unity of purpose. Mozart's Fantasia in C Minor is an example.

Modern operatic *Fantasias*, *Pots-pourris*, &c., are simply successions of Melodies, *strung together*, rather than constructed movements (see § 398). A dangerous **tendency has set in**, not to *construct new forms* of movement, but **to** repudiate **all** form as **conventional** and arbitrary. The matter cannot here be argued; but the young composer who wishes to write solid and enduring music, is cautioned against yielding to any such seductive notions. *Form,*—implying *design,*—(§ 139), not *formality,* is essential to a true work of art.

CHAPTER XXXVIII.

VOICES AND INSTRUMENTS.

Voices.

408. THERE are two principal kinds of voice of women and children: SOPRANO, or TREBLE; and ALTO, or CONTRALTO. Similarly, there are **two principal kinds of voice of men**: TENOR, and BASS. **There is also a** *medium* **voice**, in both cases: the MEZZO-SOPRANO, and the BARITONE, or BARYTONE. (See §§ 7, 250.)

The *average* compass of each of these voices is shown in Fig. 362.

Fig. 362. Bass. Baritone. Tenor. Alto. Mezzo-Soprano. Soprano.

But, while many individual voices can *exceed* these compasses, either above or below the limits here given, the majority, especially of *untrained* voices, can with difficulty take the entire range,—the extreme notes,—even of these compasses. In *Choral* writing it is desirable to keep, generally, within the limits of the staves, as here given, avoiding the use of Ledger lines. **Few** Tenors will, **with** certainty or effect, take the **low** C. Few Altos will take the low F: though when that part is sung by *men,—Counter-Tenors* (see § 7),— that note may be taken. *Solo* Tenor and Soprano singers will exceed the altitude here specified.

The Mezzo-Soprano part is now generally written, at least in this country, in the *Treble Stave;* not on the *Mezzo-Soprano Stave* **proper, as** here given. (See Foot-note, p. 258.)

409. In all voices there is a *break* between the lower and higher notes, dividing the two *registers* (as they are termed) of the voice. The lower register is termed the *chest-voice* (*voce di petto*) : the higher register is termed the *head-voice* (*voce di testa*), or *Falsetto*. The cause of this break, evidenced by a difference of quality, has not been conclusively determined.[1] The linking of the two registers, so as to modify—disguise—the effect of the break, is *one* of the various ends sought in the cultivation of the voice. There is also, according to many authorities, a *medium* register.

The character of a voice, as Soprano, Alto, &c., is determined, not by the range of notes that it *can* produce, but by those which have the best quality, and which can be produced and sustained with the greatest ease,—the least fatigue. The *Falsetto* has not the power and fulness of the *chest-voice*. The middle notes of a voice are generally the best; but, by cultivation, very good notes may be obtained from the extremes,—as from the high notes of *Soprano* and *Tenor* voices.

Musical Instruments.

410. Musical instruments are of three principal classes: —(1.) *Stringed instruments:* (2.) *Wind instruments:* (3.) *Instruments of Percussion.*

Of *Stringed* instruments there are three kinds:—(*a*.) those *struck* with a *hammer*, as the Pianoforte (*strictly* speaking, therefore, instruments of *percussion*) : (*b*.) those performed on by *friction* with a *bow*, as the Violin, &c.: (*c*.) *plectral* instruments, the strings being *plucked* by the *fingers;* as the Guitar, Harp, &c.

In some old plectral instruments, *plectra* of wood, metal, or other substances were used; as with the old *Zither*. The Violin, and other bowed instruments, are sometimes played on plectrally (*pizzicato*).

Of *wind* instruments there are two kinds:—(*a*.) those with a key-board, the wind being supplied from a *bellows*, as the Organ, &c.: (*b*.) those in which it is supplied by

---

[1] See, however, Marshall's *Outlines of Physiology*, vol. I. pp. 263, 264.

the breath of the performer. Of these latter, some are of *brass*, as the Horn, Trumpet, &c.; and others of *wood*, as the Flute, Oboe, &c.; sometimes made of other substances, however, there being Flutes of silver, &c. Some of these are blown through vibrating *reeds*, or tongues (literal reeds having, doubtless, been originally used); others simply through orifices in the instrument itself. The quality of tone,—*timbre*,—of reed instruments is distinct from that of *open pipes*, as the Flute.[1]

411. The Pianoforte, too well known to need description, was preceded by other stringed instruments with a key-board; but the keys acted, not on *hammers*, *striking* the strings, but on *jacks*, with *quills*, or other *plectra*, which *twanged* the strings. These were the *Clavicytherium*, or *keyed-cithera*, or *zither*: the *Clavichord*, or *Clarichord*: the *Virginal* (possibly so called because used by nuns to accompany hymns to the Virgin): the *Spinet*, (from *Spina*, a thorn or quill); and the *Harpsichord* (in shape, like a grand Pianoforte), also termed *Clavier*, *Clavecin*, *Clavicembalo*, *Gravicembalo* (abbr. *Cembalo*), *Flügel*. These various instruments differed in shape, and in details; but the general principle was the same. Some Harpsichords had two rows of keys, acting upon two sets of strings, and were called *Double-Harpsichords*. (See Bach's 30 Variations, many of which require two rows of keys for their performance.) The Harpsichord had originally two strings in unison, and one in 8ve, for each note. Subsequently a third unison was substituted for the 8ve string.

The *Pianoforte* (see § 37) was first constructed about the middle of last century; but did not at once displace its precursors. They were superseded gradually, as the superiority of the new instrument became evident. Many of the Sonatas of Mozart, Haydn, &c., were written for the Harpsichord.

412. The early Pianofortes were provided with *Sordini* (mutes), or *Smorzatori*,—small pieces of wood, tipped with cloth, which, by certain mechanism, under the con-

---

[1] See Tyndall on *Sound*, p. 195.

trol of the performer, were caused to touch the strings, to *lessen* the vibration. Therefore, in old Pianoforte music, the terms *con* (with) *sordini*, and *senza* (without) *sordini* are found. The *dampers* in modern Pianofortes effect a similar result, and fall on the strings immediately after the hammer has struck them. This may be averted, however, by the use of the *right Pedal* (commonly, but erroneously, called the *loud* Pedal), which *raises* the dampers. When *con sordini* is met with, then, the Pedal must not be used. When *senza sordini* occurs, the Pedal may be used, *if the same harmony continues*. Great judgment is required for its use.—The *soft* Pedal, which shifts the action or the keys, so that only one string of those in unison is struck, should *never* be used unless the words *una corda* (one string) occur, indicating that the composer desires a special effect. Its use is not the legitimate method of obtaining a genuine *piano* in tone; and its frequent use puts the instrument out of tune.

413. The *stringed instruments* performed on with a *bow* are the *Violin*, the *Viola*, the *Violoncello*, and the *Double-Bass*.

414. The VIOLIN has *four* strings, which are tuned in fifths, as shown in Fig. 363 (*a*). The intermediate sounds,

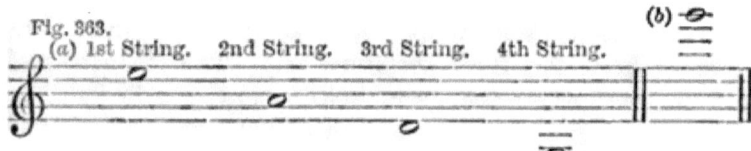

Fig. 363.
(*a*) 1st String. 2nd String. 3rd String. 4th String.

and those higher than the first string, are (as on all these instruments) obtained by *stopping* the string with the finger, shortening the length of the vibrating portion. In ordinary orchestral music it is not usual to write higher than G in altissimo (*b*); but the instrument can produce notes beyond this.

In an ordinary orchestra there are two Violin parts, the 1st and 2nd; both which are played, in unison, by a number of performers: *doubled*, that is. All the stringed instrument parts are thus doubled; but not the wind instruments.

The Viola.

415. The VIOLA (*Viola di Braccio*, resting on the *arm*), also termed the *Alto* (its part being written in the Alto Stave), and the *Tenor* (as it takes the Tenor part in the harmony of a Quartet), has four strings, tuned as in Fig. 364 (*a*); being a 5th below the Violin. It is not

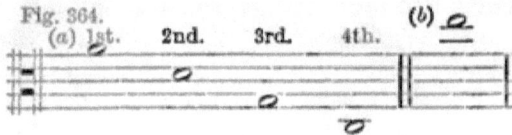

usual to write for it beyond E (*b*). Its high notes are of thin quality.

There was formerly an instrument of the same kind, the *Viola d' Amore*, with seven strings, *fretted*; of a soft, but feeble tone. *Frets* were pieces of wire placed on the finger-board, to indicate the places for the fingers to stop the strings.

There was also a *Viola di Bordone*, or *Baritono*, with seven strings of catgut, and sixteen or more of steel; for which Haydn wrote 175 pieces. Also, a *Viola Pomposa*, with five strings, invented by J. S. Bach. It was also called *Viola di fagotto;* and, in Germany, *Baryton*.

416. The VIOLONCELLO (*Bass Viol*) has four strings, tuned as in Fig. 365 (*a*). The higher notes on the 1st

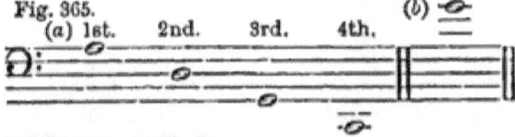

string (stopped) are sometimes written in the Tenor stave; sometimes in the Treble stave, an 8ve higher than the real sounds. In orchestral music, it is not usual to write higher than G (*b*.)

A smaller instrument of the same kind was formerly in use, termed the *Viola di Gamba* (resting on the *leg*, as distinguished from the *Viola di Braccio*). It had six, or sometimes seven strings.

417. The CONTRA-BASSO, or DOUBLE-BASS (also termed *Violone*), is the largest of the stringed instruments; and has *three* strings, in England, &c., tuned as in Fig. 366 (*a*), the sounds being an 8ve lower than written. Some-

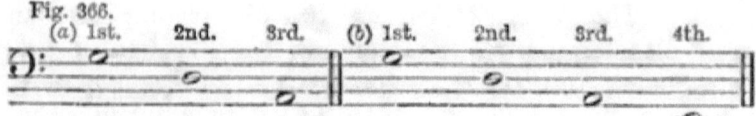

Fig. 366.

times the 3rd string is tuned down to G. In Germany the instrument has four strings, tuned as at (*b*).

In orchestral music, the *Double-Bass* part is written with the *Violoncello* part (*Cello e Basso*); the Double-Bass often merely doubling the Violoncello part in the 8ve below, especially in *full* passages. Sometimes the Violoncello plays without the Double-Bass, in light passages; and sometimes the two instruments have independent parts, written in two staves, braced. When the Double-Bass is to play in 8ves with the Violoncello, '*Col Cello*' is often written, instead of the notes: or '*unisons*,'—not strictly accurate, as the instruments play in 8ves. The Double-Bass strengthens the lowest part, like the pedals on an Organ, when not playing an independent part.

418. Of PLECTRAL instruments, the only one now in common use is the HARP, which is too well known for any detailed description to be needed. Its natural key is C♭. The Harp now used is the *Double-action Harp*; the sharpening of the pitch of the strings being effected by the *Pedals*, which can inflect them *one* or *two* semitones.

419. No adequate description of the ORGAN can be given within brief limits. Suffice it to say that it consists of a number of pipes, some of wood, and others of metal, from 32 feet to ¾ of an inch in length. The air is supplied from a bellows. In a large organ there are three (or even four or five) sets of keys for the fingers, termed the *Manuals*; and another set for the feet, termed the *Pedals*. Each set of keys acts upon a different range of pipes; so that an organ with three rows of Manuals, and a row of Pedals, is, in fact, *four* organs, enclosed (usually) in one case. Moreover, each set of Manuals acts upon a number of sets, or *registers*, of pipes, of various qualities, each series of pipes being termed a STOP; the stops being opened to the action of the key-board by means of the *Draw-stops* (commonly called *stops*) at the sides of the Manuals.

In an organ with three rows of keys, the *middle* row

acts upon that which is termed the GREAT ORGAN,—the most powerful: the *upper* row acts upon the SWELL ORGAN,—the volume of sound being susceptible of increase by the opening (by means of a pedal) of the case in which the pipes are contained, which opens like a Venetian blind, and is termed the *Venetian Swell:* the *lower* row of keys acts upon the CHOIR ORGAN, adapted for accompanying voices. These rows may be combined, by means of *couplers*. The *Pedals* act upon the PEDAL ORGAN: in some small organs, however, having no such separate set of pipes, they act upon the Manuals of the *Great Organ*.[1]

420. The HARMONIUM is an instrument with a keyboard and a bellows; the sound being produced by the vibrations of a *free metallic reed; i. e* an elastic *tongue*, fixed in a plate, with one end free, which, when a current of air is impelled against it, yields to that current; and, returning by its own elasticity, a rapid succession of puffs of air is the result, producing a musical sound (§ 1).[2]

421. The FLUTE now used is termed the *Flauto traverso*, as distinguished from the former kind, termed the *Flûte-à-bec;* which was played *long-ways*, instead of *crossways*, and, as its name implies, had a *mouth-piece:* it was also termed the *English Flute*, that in present use being termed the *German Flute*. It is made of box-wood, ebony, silver, &c. Its compass is shown in Fig. 367, but it is

Fig. 367.

not advisable to write for its highest notes, very frequently, in orchestral music.

There is also a smaller Flute, termed the PICCOLO, or OCTAVE FLUTE, which plays an 8ve higher than the notes written. Its lowest note is D on the 4th line. It is very shrill, and is used as an *extra* instrument for special effects.

---

[1] For complete information, see Hopkins and Rimbault's "*The Organ, its History and Construction.*"

[2] See Tyndall on *Sound*, chap. V.

Other Flutes are used in *military* bands, but not in ordinary *concert* orchestras. This remark applies likewise to other wind instruments.

422. The OBOE or HAUTBOY (formerly termed the *Waytes* or *Waits*,—the *watch*men who piped the night hours on it being called waits) is an instrument of wood, with a double vibrating reed. Its compass is shown in Fig. 368, but the lowest B♮ and the highest notes (above

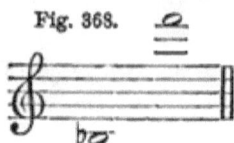

C) are somewhat hazardous, the latter, moreover, being of rather unpleasantly shrill effect. The tones of the instrument are of piercing quality; and passages are often written for it in 8ve with the Flute, which softens the effect.

The CORNO INGLESE (*English Horn* or *Vox Humana*) is almost obsolete. It is a kind of *Alto Oboe*. The part is written within the same compass as that of the Oboe (Fig. 368), but the *real sounds* are a perfect 5th lower than written. Thus, the passage written as at Fig. 369 (*a*) would sound as at (*b*).

423. The CLARIONET (or *Clarinet*) is an instrument of wood or silver, &c., with a single reed; of somewhat similar *form* to the Oboe, but of more mellow tone, and considerably greater compass.

The difficulties of producing the semitones upon the Clarionet are such, that different Clarionets are used for different keys. There are three in use in ordinary orchestras, viz.: the *C Clarionet* for the natural key: the *B♭ Clarionet* for flat keys; and the *A Clarionet* for sharp keys. But the mechanism is the same on all, the pitch, or *dia-*

pason,—range of sounds,—being different. Thus, the note at Fig. 370 (*a*) will on the C Clarionet sound as

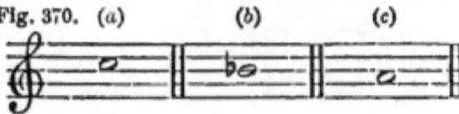

written; on the B♭ Clarionet as at (*b*); and on the A Clarionet as at (*c*). Therefore, the part for the B♭ Clarionet is written a tone higher than it is intended to sound; and that for the A Clarionet, a minor 3rd higher. And the Clarionet to be used is indicated by the composer at the commencement. Thus, if the passage at Fig. 371 (*a*)

be desired, it would be written as at (*b*), and '*Clarionet in B♭*' indicated. If the passage is desired in F, as at (*b*), the B♭ Clarionet will still be used, and the passage written in G. If the passage at Fig. 372 (*a*) be desired,

it is written as at (*b*), and '*Clarionet in A*' indicated. The compass of the Clarionet is shown in Fig. 373 (*a*, *b*, *c*); the notes in (*b*, *c*) giving the *real sounds* when written as at (*a*). The highest note is only advisable in a *Cadenza* (§ 126), or, occasionally, in a *Concerto* (§ 398), in which the capabilities and compass of the instrument are to be

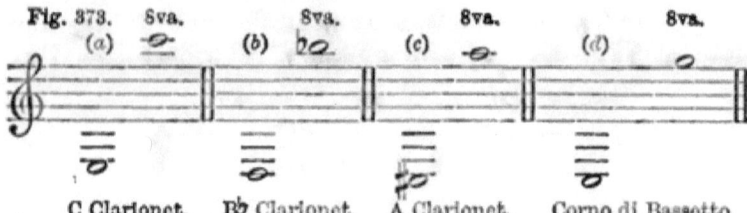

Fig. 373.
(a) C Clarionet.   (b) B♭ Clarionet.   (c) A Clarionet.   (d) Corno di Bassetto.

exhibited. Indeed, the notes above G in altissimo (§ 8) are not effective; and in orchestral music it is not desirable to write above F.

There is also a *Bass Clarionet in B♭*, an 8ve lower in compass than the ordinary B♭ Clarionet, the lower octave of which is very effective.

The CORNO DI BASSETTO in F, or BASSET-HORN, is a kind of *Baritone Clarionet*. Its compass is shown at (d); but the *sounds* are a *Perfect 5th lower* than written: F for C, whence its designation.

424. The BASSOON (or FAGOTTO, from its supposed resemblance in appearance to a bundle of faggots) is the *Bass* instrument among wind instruments of wood, used in an ordinary orchestra; and is, by some, termed the *Bass Oboe*. Its compass is shown in Fig. 374; but it is

Fig. 374.

not desirable to write above B♭, in orchestral music. Its medium notes are the best in quality. It is a double-reed instrument.

There is a smaller Bassoon (*Basson-quinte*), which is, in compass, a 5th higher than the ordinary Bassoon, and the part for which is written a 5th *lower* than the real sounds; but it is little used, at least in England.

The DOUBLE-BASSOON (CONTRA-FAGOTTO, or *Fagottone*) is an 8ve lower than the ordinary Bassoon, bearing the same relation to it that the *Double-Bass* does to the Violoncello (§ 417).

425. The FRENCH HORN (CORNO), now commonly termed *the Horn*,—the English Horn being little used, and the French Horn being that generally used in orchestras,—is a *brass* instrument (doubtless *originally* consisting literally of an animal's horn) of a curved form. It produces, naturally, simply the harmonic notes (see § 86), as shown in Fig. 375. By the insertion of the hand,

Fig. 375.

however, in the bell of the instrument, the intermediate notes, *shut-notes*, can be produced. Its natural key, as shown, is C; and *its part is always written in C*. It can play in other keys, however, by *crooks* being temporarily added to it, which change its pitch; and the composer indicates what key the Horns are to play in,—what crook is to be used,—by the term 'Corni in C,' 'Corni in D,' &c. If the natural Horn, in C, be used, the notes will be an 8ve lower than written. On other Horns, however, as in D, E♭, &c., the real sounds will be a 7th, a 6th, &c., lower. Thus, the passage written at Fig. 376 (*a*) will

sound as at (*b*, *c*, *d*), &c., according to which Horns are specified. There are Horns in A♭ bass, A♮ bass, B♭ bass, B♮, C, D♭, D♮, E♭, E♮, F, G♭, G♮, A♭ alto, A♮ alto, and B♭ alto.

Horns are used in *pairs* in an orchestra, both performers playing from the same book; as is the case with the other wind-instruments already mentioned. In some cases *four* Horns are used,—*two pairs; each pair* being in the same key, but both pairs not necessarily so.

426. The TRUMPET (or *Tromba*) is a brass (or silver) instrument, of shrill tone; and, like the Horn, produces the *Harmonic* notes only, naturally; the others, artificially. The *open* notes are most used; but, by means of modern contrivances, *valves*, &c., the intermediate notes are obtained. The *open* notes must be relied upon for power. The compass is the same as that of the Horn, but the notes do not sound *lower* than written; those on the C Trumpet (the natural key of the instrument) sounding *as* written, and those on the other Trumpets *higher* than written: different crooks being used, as in the case of the Horn. There are Trumpets in all the keys. High Trumpets are termed CLARINI.

The lowest C is only produced by Trumpets in high keys, and the high notes only on Trumpets in low keys, except with difficulty and uncertainty.

Latterly it has become very customary to use the CORNET-A-PISTONS in place of the Trumpet. There are Cornets in various keys. That in B♭ coincides in pitch with the B♭ Clarionet; and that in A with the A Clarionet; and these are written for in the same way as for the Clarionet (§ 423). Properly, the Cornet belongs to *military* bands.

427. The TROMBONE is a brass instrument, with slides, shortening or lengthening its tube. Three kinds are in use: the *Alto*, the *Tenor*, and the *Bass* Trombone, of which the respective compasses are given in Fig. 377

(a, b, c). The notes included by the small black notes are, however, the safest.

There is also a DOUBLE-TROMBONE, of deeper tone; which, however, is but little used.

428. The SERPENT (named from its shape) is made of brass, or of wood, covered with leather. Its compass is shown in Fig. 378 (a). The three notes at (b) are of

great prominence. The instrument seems to be almost superseded by the *Ophicleide*.

429. The Bass OPHICLEIDE is a powerful brass instrument. The compass is shown in Fig. 379. There

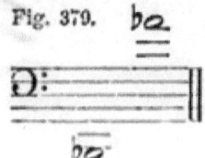

Bass Ophicleide.

are also Alto Ophicleides, but they are little used in ordinary orchestras.

430. Several other brass instruments, principally used in military bands, are occasionally used in ordinary orchestras, as the BASS-TUBA, the EUPHONIUM, &c. But the above specified are those in most common use.

431. Of *instruments of percussion*, the principal are the KETTLE-DRUM, of which a pair are customarily used in the orchestra; tuned, generally, to the *Tonic* and *Dominant* of the key. Generally, the Dominant a 4th *below* the Tonic is taken: sometimes, that a 5th above. Occasionally, the two *Drums* are tuned an 8ve apart: the Tonic and its 8ve; sometimes at other intervals. It was customary to write the Drum part in C (Fig. 380, a), and indicate the key,—'*Timpani in D, A*,' &c.; but it is now very common to write the actual notes, as at (b).

Fig. 380.

There is also the SIDE-DRUM (*Caisse-roulante*), the BIG-DRUM or BASS-DRUM (*Grosse-Caisse, Gran Tamburo*), used in large orchestras for special effect. Also the CYMBALS (*Cinelli: Piatti*),—plates of metal; and the TRIANGLE, of metal, the name of which is self-explanatory.

432. The art of INSTRUMENTATION, or SCORING, necessitates not only the knowledge of the compass and capabilities of the various instruments, as very briefly sketched above, but also knowledge and judgment as to how to *combine* and *contrast* them in a composition. This can be learned from no book, but by attentive study of the scores of the great masters, and attentive listening to performances of their works.

GLOSSARY OF MUSICAL TERMS.

BY far the largest number of musical words and phrases in common use are Italian. Few, in other languages, have extended beyond the countries in which they originated. For these latter (of which there are many modern ones in *German*, especially) a dictionary of the particular *language* would be requisite. Moreover, many words, both in Italian and in other languages, have no *special* meaning in their application to music, beyond their ordinary meaning. Many such words therefore are not included in the following Glossary, which embraces, principally, words which are commonly to be met with in music published in all countries. It is not intended as a Cyclopædia of that which is obsolete or rare (though containing some such terms), but mainly as a compendium, for *reference*, of that which is in common use.

It may be useful to remark that, in the Italian language, the affix '*issimo*' augments the power of a word: *e. g. dolce*, softly or sweetly; *dolcissimo*, very sweetly. The affix '*ino*,' or '*etto*,' diminishes the power: *e. g. Allegro, Allegretto, Allegrino*. It has not been thought necessary in this Glossary to insert the diminutives and augmentatives of such words.

Words explained in the former part of this work are, with a few exceptions, not included in the Glossary, but may be found by reference to the *Index*.

Only a few of the stops of the Organ are included · as

no verbal description can convey any idea of their quality. Many of them bear names of instruments that they are supposed to resemble.

A. At, for, with.

A BATTUTA. At the beat; in strict time: used, in Recitatives, &c., after '*senza Battuta*,' '*a piacere*,' &c.

ABBANDONE. With abandonment.

A BENE PLACITO. (See *Ad libitum*.)

A CAPPELLA. In the Church style. (See also § 24.)

A CAPRICCIO. Capriciously; in free, irregular time. (See *Ad libitum*.)

ACCAREZZEVOLE, ACCAREZZEVOLMENTE. See *Carezzevole*.

ACCELERARE, ACCELERANDO. Increasing in speed. (See *Stringendo, Affrettando*.)

ACCIDENTAL CHORDS. A term sometimes applied to Chords with Retardations or Anticipations, &c. (§§ 228, 229.)

ACCOLADE. (Fr.) The brace connecting the Staves.

AD LIBITUM. At the pleasure of the performer (with respect to time, &c.). Also applied to an *optional*, as distinguished from an *obbligato* (indispensable), accompaniment.

A DUE. *Both:* a term indicating that two instruments (*e. g.* both Oboes, in an orchestra) are to play in unison. Also applied to a composition in two parts. (See Beethoven's Variations, Op. 33.)

AFFETTUOSO, AFFETTUOSAMENTE, CON AFFETTO. Affectionately.

AFFRETTANDO. Hastened in time. (See *Accelerare*.)

AGGRADEVOLE. Agreeably.

AGRÉMENS. (Fr.) Ornaments. (See § 38.)

AGITATO. In an agitated manner.

AIR, ARIA. Melody. Also, a Vocal Solo of considerable length, in an Opera, &c.

ALLA TEDESCA. In the German style. Used by Beethoven for his Sonata, Op. 79, first movement, probably to mean in the time of a German dance.

ALLEGREZZA. Joy. *Con Allegrezza*, joyously.

ALLEMANDE. A somewhat grave movement in C time,

common in the music of Bach, Handel, Couperin, &c. Also a German dance movement in triple time.

AL ROVESCIO, or *Roverscio*. Applied to a passage or subject taken by inverse movement. Thus, there is *Contrapunto al Rovescio*: different from Retrograde Counterpoint. (See §§ 367, 368.)

ALTERNATIVO, ALTERNAMENTE. A movement played in alternation with another movement: *e. g.* the *Trio* of a *Minuet*. (See § 405.)

AMABILE. Amiably.

AMAREZZA. Bitterness, grief.

AMOREVOLE, CON AMORE, AMOROSO. Lovingly.

ANDAMENTO. Walk, or movement: *e. g. Andamento rapido*. Also applied to a long, discursive Fugue subject.

ANIMATO. Animated: usually referring to speed; as *Allegro Animato*. (Not to be confounded with *Con Anima, q. v.*)

ANTHEM. A sacred vocal composition, the words from the Bible. When for a chorus, it is termed a *Full Anthem*. When with one or more movements for Solo voices, it is termed a *Verse Anthem*. The term is supposed to be derived from ἀντί (against), φωνή (a voice); early Christian hymns having been sung *Antiphonally*, *i.e.* by responsive choirs.

A PIACERE. At pleasure. (See *Ad libitum*.)

APLOMB. (Fr.) With steadiness and firmness. applied to *touch* on the Pianoforte, &c.

A POCO A POCO. Gradually: *e. g. a poco a poco cres.*

APPASSIONATO, CON PASSIONE. Impassioned.

APPOGGIATO. Leaned upon. Also used for *Portamento di Voce, q. v.*

A PUNTA D'ARCO. With the end of the bow.

A QUATTRO. In four parts.

ARCH-LUTE. An obsolete plectral instrument (§ 410). See *Lute*.

ARCO, COLL' ARCO. With the bow (after *Pizzicato, q. v.*)

ARIA: *diminutive*, ARIETTA. See *Air*.

ARIOSO. In a melodious, singing, agreeable manner.

ARSIS (ἄρσις, *lifting up*). The unaccented (*up*) beat of the bar. (See § 367.)

A TEMPO, IN TEMPO. In time (after *Rallentando*, &c.).

A TRE. In three parts.

ATTACCA. Go on immediately (as to the next movement of a *Sonata*).

ATTACCO. A short Fugue Subject, or section thereof (See *Motivo*: also § 394.)

AUBADE. Music performed under a window at daybreak.

BAGPIPE. A well-known instrument; not, as commonly supposed, of Scottish origin, but of great antiquity.

BAGUETTE. Drum-stick.

BALLAD. In England, a simple song, with simple accompaniment; the different stanzas being set to the same music. In Germany, the term being applied to poems of a lengthened and elaborate character, it has also been used, there and elsewhere, as the title of compositions, both Vocal and for the Pianoforte (as by Chopin), of an extended, and by no means simple kind.

BALLET. Formerly, a light vocal composition, danced to, while sung. In modern times, a fabulous story, represented by dancing, accompanied by music. Probably *Ballad* and *Ballet* originally had the same signification. It is said that *Ballets* were sung to in France.

BALLO, BALLETTO. An old Italian dance air. (Found in D. Scarlatti's works.)

BARCAROLLE (Fr.), BARCAROLA (Ital.). A song or Chorus in $\frac{6}{8}$ time, sung in a Gondola, with the movement of which its rhythm coincides.

BAS-DESSUS. (Fr.) Mezzo-Soprano.

BASSO-OSTINATO. Ground-Bass. (§ 247.)

BEN. Well; *e. g. Ben Marcato*.

BOLERO. A Spanish song and dance, accompanied with castanets, in $\frac{3}{4}$ time, and generally in the Minor key.

BOMBARDO. An obsolete wind instrument of the *Oboe* kind.

BOURDON. The burden, or *drone*-bass, in such instruments as the Bagpipe.

BOURRÉE. An old French dance of cheerful character, in duple time.

BOUTADE. (Fr.) A little impromptu dance.

BRANLE. A gay French dance; the music in *Rondo* form (see § 404). Supposed, by some, to be identical with the *Braule*, an old dance.

BRAVURA. Bravery, spirit. Thus, *Aria di Bravura*, as contrasted with *Aria Cantabile*, &c.

BRILLANTE. Brilliant.

BRINDISI. A drinking song; the term being used in drinking healths.

BRIOSO, CON BRIO. With briskness, life.

BUFFO. Comic; *e. g. Opera buffa (fem.)*.

BUGLE. A short horn (*bucula*, a heifer), much used by the Germans in hunting; and by them termed, therefore, *Waldhorn*, wood-horn. A *keyed-bugle* is now in use in brass bands.

BURDEN. Formerly, the Bass added to a song; also, a *Refrain*, or *Ritornello, q. v.*

BURLETTA. A light musical drama.

CABALETTA. A certain brilliant passage occurring towards the close of *Arias*, &c., in Italian Operas.

CACCIA. The chase.

CACHUCHA. A Spanish dance in triple time.

CALANDO. Literally, *falling away*, and applicable to *tone*; being then synonymous with *Diminuendo*; in which case it is occasionally written *Calando nel forza*. More frequently, however, it is used to signify *slackening of time*; being then sometimes (but seldom) expressed *Calando nel tempo*. It is most frequently used in this latter sense; as is shown, often, by its being succeeded by the words *a tempo*.

CALCANDO. Equivalent to *Pesante, q. v.*

CALMATO. Calmly.

CANARY. An old dance, in jig form, in $\frac{6}{16}$, or $\frac{3}{8}$, or $\frac{6}{8}$ time. The movements by Couperin, bearing this name, seem intended to imitate the birds.

CANTABILE, CANTANDO, CANTANTE. In a singing manner.

CANTATA. A long Vocal Solo of a dramatic character. Also, a composition for voices, with accompaniment, consisting of choruses interspersed with solos, &c.

CANTILENA. A sustained melodious passage.

CANTIQUE. A sacred song.

CANTORIS. That part of Antiphonal church music sung by the choir who are on the same side of the cathedral as the *Cantor*, or Precentor.

CANZONE, CANZONET, CANZONETTA (*dimin.*). A song, or duet, of a flowing character.

CAPRICCIO, CAPRICE. An instrumental solo without prescribed form. (See § 407.)

CAPRICCIOSO. See *A Capriccio*.

CAREZZEVOLE, CAREZZANDO. In a caressing manner.

CARILLONS. A set of tuned bells, played with keys and pedals; common in Holland and Belgium. See Cramer's *Studio*, vol. I. No. 10, ' en Carillon.'

CAROL. A song of joy, or of devotion.

CAROLA. A dance, accompanied with singing.

CASTAGNETTES, CASTANETS. Hollow shells, or pieces of wood, &c., rattled in Spanish dances.

CATENA. A chain. *Catena di trilli*, a series of shakes or trills.

CAVATINA. A short song, without episode, or return to the subject.

CHACONNE, CIACONNA. A dance of Italian or Spanish origin; the music, in triple time, consisting, generally, of Variations on a *Ground-Bass*. (§ 247.)

CHALUMEAU. An old reed-instrument. Also, the lowest register of the Clarionet diapason. The term *en chalumeau*, in Clarionet music, signifies that the passage is to be played an 8ve lower than written.

CHANT. A short composition, adapted for the musical *recitation* of the Psalms, &c.

CHANTERELLE. The 1st string of the Violin.

CHITARRONE. An old instrument of the Guitar kind. A Theorbo.

CHORALE. A German hymn-tune.

CHORUS, CHOIR. A body of voices singing together, several to each part. A composition sung by such a body is also termed a *Chorus*.

Glossary of Musical Terms. 237

CITHER. See *Zither*.

COLLA PARTE. The accompanist to follow the Solo part, closely: used in *ad lib.* passages, &c.

COME SOPRA. *As above:* referring, generally, to the manner of performance of a reiterated passage.

COMMA. A fraction of a *Diesis, q. v.*

COMODO, COMODAMENTE. Conveniently, properly: used, generally, as an adjunct to *Allegro,* to indicate moderation of speed.

CON AMORE. See *Amorevole*.

CON ANIMA. With soul. (Compare with *Animato*.)

CON DELICATEZZA. See *Delicatamente*.

CON DOLCEZZA. See *Dolce*.

CON FUOCO. With fire.

CON GIUSTEZZA. See *Tempo Giusto*.

CON GRAZIA. See *Grazioso*.

CON GUSTO. See *Gustoso*.

CON IMPETO. With impetus.

CON LEGGEREZZA, or LEGGIEREZZA. With lightness and agility.

CON LEGGIADREZZA. With grace, elegance, gentleness.

CON MAESTA. See *Maestoso*.

CON MOTO. With motion, or impulse.

CON SPIRITO. See *Spiritoso*.

CON TENEREZZA. See *Teneramente*.

CONTREDANSE. (Fr.) A dance so named from the dancers being ranged *opposite* (*contre*) to, and encountering one another. Not, as frequently, to be confounded with *Country-dance, q. v.*

CORNEMUSE. (Fr.) Bagpipe.

CORONA. A Pause. ⌢

COTILLON. An old dance, in $\frac{6}{8}$ time.

COUNTRY-DANCE. The general name for a variety of old English dances. (Compare with *Contredanse*.)

COURANTE, CORANTE. An old French dance, in triple time.

CRWTH. An old Welsh instrument, of the Violin kind.

DECANI. The choral priests in a Cathedral, as distinguished from the lay choristers. The term is used in antiphonal music, in opposition to *Cantoris*, *q. v.*

DECISO. Decided.

DELICATAMENTE, DELICATO, CON DELICATEZZA. Delicately.

DESSUS. (Fr.) Soprano.

DIAPASON (§ 8). The tuning-fork—an instrument for fixing the pitch—is so termed by the French. The term also signifies the range or compass of a voice or instrument (§ 423). Also, a stop on the organ (§ 419), of which there are two kinds: the *Stopped Diapason*, the pipes being open at *one* end only; and the *Open Diapason*, the pipes being open at both ends. Most organs have both. They are called *Foundation* stops.

DIÈSE. Sharp.

DIESIS. The enharmonic difference between a diatonic and a chromatic semitone. This term, and *Comma* (*q. v.*), are used in the mathematical computation of intervals.

DI MOLTO. See *Molto*.

DITHYRAMBUS, DITHYRAMBIC. Originally, a song to Bacchus. Also applied to a wild enthusiastic poem, or musical composition.

DITONE. Major third.

DIVERTIMENTO. A light piece of music.

DIVISI. *Divided:* applied when the first violins (for example), in an orchestra, are to divide, playing two parts, instead of all in unison.

DIVISIONS. Several notes, in one part, to one continued harmony in the others; as in the third species of Counterpoint.

DOLCE, DOLCEMENTE. Softly, sweetly.

DOLENTE, CON DOLORE, DOLOROSO, DUOLO. With grief.

DOUBLE. An old dance in triple time. Also, formerly, a **Variation**. (§ 406.)

DRONE. See *Bourdon*.

DUET, DUO. A composition for two voices or instruments.

DUE VOLTE. Twice.

DULCIMER. An instrument consisting of strings stretched

across a sounding-board, struck with hammers, or plucked by *plectra*. The Psaltery is supposed to have been an instrument of this kind.

DUR. (Germ.) Major, as applied to *Mode* or *Key*: e. g. G *dur*. (See *Moll*.)

ECOSSAISE. A lively dance, in duple time. Formerly, a slow dance, in triple time.

EGUALMENTE. Equably (in *touch*).

EMBOUCHURE. The mouth-piece of a wind-instrument. Also applied to the performer's aptitude of lip, natural or acquired; it being said of a skilful performer, that 'he has a good *embouchure*.'

ESPRESSIVO, CON ESPRESSIONE. With expression. A performer may play or sing with great artistic *finish*, by observing all the *marks of expression*, as they are often termed,—such as the *pianos, fortes*, &c.; but to play with *expression* necessitates inward susceptibility to the sentiment of the music.

FANDANGO. A Spanish dance, in $\frac{3}{4}$ time, accompanied by Castanets.

FANFARE. A flourish of Trumpets. A short composition for military instruments.

FARANDOULE. A French dance in $\frac{6}{8}$ time.

FASTOSO. Pompously.

FERMATA, FERMATE. Pause.

FIDDLE. From Anglo-Saxon *Fithele*; thence *Fiele, Vielle, Viol, Violino* (diminutive), *Viola*, &c. Fiddle, therefore, is not a *vulgarism*, but the archaic form of the word Violin.

FIFE. A small, shrill instrument, shaped like a Flute.

FIFTEENTH. A stop on the Organ, giving the sounds two 8ves above the *Diapasons*.

FINALE. The last piece in an act of an Opera. The last movement of a Sonata, &c.

FLAGEOLET. A shrill wind instrument, blown from the end. The Harmonic sounds on the Violin, produced by a peculiar treatment of the strings.

FORZATO. See *Sforzato*.
FUOCO. See *Con Fuoco*.
FURLANA, FORLANA. A Venetian dance, in $\frac{6}{8}$ time.

GAGLIARDE. See *Galliard*.
GAIO, or GAJO. Gaily.
GALLIARD. An old Italian dance, in triple time, also called *Romanesca*.
GALOP. A quick dance, in duple time.
GALOUBET. An acute instrument of the Flute kind, almost obsolete, though still played in some parts of France. It is played in conjunction with the *Tambourine, q. v.*
GARBO. Elegance, grace.
GAVOT, GAVOTTE, GAVOTTA. An old dance, in ¢ time; of lively, but stately character; always beginning at the half-bar.
GIGA, GIGUE. Jig. A lively dance, of a pastoral character, generally in $\frac{6}{8}$ or $\frac{12}{8}$ time; but specimens are to be found in $\frac{3}{8}$, and likewise in ¢ time, in old music, by *Muffat*, &c.
GIOCOSO. Jocosely.
GIOJOSO. Joyously.
GIUSTO. Exact, just. (See *Con Giustezza, Tempo Giusto*.)
GLEE. A composition for several voices; not always, as its name would indicate, of a lively character, some Glees being sentimental and pathetic; and some expressly termed *Serious Glees!* The word is from *Glew, Glie (Anglo-Sax.)*, which signified music generally, as well as mirth.
GLISSANDO. Gliding: applied to the playing of several notes successively, on the Pianoforte, by the same finger, sliding from one to the other.
GORGHEGGIO. A florid vocal passage, or exercise.
GRACES. Ornaments, such as the Appoggiatura, &c.
GRADUALE. Hymn sung at a certain part of the Roman Catholic service, upon the *steps (gradi)*, or an elevated place.
GRANDIOSO. Grandly.
GRAZIOSO. Gracefully.

GRUPPETTO. A little group of ornamental notes, preceding an essential note.
GUSTOSO. With taste.

HALLING. A Norwegian dance, in duple time.
HARMONICA. A musical instrument consisting of a series of glasses, tuned in order, and played on by the moistened finger. It was invented by Dr Benjamin Franklin.
HAUT-DESSUS. (Fr.) First Soprano.
HAUTE-CONTRE. (Fr.) Counter-Tenor.
HAUTE-TAILLE. (Fr.) Tenor.
HEMITONE. Semitone.
HOMOPHONY. The unison of several voices or instruments.
HORNPIPE. An instrument, common in Wales, consisting of a wooden pipe with a horn at each end, into one of which the performer blows; the sound proceeding from the other: also called *Pip-corn,* or PIBGORN. Being used to accompany a certain national dance, that dance, and the tune played,—which is in triple time,—both bear the name *Hornpipe.* Some modern Hornpipes are in duple time.

IMPETUOSO. Impetuously.
IMPROMPTU. A piece of music bearing an improvised character. (See, however, § 407.)
INTERLUDE, INTERMEZZA. A short movement introduced between other movements; the former term being applied, generally, to the short passages played by an Organist between the verses of hymns.
INTRADA. Introduction.
INTROIT. A short anthem, sung, in the Roman Catholic Church, as the priests, or the Pope, advance towards the altar.
ISTESSO. See *L'istesso.*

JIG. See *Gigue.*
LONGLEURS. (Fr.) The itinerant minstrels of the middle ages.

KALAMAIKA. A lively Hungarian dance, in triple time.
KISSAR. An ancient instrument of the Lyre kind.
KIT. (POCHETTE: Fr.) A small, pocket Violin.

LAGRIMOSO, LAGRIMANDO; sometimes LACRIMOSO, LAMENTEVOLE. In a weeping manner.
LANDLER. An old Austrian dance, of Waltz character, in triple time.
LANDU. See *Lundu*.
LANGSAM. (Germ.) Slowly.
LANGUIDO, LANGUENTE. In a languid manner.
LARGAMENTE. In a broad, large style.
LIED. (Germ.) A song.
L'ISTESSO, or LO STESSO TEMPO. The same time: *e. g.* when a change is made from $\frac{2}{4}$ to $\frac{6}{8}$, the term is used to indicate that the dotted crotchets are to be of the same length as were the crotchets; the rate of movement not being altered.
LUNDU. A Portuguese dance in duple time.
LUOGO, LOCO. (§ 32.)
LUSINGANDO, LUSINGANTE. Coaxingly, flatteringly.
LUTE. An early plectral instrument; one form of the *Cithara*, or *Zither*, q. v.
LYRE. An ancient instrument of the Harp kind: originally triangular, with only three strings.

MA. But: as, *Allegro ma non troppo:* quick, but not too much so.
MADRIGAL. A word whose etymology is quite uncertain though it has been the subject of much conjecture. It is applied to short poems, generally of an amatory character, and to the music set to those words. Madrigals are usually compositions of a contrapuntal, imitative character, for three, four, five, or more voices. They originated with the Flemings in the 16th century; the Italians and the English following, with great success. Palestrina and others wrote sacred Madrigals (*Madrigali Spirituali*): being, in fact, *Motets*. The Madrigal gave place to the *Glee;* and that to the

Part-Song, now in vogue; a much inferior style of composition. The Madrigal style is not now cultivated.

Maestoso, Con Maesta. In a majestic manner.

Mancando. Failing, waning: used in the same sense as *Diminuendo*, generally towards the close of a movement.

Mandoline. An early instrument of the guitar kind, played with a *plectrum*.

Marcato, Marcando. In a marked, emphatic manner.

March. A composition of rhythmical character, in simple quadruple or duple time, to give the time to soldiers, &c., in their marchings. Marches are not always military, however: there is a *March of Priests* in Mozart's Zauberflöte, &c. Not only are there marches of different character, as *Funeral*, *Wedding*, &c., but they may be marked by *national* character, as *Turkish*, &c.

Martellato. (Lit. *hammered*.) Applied to the rapid repetition of the same note.

Mask, Masque. A kind of musical drama, formerly in vogue, in which the performers wore masks. Milton's *Comus*, and the Masques of Ben Jonson, were set to music for performances of this kind.

Mass. A composition for voices, with accompaniment, in several movements, performed at the celebration of the Eucharist in the Roman Catholic Church.

Mazurka. A Polish dance, of a sentimental character, in triple time.

M.D. *Mano destra*. The right hand.

Mean. Old term for the *Tenor*, or *middle* voice. (See § 250.)

Medesimo. The same. (See *L'istesso tempo*.)

Meno. Less: *e. g. meno mosso*, less motion.

Messa di Voce. Putting forth the voice: applied to the swell, < > on a single note.

Mesto. Sad, pensive.

Metre. See Chapter xxxiii., on *Rhythm*.

Mezzo. Middling; as *mezzo-forte, mezzo-piano*. (*mf. mp.*)

Minuet. An antiquated French dance, in triple time, of stately character: said to have originated in the 17th century, in Poitou. (See § 405.)

MODERATO. At a moderate pace.
MODINHA. A little Portuguese song, accompanied by the Guitar.
MOLL. (Germ.) Minor, as applied to *Mode* or *Key*: e. g. A *moll*. (See *Dur*.)
MONFERINA. A gay dance, in $^6_8$ time, common in Piedmont and Lombardy.
MONOCHORD. A one-stringed instrument, used for experiments on the vibrations of strings. Also, an old instrument of the *Clavichord* kind (§ 411); which, however, should be *Monichord*, many-stringed.
MORDENTE. (*Nipping*, &c.) A little ornament preceding a principal note to give it point; such as the *trill*, &c. (§ 38.)
MORENDO. Dying away.
MORISCO. In the Moorish style. The *Morris-dance*, formerly common in England, is said to have been of *Moorish* origin; whence its name.
MOSSO. Motion. *Più mosso*: more motion, faster.
MOTET. Formerly, certain crude counterpoint, added to a plain chant. Now, signifies a sacred vocal composition, the words generally from the Bible, in one or more movements, with or without accompaniment, for any number of voices.
MOTIVO. A short musical subject. See *Attacco*.
M.S. *Mano sinistra*: the left hand.
MURKY. An obsolete form of composition, on a sort of Ground-Bass.
MUSETTE. A kind of Bagpipe with a double-drone; generally the Tonic and Dominant. Hence applied to a pastoral dance-tune, in $^6_8$ time, with a Double-pedal Bass (§ 237); or in ₵ time, after a Gavotte.
MUTE. (Ital., *Sordino*.) A small piece of metal sometimes placed on the bridge of Violins, &c., to subdue the sound. (See § 412: also *Sordino*.)

NACCARE. Large Castanets.
NOCTURNE, NOTTURNO. A piece of music for performance in the open air at night.

O, over a note in a Figured-bass, signifies that it is to be unaccompanied.

OBBLIGATO. Compulsory. An *obbligato* accompaniment is one that is *essential*, as distinguished from *ad lib.* The term is often applied when some particular instrument has a specially prominent part : *e. g.* ' *Clarinetto obbligato*.'

OFFERTOIRE, OFFERTORIUM. A composition performed during the *offertory*, in the Roman Catholic Church. Formerly, it was a vocal piece : latterly, an organ piece has been substituted.

OLLA-PODRIDA. Equivalent (as a term applied to music) to *Pot-pourri, q. v.*

ONDEGGIAMENTE. In a waving manner.

OP. *Opus*, or *Opera:* work. Used to designate the *number* of a composition in the order of its composer's published works.

OPERA. A musical drama.

ORATORIO. A sacred musical drama, or series of Choruses, Airs, &c., connected with one another, and constituting a complete whole. The term is said to have been applied to them on account of their having been performed in *Oratories;* or because performed at *Orations*, or sermons. They were first introduced by Filippo Neri, founder of the *Congregatione dell' Oratorio*, in 1548.

ORCHESTRA. A band of instruments of mixed kinds. Also, the platform on which they perform.

ORGAN POSITIVE. A small Organ without Pedals. Formerly, a table-organ.

O SIA. *Or else:* sometimes used where a passage may be performed either of two ways.

OTTAVINO. The Octave Flute, sounding an 8ve higher than the ordinary Flute. Also, a small spinet, the compass of which was an 8ve higher than the Harpsichord.

OTTETTO, OCTET. A composition for eight instruments or voices. (See § 316.)

OVERTURE. An Orchestral movement, prefixed to an

Opera or Oratorio; frequently, especially in the case of Operatic Overtures, intended to foreshadow some of the dramatic incidents of the work. There are also Concert Overtures: e. g., Mendelssohn's *Isles of Fingal*, Bennett's *Naïades*, &c. The term was formerly used to designate a *Symphony* (§ 398), with which to *open* an Orchestral Concert.

PANDOR, PANDURA. An old instrument of the *Zither* kind.

PARLANDO, PARLANTE. In a speaking manner.

PARTIMENTO. A Figured-bass.

PARTITUR. (Germ.) Score. Music was not printed in Score till, probably, the early part of the 17th century.

PART-SONG. A Choral composition, of simpler, less imitative structure, than that of a Madrigal.

PASSACAGLIA, PASSECAILLE. A rather slow, dignified dance, in triple time, of Spanish origin.

PASSAMEZZO. An old slow dance.

PASSEPIED, PASPY. An old dance, in triple time, of brisker movement than the *Minuet*, of which it was the precursor.

PASTICCIO. A little opera made up of pieces from different composers. Also, a *Pot-pourri;* a piece made up of different extracts, or tunes strung together. (§ 407.)

PASTORALE. A simple piece of music of a pastoral character, generally in $\frac{6}{8}$ time.

PAVAN. An old dance, of Spanish or Italian origin, in triple time.

PERDENDOSI. (*lit.* losing.) Equivalent to *Mancando,* &c.

PESANTE. Heavily. Rather dragged, and leaned on.

PIACEVOLE. Agreeably.

PIANGEVOLE, PIANGENDO. In a weeping manner.

PIFFERO. The fife.

PIÙ. More. *Più tosto* (more soon). Rather: e. g., *Andante più tosto Allegretto.*

PLACIDAMENTE. Placidly.

POCHETTE. See *Kit.*

POCO. Little: e. g., *Un poco forte.* See *A poco a poco.*

POGGIATO. See *Appoggiato.*

Poi. Then.

Polacca, Polonaise. The Polish National dance, in triple time; rather slow and sentimental, with a peculiar rhythm,—the phrases always terminating with the third beat of the bar.

Polka. A dance in $\frac{2}{4}$ time, probably of Polish origin.

Polska. A Swedish dance, in triple time.

Pomposo. Pompously.

Ponticello. The bridge of the Violin, &c.

Portamento della Mano. Management of the hand, and touch, on the Pianoforte.

Portamento di Voce. The management of the voice, in singing; especially in gliding from one note to another: often done most affectedly.

Positive. See *Organ Positive*.

Pot-pourri. See *Pasticcio*.

Prelude. An introductory movement.

Principal. A stop (§ 419) on the Organ, the pitch being an 8ve above the Diapasons.

Principale. A third (solo) Trumpet, used in some bands.

Pulsatile. Instruments of percussion are also termed Pulsatile.

Puntato. Pointed.

Quadrille. A well-known set of dances.

Quartet, Quatuor. A composition for four voices or instruments.

Quasi. As if: like:—*e. g.*, *Andante quasi Allegretto*, rather faster than *Andante*, verging towards *Allegretto*.

Quintet, Quintuor. A composition for five voices or instruments.

Quodlibet. (*Latin:* "What you please.") An indefinite term, applied formerly to little free vocal compositions, often of a jocose character: also applied to any composition of undefined form. Bach so terms No. 30 of his 30 Variations.

Raddolcendo, Raddolcente. Increasing in softness. See *Dolce*.

Rallentando. Gradually slackening in speed.

RANT. An old English dance.
RANZ DES VACHES. Alphorn melodies, played by the Swiss herdsmen to collect the cattle.
RAVVIVANDO. Reviving; as, for example, after *Calando* or *Morendo*.
REBEC. An old rustic fiddle.
RECITATIVE. A musical declamation. It is termed *Simple*, or *unaccompanied* (Ital. *secco*), when only supported by plain chords, on the Violoncello, or Pianoforte, &c.; *Obbligato*, when with more elaborate, prominent accompaniment for all the instruments in *strict time:* e. g., "*Comfort ye, my people*": such a Recitative being also termed *Recitativo Arioso*.
RECORDER. An old kind of flute.
REDOWAK. A Bohemian dance, rather slow, in triple time.
REEL. A lively dance.
REFRAIN. A burden, or *Ritornello*, q. v.
REGAL. A small portable Organ, formerly in use: also, a kind of small *Cembalo* (§ 411).
REGISTER. The compass, or part of the compass, of an instrument: thus, a passage changed from one pitch to another, e. g., an 8ve higher, is said to be in a different *Register*. Also, a stop, or range of pipes, on the Organ. (See §§ 8, 409, and 423.)
REPLICA, REPRISE. A repeat. Applied, also, to the return to the Subject (§ 401).
REQUIEM. A mass for the dead.
RIFFIORAMENTI. Extemporized embellishments.
RIGAUDON, RIGODON. An old gay French dance, in duple time.
RINFORZANDO. Re-inforcing the tone.
RIPIENO. The subordinate stringed instruments in an Orchestra are sometimes termed *Ripieni*, as distinguished from the *Principals*. Sometimes, in accompaniments, they cease to play; the Principals only playing: a fashion less common than formerly.
RIPRESA. The *Renvoi*, :S:. (See § 30.)
RISOLUTO. In a resolute manner.
RISVEGLIATO. In an animated, revived manner (*lit.* awaked). See *Ravvivando*.

Glossary of Musical Terms.

RITARDANDO. Retarding the speed.

RITENENTE, RITENUTO. Keeping back the time.

RITORNELLO. A passage occurring at the conclusion of a melody, &c., at each repetition; or between the Variations to a Theme.

ROMANCE, ROMANZA. A little simple, elegant song. Also, an instrumental piece of similar character. The term is indefinitely applied, however.

ROULADE. A florid vocal passage.

ROUNDELAY. A little vocal solo, in Rondo form. (See

RUBATO. See *Tempo Rubato*. [§ 404.)

SACKBUT. An old wind instrument, resembling the Trombone. That mentioned in the Bible is by some believed to have been a stringed instrument of the guitar kind.

SALTERELLO. (From *Saltare*, to leap.) A peculiar *leaping* dance in duple time.

SANTIR. A kind of Dulcimer.

SARABAND, ZARABANDA. A slow, serious dance, in triple time; probably of Moorish origin.

SAUTEUSE. A kind of leaping *Valse à deux temps*, very rapid, formerly in vogue.

SCEMENDO. Equivalent to *Mancando*.

SCENA. A dramatic solo for the voice.

SCHERZANDO, SCHERZOSO. Playfully. (See § 405.)

SCIOLTO. Free, separated; opposed to LEGATO. Formerly applied to Free Counterpoint.

SCORE. See *Partitur*.

SDEGNOSO. Disdainfully.

SDRUCCIOLATO. Gliding. See *Glissando*.

SEGUE, SIEGUE, SEGUITO. It follows: used to indicate that the next movement is to be immediately begun. See ATTACCA. *Segue la parte:* a direction to an accompanist, to follow the voice, or other instrument, closely.

SEGUIDILLA. A Spanish song and dance, in triple time, accompanied with Castanets.

SEMI-CHORUS. A section of a full chorus, singing some portions, often of an episodical kind.

SEMPLICE. Simply, without ornament.
SEMPRE. Always: *e. g., Sempre più cres.*; constantly increasing in tone.
SENTIMENTALE. In a sentimental manner.
SENZA. Without: *e. g., Senza repetizione*, without repeats.
SEPTET, SEPTUOR. A composition for seven instruments or voices.
SERENADE, SERENATA. Strictly, music performed on a *serene night*. Applied, however, to open air music, generally, or music, the scene of which is laid in the open air: *e. g.*, Handel's *Acis and Galatea* is termed a *Serenata*. The term is generally applied to love-songs, or other music, performed under a window at night or morning. See *Aubade*.
SERINETTE. A little organ, formerly used by French ladies, to teach tunes to the little bird called the *Serin*.
SERIOSO. Seriously.
SESQUIALTERA. A *compound* stop on the Organ (that is, consisting of several *ranks*, or registers of pipes), giving the Triad of the note struck. (§ 409.)
SESTET, SEXTUOR. A composition for six instruments or voices.
SEXTOLE. A group of six notes, to be played in the time of four.
SFORZANDO, SFORZATO. *Sf.* This term signifies *weakening, enervating*; but is applied in music in quite the reverse sense, to indicate *force*, especially to a particular note or chord (§ 36).
SHAWM, SHALM. An early form of reed wind instrument, the precursor of the Clarionet, &c.
SICILIANA. An old Sicilian dance in $\frac{6}{8}$ time, with a *Saltarello* movement.
SIMILE. In the same manner (§ 32).
SINFONIA, SYMPHONY. An introductory or intermediate passage, by the accompanying instrument or instruments, to a song or solo. (See also § 398.)
SINGHIOZZANDO. In a sobbing manner.
SINISTRA. See *M.S.*
SISTRUM. An Egyptian instrument, of a rattling kind.

SLARGANDO. Slackening in speed, and increasing in largeness of manner.
SLEGATO. Separate, disconnected.
SLENTANDO. Slackening.
SMORZANDO. Smotheringly. Equivalent to *Diminuendo, Morendo,* &c.
SMORZATORE. *Sordino, q. v.*
SOAVE. Sweetly, agreeably.
SOL FA. *Solmisation.* Singing with the Italian syllables (§ 5).
SOLFEGGIO. A vocal exercise to be sung to the Italian syllables.
SOLO. A composition for one principal voice or instrument, with or without accompaniment. Those passages in a Concerto (see § 398) in which the principal instrument plays, as distinguished from the *Tuttis, q. v.* The principal voices in an Oratorio or Opera are termed the Solo voices, as distinguished from the chorus.
SONG. A vocal Solo, generally of concise rhythmical construction. See *Ballad, Romance,* &c.
SORDINO. A *Mute, q. v.* Also, an ancient *Kit* or POCHETTE, *q. v.*
SOSTENUTO. In a sustained manner.
SOTTO VOCE. With subdued tone.
SPANIATO. Disentangled, clear.
SPIANATO. Simply, unaffected.
SPICCATO. Equivalent to *Staccato.* When used in Violin music it signifies with the point of the bow.
SPIRITOSO, CON SPIRITO. In a spirited manner.
STENTANDO, STENTATO. Holding back the time, and in a somewhat heavy, laboured manner.
STRACCIANDO. With commotion.
STRATHSPEY. A Scotch dance, in ₵ time.
STREPITOSO. Boisterously.
STRETTA. A coda, in which the materials of the movement are brought together with somewhat rapid recapitulation; also especially applied to the termination of an Opera *Finale,* even when no such recapitulation takes place.

STRETTO. (See § 387.) *Più stretto* is equivalent to *più mosso*, more motion.

STRINGENDO. Urging on the speed.

STUDY. A composition intended to assist in the overcoming of some special difficulty, or in the attainment of some special excellence in musical performance.

SUBITO. Quickly. *V. S., Volti Subito*, turn over quickly.

SVEGLIATO. Awakened: equivalent to *Ravvivando*.

SYREN. A beautiful instrument for measuring the vibrations of the air. (See Tyndall on *Sound*, chaps. ii. & viii.)

SYRINX. Pan's pipes.

TABLATURE, ENTABLATURE. A method formerly in use of representing musical sounds by letters of the alphabet, or other signs, instead of by musical characters. It was especially adopted for music for the Lute, &c.

TABOR. A small drum, to accompany a pipe.

TACET. Be silent: used in the separate voice or instrument parts of a composition, when one of the parts is not to perform during a movement.

TAMBOUR, TAMBURONE. The great drum. (§ 431.)

TAMBOURINE, TAMBOUR DE BASQUE. A hand drum. Also an old Spanish dance, in ¢ or $\frac{2}{4}$ time, the time of which was marked by the instrument so named.

TANTO. See § 39.

TARANTELLA. A lively Neapolitan dance in $\frac{6}{8}$ time, generally accompanied by the Tambourine. Its name is from the *Tarantula*, spider; the effect of whose poisonous bite was supposed to be counteracted by dancing this dance.

TEMA. A theme or melody.

TEMPO GIUSTO. In exact time.

TEMPO PRIMO. The first time (after *Rallentando*, &c.).

TEMPO RUBATO. (*Robbed* time.) The slight deviations from strict time which a performer makes, to obtain expression, by taking from the value of one note and adding to another; or by accelerating in one place, and retarding in another. The term is also applied to the writing a common time passage in triple time, or *vice versâ.* Also to a cross accenting of a passage.

TENERAMENTE. Tenderly.

TENUTA, TENUTE, TENUTO. Held on.

TERZETTO. A short Trio: generally applied to *Vocal* Trios.

THEORBO. A kind of *Lute.*

THESIS. (θέσις, a placing.) The down-beat. See *Arsis.*

TIRANA. A Spanish air in triple time, with syncopation.

TOCCATA. (From *Toccare,* to touch.) A composition to *touch* or try an instrument with ; usually of a character to exhibit the resources of the instrument, and the powers of the performer. Applied principally to movements for keyed instruments.—A fourth Trumpet, used in some bands.

TOSTO. See *Più tosto*

TRANQUILLO, TRANQUILAMENTE. Tranquilly.

TREMOLANDO, TREMOLO. The rapid repetition, or alternation of notes, to give a trembling effect. Also, a certain trembling manner of putting forth the voice, far too much resorted to by singers.

TRENCHMORE. An old English Court dance.

TRIO. A composition for three instruments or voices. (See also § 405.)

TROPPO. See § 39.

TUTTI. All. Used when all the voices or instruments are to perform, in contrast with *Soli.* Also, the Orchestral passages without the Solo instrument, in a Concerto, are termed *Tuttis.* (See *Solo.*)

TWELFTH. A stop on the Organ, giving the sounds a 12th above the Diapasons.

TYROLIENNE. A kind of Waltz movement in vogue in the Tyrol; founded on two harmonies, alternated.

VALSE. See *Waltz.*

VAUDEVILLE. Formerly, a little French song. In modern times, a short and light musical drama.

VELOCE. Rapidly.

VIBRATO. With much vibration or tone.

VIELLE. The *Hurdy-gurdy;* formerly termed *Rote* or

Riote (*Rota,* a wheel). Its sounds are produced by the friction of a wheel upon strings.

VILLANELLA. An old Neapolitan air, of a rustic kind, to be sung and danced to.

VIVACE, VIVO. In a lively manner.

VOCALISE. To sing with several notes to one vowel, as distinguished from *Sol-faing,* or *Solmisation, q. v.* Also applied to vocal exercises, generally, without words.

VOICING. The process of regulating the tone and pitch of Organ pipes.

VOLANTE. In a light, *flying* manner.

VOLTE. An obsolete dance, of the *Galliard* kind.

VOLTI, V. S. See *Subito.*

VOLUNTARY. An Organ composition, of an extempore character.

WALTZ. A well-known dance, in triple time. The *Valse à deux temps* is not written in duple time, but with a cross accent.

ZITHER. An old instrument of the Guitar kind. A modern instrument of the Dulcimer kind.

ZOPPA. A certain kind of syncopated, *limping* Counterpoint, was formerly termed *Contrapunto alla Zoppa.*

EXERCISES IN
HARMONY AND COUNTERPOINT.

INTRODUCTORY OBSERVATIONS.

The following Exercises are intended to be filled up by the student as he proceeds with the perusal of the foregoing chapters. With this view, they are arranged under the headings of the chapters to which they respectively refer; and, in various cases, with references to particular paragraphs. They consist, after some Preparatory Exercises, firstly, of *Figured Basses*, to which the student is to add the harmonies indicated: secondly, of *Unfigured Basses*, to which the student is to add both the harmonies and the proper figuring thereof: thirdly, of *Melodies* to be harmonized: fourthly, of *Canti Fermi*,—subjects for contrapuntal treatment: fifthly, of Exercises on *Modulation*; and, sixthly, of *Fugue Subjects*, to which the student is to write the Answers and the Counter-Subjects; afterwards proceeding, if he pleases, to write the entire Fugues, preparatory to writing Fugues on his own subjects.

But, while the Exercises are thus arranged, to correspond with the order of the chapters, this arrangement is by no means intended to indicate the order in which they should be written. On this subject—the order in which the work should be studied—the student is referred to the remarks in the Preface. (See § 81.)

The Figured and Unfigured Basses are to be filled up—in the first instance, at least—in *four parts: i. e.*, three parts added to the Bass; with the exception of some, in regard to which other directions are given; *viz.*, those on the Dominant ⁹⁷, on the chords of the 11th and 13th, on Pedal Basses, &c. In many cases, the Melody, as well as the Bass, is given; and only the *inner* parts have to be added. These four parts should be for the four voices, Soprano, Alto, Tenor, and Bass. To write for voices is likely to cultivate a pure style of part-writing: melodious, and free from crude progressions. (See § 108.)

All these Exercises, in four or more parts, should be written in *Score*, with some exceptions which are indicated. This is desirable, as giving the student a clear view of the *walk*, or *progression*, of each individual part; and, in addition, as accustoming him to the habit of *reading a score*,—an indispensable part of a thoroughly furnished musician's qualifications. If, at first, the student should find it difficult to do this, he may write the earlier Exercises in *Short Score*, afterwards translating them into Score. In all such cases of writing in Short Score, the parts should be *equally distributed* between the two staves; the Soprano and Alto being written in the upper stave, and the Tenor and Bass in the lower. And, when other notes than semibreves are used, the *stems*, on each stave, should be turned contrary ways, as in Fig. 95, p. 65. This is especially desirable when the notes are of *various* lengths. In such cases, however, the *figuring* must be *under* the Bass, as in Figs. 112, 113. In Fig. 114, as the figuring is *above* the Bass, the *three* other parts are written in the upper stave.

When only a single part is written on a stave, as in a Score, the general rule is to turn the stem *up* if the note be in the *lower* part of the stave, and *down* if it be in the *upper* part. This avoids the projection of stems beyond the stave. Exception would be made to this, in the case of a *group* of notes; and in the case of a series of notes included in one *phrase*, especially if *slurred*. When copying the Exercises for *Short* Score, *all* the stems in the Bass must be turned *down,* and those in the Treble, *up.*

The Exercises in Score should be written with the appropriate *Clefs: i. e.,* in the proper *Staves* for the different voices (§ 7). This is desirable, because any other method is likely to lead either to the inconvenient use of Ledger lines, or else to writing out of the proper range of the voices. To obviate the former evil, a most reprehensible practice has arisen of writing the *Tenor* part in the *Treble* stave an 8ve higher than it is to be sung; a practice in utter violation of the scheme of the stave, &c., as explained in §§ 6, 7, and, in a Score, productive of confusion. The practice has been defended on the ground of its being easier to read a part so written than in the proper stave, for those who *do not understand the clefs!* in other words, persons who have not properly learned the first principles of musical notation: persons to whom there can surely be no good reason to make any concession at the sacrifice of propriety. It is presumed that those who study this book will repudiate any idea of writing, or doing anything else, inaccurately, to save themselves a few hours' application.

Undoubtedly, however, *facility* in writing, and reading from, four different staves of five lines—a Score, *in the Clefs,* as it is commonly called—is not *quickly* attained; and, as it is exceedingly important that the student should have a clear idea of exactly what notes he is writing, their pitch, the relation of part to part, &c.; and, moreover, as it is undesirable that he should have to combat more difficulties at a time than are inevitable, he may proceed progressively in this matter.

Thus, if he writes the early Exercises in *Short Score,* and then re-writes them in Score, as above recommended, he may proceed to write the succeeding Exercises in Score, in the first instance, with the *Tenor* only in the C clef; afterwards writing the Alto also in its proper stave; still writing the Soprano in the Treble Stave. The professional student is recommended ultimately to write the

17

Soprano in the [Mezzo-]Soprano Stave;[1] as, though not now much in use in this country, it was formerly used, and much music still exists with it; and it is still in use in Germany. It is desirable, therefore, that the professional student should familiarize himself with it. So that, ultimately, the Scores of the Exercises will be as in Example 1 (*b*); which is the Score of the Chant given in Short Score at (*a*).

After the student has written an Exercise, he should carefully examine it, to ascertain whether he has infringed any of the Laws of Part-writing; either those given in chap. xii., or those relating to the particular Chord or Subject on which the Exercise is given. In this ex-

---

The Stave with the C clef on the 2nd line (not now used) was *formerly* termed the *Mezzo*-Soprano Stave. See Preface to 6th Edition.

amination it may assist him to remember the principal forms of error which are most likely to occur in the connection of any two Chords.

(1.) Forbidden Consecutives (§ 103). To ascertain these, each part must be compared with each other part. *Hidden* Consecutives will be discovered by comparing the *extreme* parts (§ 104).

(2.) An objectionable interval of melody (§ 108). To ascertain this, each individual part must be examined, separately. The Augmented 2nd is the most likely to occur, of these bad intervals.

(3.) A neglect of a fixed progression : *e. g.*, that of the *Leading-note* (§ 109), or that of a *Dissonant* note.

(4.) A False Relation (§ 110).

The habit of carefully examining Exercises, to ascertain whether either of these errors occur, will be excellent discipline for the student, and will train him to avoid them. Though a slow process, he will acquire facility by practice.

After he has revised his Exercise in this way, and made the necessary corrections in it, he should play it on the Pianoforte, and judge of its effect. When he comes to anything which has an ill-effect, he should again examine the progression, to ascertain whether he has overlooked any infringement of a rule. In any case, that which is flagrantly ugly should be altered. Rules cannot reach all kinds of objectionable writing ; and although, in his early efforts, the student will be principally concerned to get his Exercises *correct*, yet, as he advances, he must try to make them musical and agreeable in every way. He must not grudge time and trouble in making corrections. Frequently, the correction of some one error may necessitate the alteration of several bars ; or even the re-writing of an entire Exercise, otherwise not faulty. At this, the student must not be discouraged.

In all cases, the student is advised to read *through* the chapter with which the Exercises correspond, in order to obtain a general view of the Subject, before attempting to write any of them ; and afterwards to read it a second time, writing them at the several stages indicated by the numbered paragraphs to which reference is made. And it is especially important that, before attempting any of the Exercises on Harmony, chap. xii. be thoroughly mastered: read and re-read.

After the Exercises in which the Melody is given have been filled up, they should, for practice, be re-written with a different melody. Not that the student should write a new melody, before writing the inner parts; which requires experience to do well. But he should recommence the Exercise in a different position, and then proceed without reference to the first filling up. And it will be excellent practice for the student to *transpose* the Bass of some of the Exercises—especially those which give him the most trouble in the first instance—into other keys, and fill up the harmonies, without reference to the former filling up. The new key will necessitate, in most cases, a new position of the Chords, to suit the voices; and thus new exigencies of part-writing will arise, exercising the student's thought. In transposing, he must be careful to preserve the correct notation; bearing in mind that *accidentals*, both in the parts and (of course) in the figuring, will, in many cases, be different in the new key;—sharps sometimes becoming naturals, &c. This will be especially necessary to observe in Exercises that *modulate*, and in those in the *Minor* key. (See Example 2, *a*, *b*.) A little consideration of the notation of the *Minor scales* will show this; as well as of the fact that a *natural* may either *lower* or *raise* a note, according to whether the note be *sharp* or *flat* in the first instance. Beyond these remarks, no special directions for transposition need be given; it being a very simple application of general musical knowledge.

Ledger lines, forming a continuation of the stave, should be written at the same distance from one another as the lines of the stave itself.

Dots should be written on the same space as the *head* of the note to which they apply; or on the space above or below, if the head be on a line.

Example 2. (a)

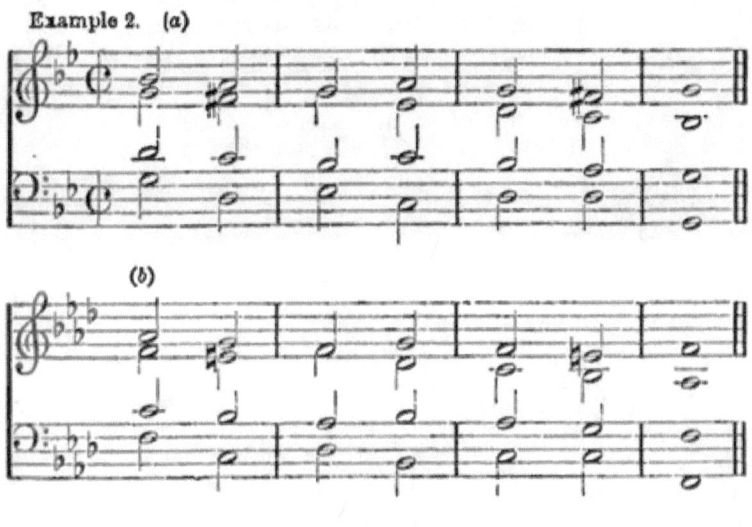

(b)

PREPARATORY EXERCISES ON THE RUDIMENTS OF THEORY.

CHAPTER V.   THE DIATONIC SCALE: MAJOR MODE.

§ 49. Write the Major Scale to every Tonic, placing the necessary sharps or flats *before the notes* to which they apply.

§ 51. Without reference to the book, arrange the sharps or flats for the *Signatures* to the above written scales; and then compare with Fig. 43.

CHAPTER VI.   THE DIATONIC SCALE: MINOR MODE.

§ 59. Write the Relative Minor Scale, ascending and descending, to each of the above-written Major Scales; *prefixing* the signature, and afterwards making the alterations, as explained in § 58, Fig. 47; and in § 59, Figs. 48, 49; *i. e.*, writing them according to *both* models. Compare the Tonics with the list in § 60.

Preparatory Exercises.

CHAPTER VII. THE CHROMATIC SCALE.

§ 64. Write all the *Major* Scales, with their signatures, ascending and descending, leaving space between all the notes for the Chromatic Semitones; which **afterwards** insert, according to the models, Figs. 51, 52; with which **compare the** Chromatic Scales so written.

§ 66. Write examples of Diatonic and Chromatic **Semitones,** above and below C♯, D♭, B, C♭, &c., as in Fig. 54.

CHAPTER VIII. INTERVALS.

§ 73. Write the Diatonic Intervals in the Scales of D, E♭, F♯, G♭, &c., according to the Model, Fig. 57, which gives those in the scale of C.

§ 76. (1.) Write columns of Intervals, according to the Model, Fig. 59, on G, B, C♯, D♭, &c.; *first of all* writing the centre column of Diatonic Intervals, leaving space on both sides for the Chromatic, **which** afterwards add. (2.) Write several specimens of all the Diatonic and Chromatic **Intervals on various notes.**

CHAPTER X. HARMONICS.

Write the Harmonic Chord to various notes, **according to the** Model, Fig. 61.

EXERCISES ON HARMONY.

CHAPTER XIII. THE TRIAD, OR COMMON CHORD.

§ 113. Write examples of Major, Minor, and Imperfect **Triads,** on C, D, D♯, E♭, &c.

§ 116. (1.) Write Triads, in four parts, in various **good positions** (see § 101), on different notes, in Short Score. (2.) **Add the inner parts to** the successions of Triads, Exercise 1, connecting **each two Chords** enclosed by Double-bars, according to the principles explained in chap. xii.; especially observing §§ 103, 105, 106, 109. In this, as in similar subsequent Exercises consisting of *couplets* of Chords, *only those within the Double-bars* are to be connected. (3.)

Exercises on the Triad.

Exercise 1.

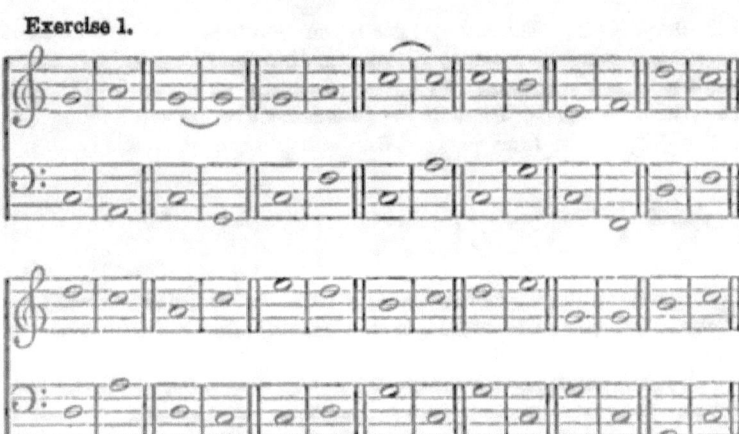

Fill up, with the *three* additional parts, the couplets of chords, Ex. 2.

Ex. 2.

Observe the progression of the Leading-note, in the third and fourth couplets. (4.) Add inner parts to Exercises 3 and 4, which are *con-*

Ex 3. [See § 120.]

Ex. 4.

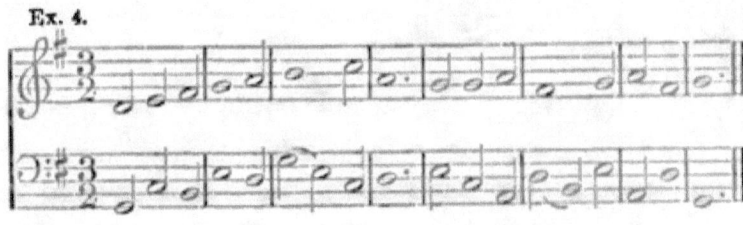

tinuous, not in couplets. Before writing them, study §§ 126, 127,

128, chap. XIV. When any note is common to successive chords, it may be written as a sustained note, as the first note in the melody, and the other tied notes, Ex. 3; or repeated, as in bar 5 of Ex. 4. In writing to *words*, this will be determined by the *syllables*. (5.) Fill up Ex. 5, in four parts. Generally, when the melody is not

Ex. 5.

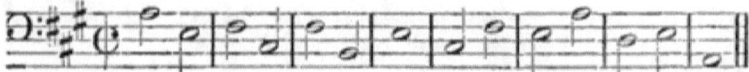

given, endeavour so to dispose the parts as to terminate with the Tonic (the 8ve to the Bass), in the Treble; preceded either by the Leading-note (as in Ex. 4), or by the Super-tonic (as in Ex. 3).

In commencing an Exercise in which the melody is not given, observe the early progression of the Bass. If it *ascends*, be careful not to begin with the parts so near to it as to *force* too much similar motion. If, on the other hand, the Bass *descends*, begin sufficiently near to it to prevent the parts becoming too much separated from it. In *all* cases, throughout the Exercises, *look forward*, endeavouring to trace the consequences of each position and progression, as much as possible.

The Parts should not be *crossed* in any of the earlier Exercises: i. e., the Tenor should not be above the Alto, &c. In later, elaborate Exercises, as those on Passing-notes, it may be desirable to cross the inner parts, sometimes.

§ 125. (1.) Add the inner parts to the couplets in Ex. 6; espe-

Ex. 6.

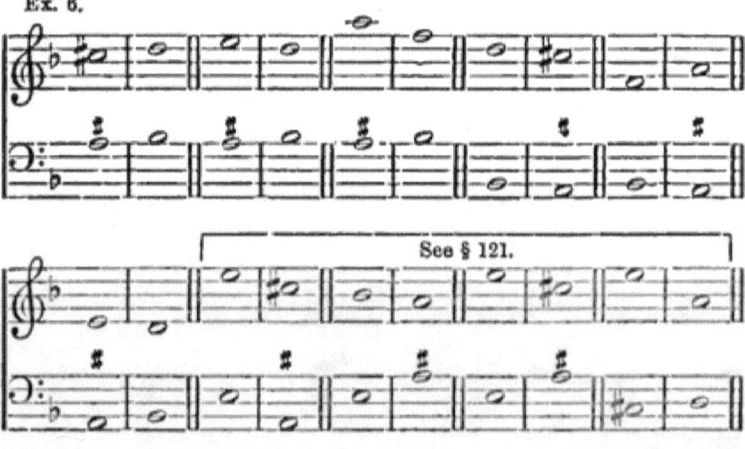

cially observing § 119. (2.) Add three parts to the couplets, Ex. 7;

Ex. 7.

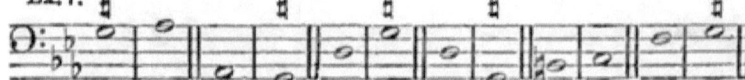

the first three couplets in three different positions. (3.) Fill up Exercises 8 and 9. Before writing the latter, study chapter XV., on

Sequences; and observe the application of § 138 to the first and third bracketed passages.

When the same chord is repeated, either with the same Bass-note, or the 8ve higher or lower, as in the fourth complete bar of Ex. 9, the position of the upper parts can easily be changed, should the previous context have brought them too near to, or too far from the Bass. Likewise, on a long note, such as a Minim, a change of position can be effected; two notes being taken, in one or more of the upper parts, to the one note in the Bass. The same Bass-note, repeated, bears the same harmony, till the figuring is changed.

CHAPTER XIV. CADENCES.

§ 128. Write *Perfect Cadences* in several Major and Minor keys; prefixing the signatures.

129. Add *Plagal Cadences* to the above Perfect Cadences.

§ 130. Write *Imperfect Cadences* in several Major and Minor keys.

§ 131. Write *Interrupted Cadences* in several keys, preceding them by a few chords.

CHAPTER XV. SEQUENCES.

Fill up Exercise 10. The sharpened 3rd in the sixth bar effects a brief transition into the Relative Minor (see § 339); and its progression as the temporary Leading-note must be observed.

266 *Exercises on Inversions of the Triad.*

Ex. 10.

CHAPTER XVI. INVERSIONS OF THE TRIAD.

First Inversion: the Chord of the Sixth.

§ 145. (1.) Fill up the (isolated) Bass-notes, Ex. 11. Place a

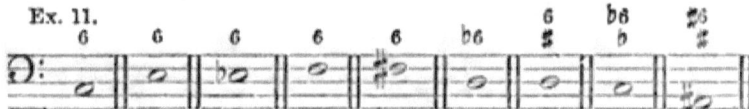

Ex. 11.

Direct under them, to indicate the Roots (as in Fig. 103). Write under each Chord whether it is the inversion of a *Major* or of a *Minor* Triad. (2.) Write the 1st inversion of the Triads of A Major, B Major, G Major, F Minor, E Minor, C♯ Minor; and figure the Bass. (3.) Fill up Exercises 12 and 13.

Ex. 12.

Ex. 13.

§ 150. Fill up Exercises 14 and 15.

Second Inversion: Chord of the Sixth and Fourth.

§ 153. (1.) Fill up the (isolated) Bass-notes, Ex. 16. Place a

Exercises on Inversions of the Triad. 267

Direct to indicate the Root (as above); and write under each Chord whether it is *Major* or *Minor*. (2.) Write the 2nd Inversion of the Triads of F, B♭, C♯ Major, D, G, F♯ Minor, and figure the Bass.

§ 159. Fill up Exercises 17, 18, 19, 20, and 21; Ex. 20 being a

268 *Exercises on the Dominant Seventh.*

Ex. 21.

transposition of the Bass of Ex. 8, with varied figuring. (See introductory observations on transposition, page 260.)

CHAPTER XVII. CHORDS OF THE SEVENTH.

§ 165. Fill up the Bass-notes, Ex. 22, and write the letter D

under those Chords which are *Dominant* 7ths, and the letter S under the Secondary 7ths.

The Chord of the Dominant Seventh.

§ 166. Write the Chord of the Dominant 7th in E, A♭, D♭ Major; and C, B, and G♯ Minor; prefixing the Signatures, and figuring the Bass.

§ 167. (1.) Fill up the couplets, Ex. 23, in various positions.

(2.) Resolve the Chords written under § 166, in different ways. Write some in *five* parts,—2 Sopranos, Alto, Tenor, and Bass;—resolving them to the Tonic Triad. (See § 167, (1, 2).) (3.) Fill up Exercises 24, 25, 26, and 27. Ex. 27 is the same Bass, transposed, as Ex. 8 and Ex. 20, with varied figuring.

Ex. 24. DOUBLE CHANT.

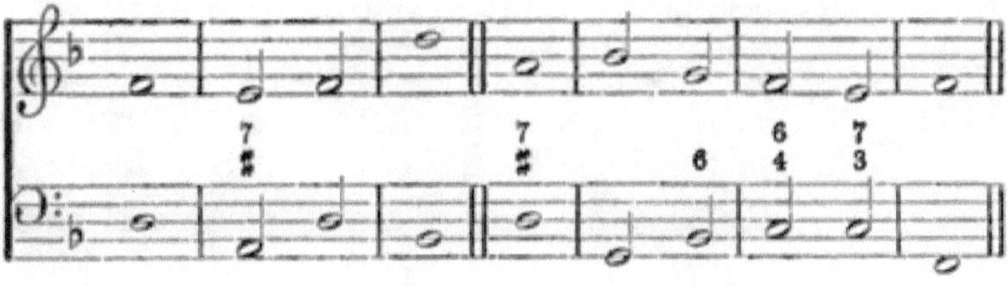

Exercises on the Dominant Seventh.

Ex. 25.

Ex. 26.

Ex. 27.

§ 168. Fill up Ex. 28.

Ex. 28.

Secondary, or Non-Dominant Chords of the Seventh.

§ 170. (1.) Fill up Ex. 29 (*a, b, c*). (2.) Fill up the Bass-notes,

Ex. 29. (*a*)   (*b*)   (*c*)

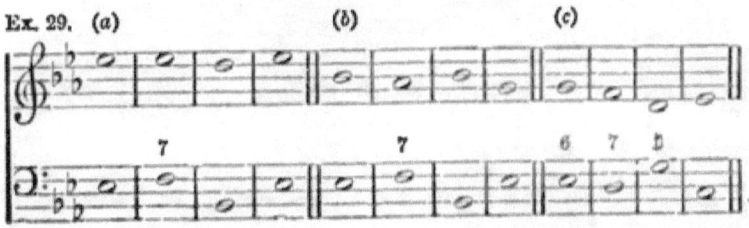

270 Exercises on Secondary Sevenths.

Ex. 30, in four and in five parts, preparing and resolving the dis-

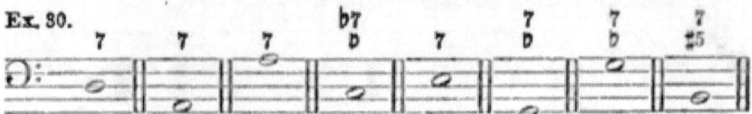

cords: *i. e.*, preceding and following each chord by appropriate chords.

§ 172. Fill up Exercises 31, 32, and 33.

Ex. 31.

Ex. 32.

Ex. 33.

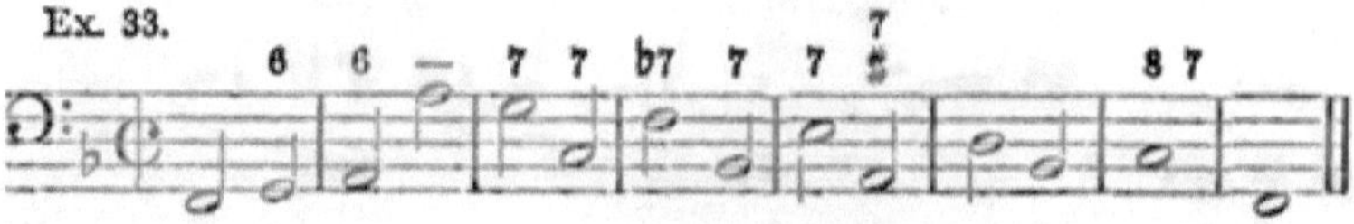

CHAPTER XVIII. INVERSIONS OF CHORDS OF THE SEVENTH.

Inversions of the Dominant 7th.

§ 176. Fill up the couplets, Ex. 34, and indicate the Roots of the Inversions by a *Direct.*

Exercises on Inversions of the Seventh.

§ 177. Fill up Exercise 35, indicating the Roots, as above.

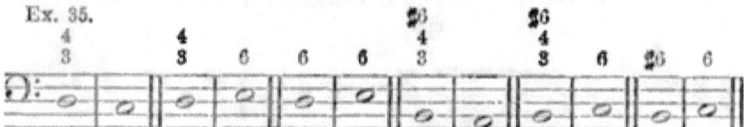

§ 178. (1.) Fill up Ex. 36, in like manner. (2.) Write the three

inversions of the Dominant 7th in F Major and F Minor, and in E Major and E Minor; prefixing the signatures, figuring the Bass, and resolving the dissonances.

§ 180. (1.) Fill up Exercises 37, 38, and 39. (2.) Transpose

272   *Exercises on Inversions of the Seventh.*

Exercises 37 and 38 into their Relative Minors, and fill up afresh. Be careful that the Chords of the 7th, and the inversions, are *true Dominant* Chords. (See §§ 113, 166.)

Inversions of Secondary Chords of the Seventh.

§ 181. (1.) Fill up Ex. 40 (*a, b, c, d, e, f*), being careful to pre-

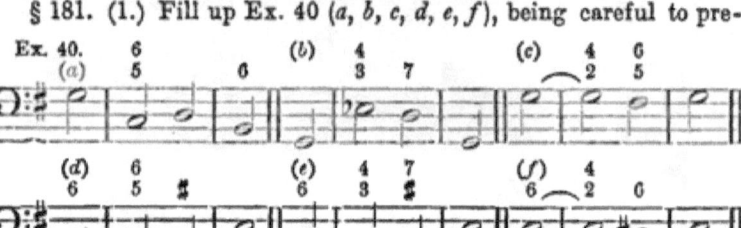

pare and resolve the dissonances. (2.) Fill up Ex. 41 (*a, b, c*); and

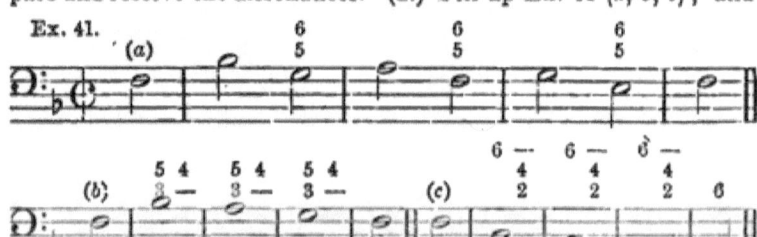

afterwards re-write (*a*), substituting the Chords of the 7th of which the first inversions are there given. (3.) Fill up Ex. 42 (*a*); and

then complete the three series of inversions thereof, commenced at (*b, c, d*). (4.) Fill up Exercises 43 and 44, indicating which of the Chords of the 7th, and inversions thereof, are Dominant, and which Secondary, as in Ex. 22, chap. xvii.

CHAPTER XIX.   THE CHORD OF THE DOMINANT $\frac{9}{7}$.

§ 187. (1.) Fill up Ex. 45 (*a, b, c, d*), in four and in five parts.

Exercises on the Dominant $^9_7$.

(2.) Write the Dominant $^9_7$ in B♭ Major and B♭ Minor, in four and in five parts; prefixing the signatures, figuring the Bass, preparing the 9th, and resolving both dissonances. (3.) Fill up Exercises 46 and 47, in four and in five parts.

274 *Exercises on Leading and Diminished Sevenths.*

CHAPTER XX. CHORDS DERIVED FROM THE DOMINANT $\frac{9}{7}$.

§ 191. (1.) Fill up Ex. 48 (*a, b, c*), in four parts; indicating the

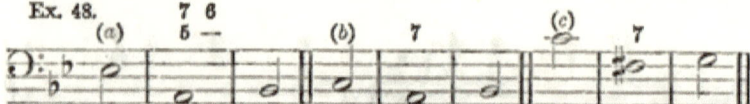

Roots of the Chords of the 7th by a *Direct*. (2.) Write the Chord of the Leading 7th in F Major, and the Chord of the Diminished 7th in F Minor, prefixing the signatures, preparing and resolving the dissonances, figuring the Bass, and indicating the Root. (3.) Fill up Ex. 49.

§ 192. (1.) Fill up Ex. 50, and indicate the Roots of all the in-

versions. (2.) Write the inversions of the Leading 7th in A Major, with signature; and of the Diminished 7th in A Minor; figuring, &c., as in former Exercises. (3.) Fill up Exercises 51, 52, 53 and 54.

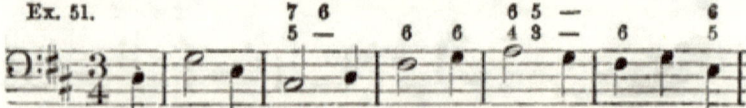

Exercises on Leading and Diminished 7ths. 275

[musical examples Ex. 52, Ex. 53, Ex. 54]

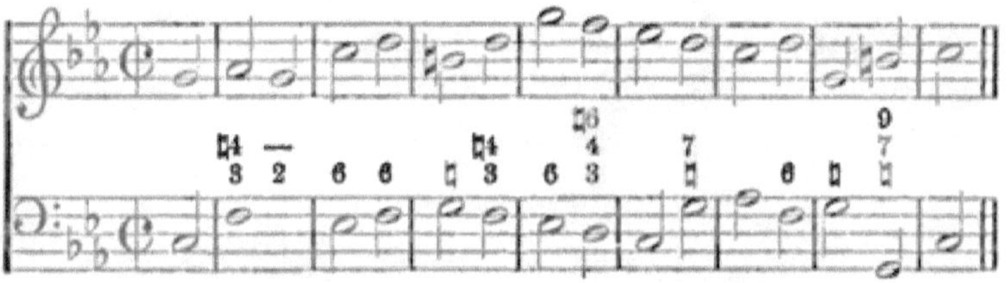

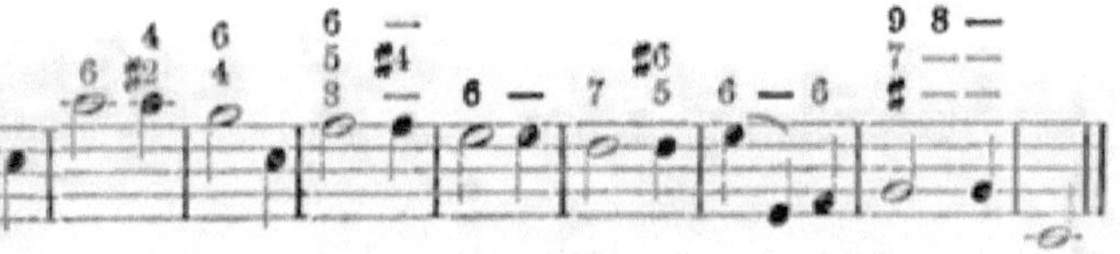

§ 195. (1.) Find the Roots of the Chords in **Ex. 55**, and the keys in which they severally occur. Then write them in Score with the signatures, and resolve them. (2.) Change the notation, in the same manner, of the Chord, **Ex. 56**, and then proceed similarly.

Ex. 55.

276 *Exercises on Chords of the 11th and 13th.*

Ex. 56.

CHAPTER XXI. THE CHORDS OF THE ELEVENTH AND OF THE THIRTEENTH.

Fill up Ex. 57 (*a*) and (*d*) in *five* parts: (*b*) and (*c*) in four parts.

Ex. 57.

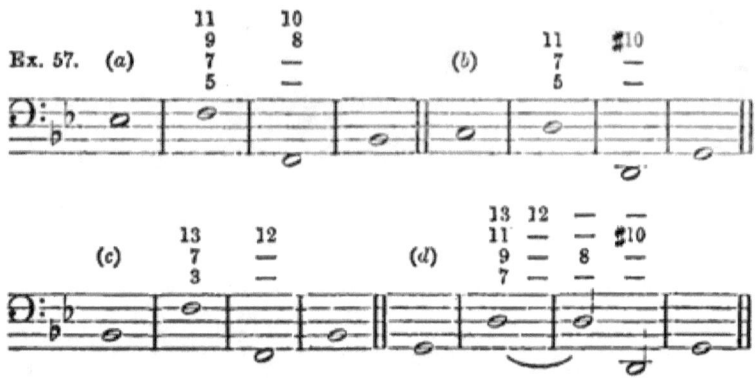

CHAPTER XXII. DISCORDS BY SUSPENSION.

§ 209. (1.) Transpose the *Bass* of Fig. 159 into F Major, and fill it up afresh, according to the figuring, in *four* parts; except (*l*) and (*m*), which will be in five parts: (*g*) and (*m*), moreover, will be in D Minor. (2.) Fill up Exercises 58, 59, and 60.

Ex. 58.

Exercises on Discords by Suspension. 277

§ 210. (1.) Transpose the *Bass* of Figs. 162 and 163 into F Major, and fill them up afresh. (2.) Fill up Exercises 61, 62, and 63.

278 *Exercises on Discords by Suspension.*

§ 211. (1.) Transpose Fig. 165 (*a, b, c*) into F Major, and (*d, e*) into D Minor, and fill it up afresh.   (2.) Fill up Ex. 64.

§ 212. (1.) Transpose the Bass of Figs. 166, 167, and 168, into F Major, and fill them up afresh.   (2.) Fill up Exercises 65, 66, and 67.

Exercises on Discords by Suspension.

Ex. 66.

Ex. 67.

Ex. 65 furnishes examples of the resolution of *fundamental* discords being delayed by suspension: the D in the Bass, bar 3, and the A in the $\frac{6}{5}$, bar 4. In Ex. 66, the resolution of the 7th, in the second complete bar, is similarly suspended.

§ 213. (1.) Transpose Fig. 169 into **F**, and fill it up afresh. (2.) Fill up Ex. 68, in five parts. Observe that the $\frac{9}{7}$ in fifth and sixth

Ex. 68.

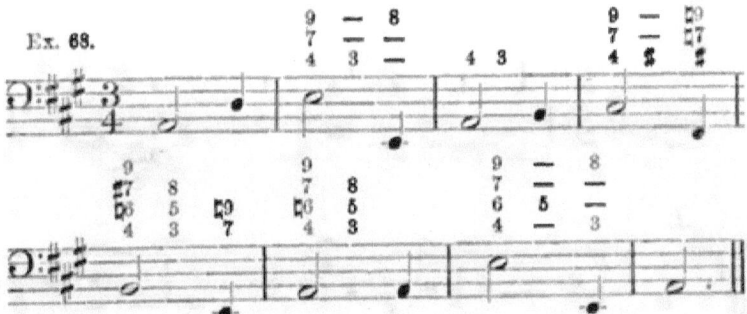

bars are *quadruple Suspensions* **on the** *Triad*: that in bar 7, is a double suspension on the $\frac{9}{7}$ (resolved as explained in § 214). (See Fig. 159, *m*.)

§ 214. Fill up Exercises 69 and 70.

§ 215. Fill up Ex. 71. The Tenor passage written **is in** *imitation* of the Soprano. (See chap. **xxxv**.)

280 *Exercises on Discords by Suspension.*

Exercises on Unessential Discords. 281

§ 216. Re-write Exercises 8, 13, 15, 17, 25, 26, 31, 34, 41 (a), 49, introducing Suspensions, single, double, with deferred resolution, &c., on the harmonies indicated, wherever they can be properly prepared and resolved. Do not figure the Bass till after the Exercise is completed: then figure, according to the Suspensions introduced. Often, in order to prepare a Suspension effectively, some change of position in the upper parts is necessary, on a single Bass-note.

CHAPTER XXIII. UNESSENTIAL DISCORDS.

§ 224. (1.) Add *one* inner part to Ex. 72. (2.) Fill up Exercises 73 and 74, in four parts. Ex. 73 is a Variation, by Passing-notes,

Ex. 74.

&c., of Ex. 21. Passing-notes may be added in the inner parts.
(3.) **Fill up Ex. 75**, adding Passing-notes. This Bass is the Melody
of Ex. 74. (4.) Vary Exercises 12 and 13, by Passing-notes.

Ex. 75.

CHAPTER XXIV. CHROMATIC CHORDS, AND CHROMATIC ALTERATIONS OF CHORDS.

§ 231. Fill up Exercise 76.   § 232. Fill up Exercise 77.
§ 236. Fill up Exercises 78 and 79. (See also Appendix I.)

Exercises on Chromatic Chords.

CHAPTER XXV. PEDAL NOTES.

(1.) Fill up Ex. 80, in two staves, as for the Organ. (2.) Fill

Ex. 80.

up Ex. 81 in Score. (3.) Fill up Ex. 82 (*a, b, c, d, e, f, g,*) in two staves. This Exercise is from C. P. E. Bach's "*Versuch,*" &c., with slightly altered figuring. In those written in two staves, the number of parts is not restricted to four, nor necessarily uniform in all the chords. (4.) Fill up Ex. 83 in Score. In the first three bars, Passing-notes may be introduced. In all these Exercises, indicate the Roots of the Chords, on a stave below the Bass.

Exercises on Pedal Notes.

Rule of the Octave.

Ex. 83.

UNFIGURED BASSES.

To these the student is to add harmony and figuring. In doing so, he should give special attention to all that is said in the chapters respecting the usual *context* of the various Chords, and the degrees of the Scale on which they respectively occur; also, to the chapter on *Cadences*, in connection with that on *Rhythm*. Before proceeding to these Unfigured Basses, however, it is desirable that the student should understand how to harmonize the Scales, Major and Minor.

Exercise 84 (*a*, *b*) furnishes the formula termed the RULE OF THE

Ex. 84. (*a*)

OCTAVE; a method of harmonizing the Scales,—the *Octave* of Sounds,—recognized by musicians as one of the most natural. It is capable of considerable variation, however, and the student can exercise himself by harmonizing the Scales in other ways.

Ex. 85 exhibits the Chromatic Scale harmonized. This, also, may be done in other ways. See Appendix I.

All the Unfigured Basses are susceptible of being harmonized in various ways; with Suspensions, Passing-notes, &c. (See § 247.) In these devices, the student should, progressively, exercise himself.

Exercises 86, 87, 88, give the Basses for the Major and Minor Scales when in the Melody. Exercise 89, that for the Chromatic Scale. See Appendix I.

288 *Unfigured Basses.*

UNFIGURED BASSES.

No. 1.

No. 2.

No. 3.

No. 4.

No. 5.

No. 6.

No. 7.

Unfigured Basses.

MELODIES TO BE HARMONIZED.

In harmonizing these, **the same attention is required as in the** Unfigured **Basses,** to Cadences, Rhythm, **and Modulation.** The *Sections* of Chants and the *Periods* of Psalm Tunes generally terminate with one of the various forms of Cadence. The first and third *Sections* **of** (four-line) Psalm Tunes do not always so terminate, nor **even end with a Concord;** the *words* of the **Hymns frequently** having more immediate connection between the **first and** second lines, and between the third and fourth; *repose*, therefore, not being so necessary.

Numbers 13 and 14 of these Melodies may be harmonized in four parts; also as Vocal Solos, with Pianoforte accompaniment, in Arpeggio. (See §§ 245, 246.)

Melodies to be Harmonized.

No. 6. DOUBLE CHANT.

No. 7. PSALM TUNE. C. M.

No. 8. PSALM TUNE. C. M.

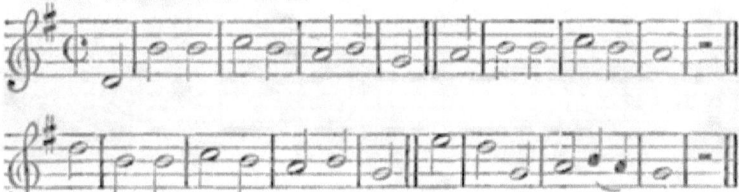

No. 9. PSALM TUNE. S. M.

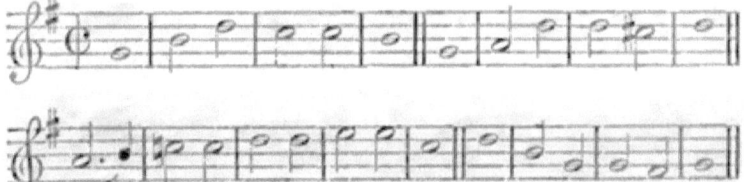

No. 10. PSALM TUNE. L. M.

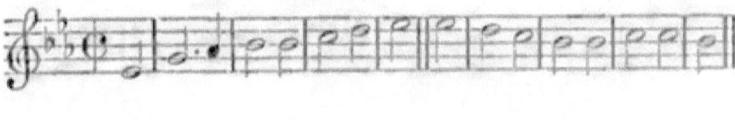
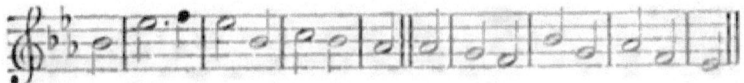

Melodies to be Harmonized.

No. 11. Psalm Tune. 8. 7. 4., or 8. 7., 6 lines.

No. 12. Psalm Tune. L. M.

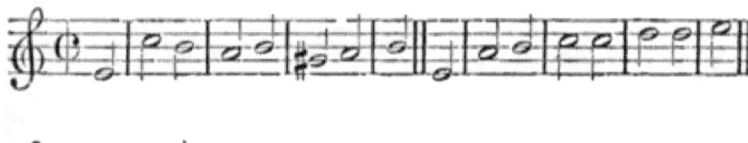
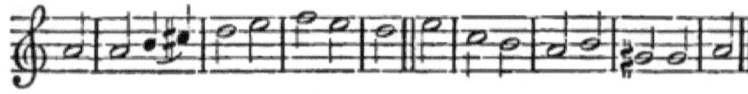

No. 13.

No. 14.

SUBJECTS FOR COUNTERPOINT.

CHAPTERS XXVII. TO XXXII.

These Canti Fermi are to be used throughout the course of Contrapuntal study, in all the Species, and in two, three, and more parts; being taken as lowest, inner, and highest parts, as explained and illustrated in the chapters. If they are not *all* used, it is desirable that the *same* should be used throughout, to illustrate different treatments of a given Subject. They are, all but the last two, taken from the works of old writers (most of whom were Italian), whose names are indicated. The authorship of the Canti is, however, uncertain. The two from Beethoven's *Studien* may have been given him by Albrechtsberger; as the book consists of notes, &c., made while he was studying with that eminent theorist.

CANTI FERMI FOR CONTRAPUNTAL TREATMENT.

294 *Canti Fermi for Contrapuntal Treatment.*

Canti Fermi for Contrapuntal Treatment. 295

EXERCISES ON MODULATION.

CHAPTER XXXIII.

Natural Modulation.

§ 340. (1.) Transpose Figs. 288 and 289 into E Major and Minor. (2.) Modulate, in similar manner, by the Dominant 7th and its inversions, from various other Major and Minor keys, to their attendants.

341. (1.) Transpose **Fig. 290, as above;** and then proceed simi-

Examples of Modulation.

larly, in other keys. (2.) Fill up Examples 1 to 10, which are from C. P. E. Bach's "*Versuch;*" and consist of Modulations, somewhat extended, from C Major and A Minor to their attendants. Example 5 is an *Enharmonic* Modulation by changed notation of the Diminished 7th. (See §§ 195, 348.) (3.) Write Examples of Modulations *through* the attendants of various keys: thus, D Major, A, F♯ Minor, B Minor, G, E Minor, D. Proceed similarly from other keys.

EXAMPLES OF MODULATION.

Extraneous Modulation.

§ 342. Transpose Figs. 291 to 294.

§ 345. (1.) Fill up Examples 11 to 15, which are from C. P. E. Bach's "*Versuch;*" and carefully analyze them. (2.) Write examples of Extraneous Modulation, in the various methods explained in the paragraphs.

Examples of Modulation.

Enharmonic Modulation.

§ 347. Transpose Fig. 295.

§ 348. Modulate, by means of the changed notation of the Diminished 7th, from E Minor to G Major and Minor, A Major and Minor, C♯ Major and Minor, B♭ Major and Minor.

§ 349. Modulate, by the Enharmonic change of the Dominant 7th, from D Major to C♯ Major and Minor, and to A♭.

§ 350. Modulate, by the Enharmonic change of the Augmented Triad, from D to B♭.

All these various directions can be carried out in other keys, and in various positions, &c., to afford ample practice.

CHAPTER XXXVI. FUGUE SUBJECTS.

300   *Fugue Subjects.*

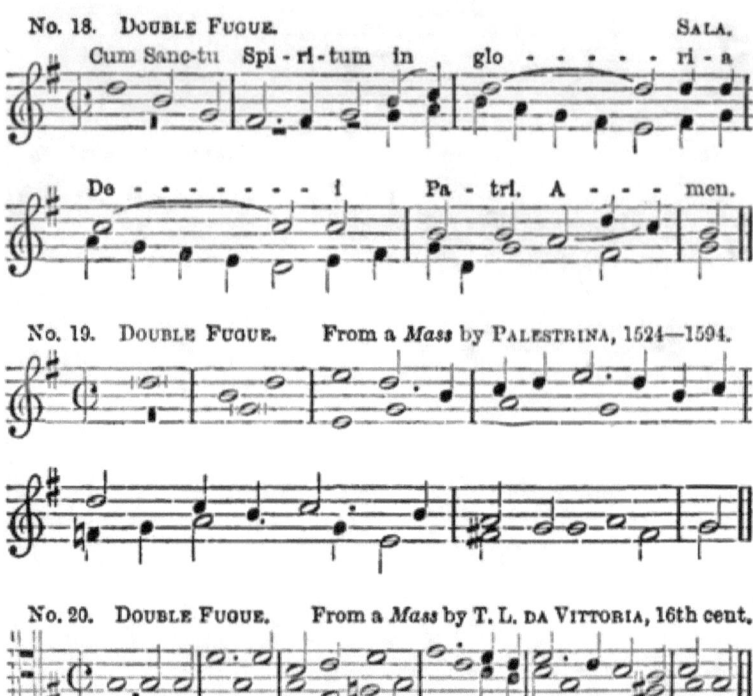

The Student should exercise himself with the above Subjects,—firstly, by writing the *Answers*, tonal or real, as the case may be, both direct and inverse: secondly, by writing Counterpoint, of course florid, to each Subject; which, for fugal purposes, should be *double :* and, ultimately, by writing complete Fugues on some or all of them, in two, three, and more parts. It is excellent practice to take the same Subject, and write more than one Fugue on it; beginning, firstly, with the Subject in the Bass, afterwards in the Treble, and so on. For patterns, see Bach's *Art of Fugue.* Before commencing a Fugue, it is advisable to ascertain what *Strettos* can be obtained from the Subject: also, of what Fugal *devices* it is most susceptible. (See § 394.)

APPENDIX I.

THE notation of the Chromatic Scale given in Fig. 53 is inseparable from that theory of Harmony[1] which regards every note of this scale as integral to the key: not as a Chromatic alteration of the proximate diatonic note; and which, moreover, very justly regards the Major and the Minor Scales from the same Tonic as being *different Modes* of the *same Key*. (See § 61.)

This theory enunciates that there are *three* FUNDAMENTALS or *Roots* in the Scale, the *Dominant, Tonic,* and *Super-tonic*, on each of which *Fundamental Discords* have place. These are shown in Example A.

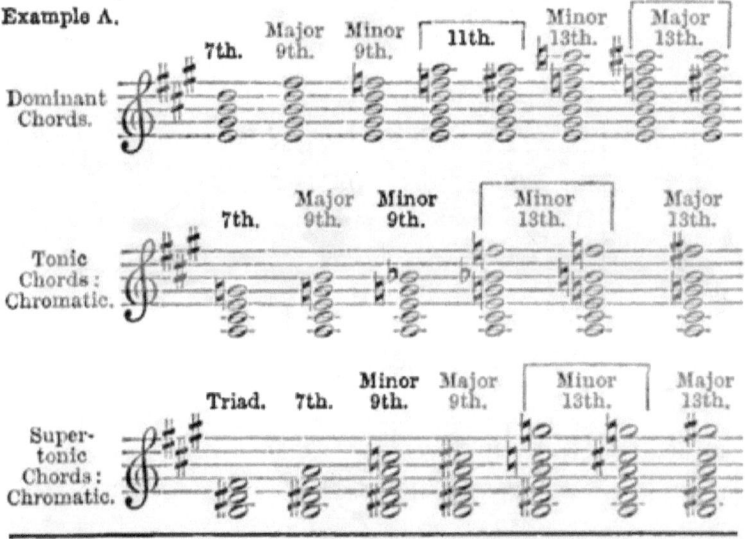

[1] Generally known as the *Day Theory;* having been propounded by Dr. Alfred Day.

302   *Appendix I.*

The *Tonic* and *Super-tonic* dissonant chords are termed *Chromatic Chords*. Each of the Chromatic notes may take the progression proper to it in the Chromatic Scale, ascending or descending: *i.e.* one semitone. Thus, the various resolutions of these Chords and their inversions will be as in Examples B, C, D.

Appendix I. 303

304 Appendix I.

Appendix I.   305

Some of the resolutions of *Dominant* Chords are the same as given in Chapters XVII. to XXI. inclusive; but are given here also, for completeness. The inversions are not all given, where the progressions would be the same as in the Fundamental Chords. The last inversion of the Major 9th (see § 192), the 1st inversion of the Chord of the 11th, and the 2nd, 5th, and last inversions of the 13th, are not inserted, being rarely or never used.

All these Discords, being Fundamental, may be taken unprepared. It will be seen that *Dominant* dissonant harmony proceeds to *Tonic* harmony: *Tonic* dissonant harmony proceeds either to *Dominant* dissonant harmony (Example C. *a, c, e, f, g, h, j*), or to *Super-tonic* dissonant harmony (*b, d, i*): *Super-tonic* dissonant harmony proceeds either to *Tonic* harmony (Example D. *a, c, f, g, h, i, k, m, o*), or to *Dominant* harmony (*b, d, e, j, l, o*). The Tonic Discords *may* also be resolved on Sub-dominant harmony, in context not suggesting modulation.

The Chords of the 11th and 13th and inversions are given incompletely, rarely occurring in their entirety. (See § 197.) The 3rd or 5th may be omitted from the Chord of the 11th. The 3rd may not be omitted from the Chord of the Super-tonic 13th.

The resolutions of the **dissonant** note by *skip* to another note of the same harmony, Example B. (*f, i*), by *rise* of a 2nd, Example B. (*g, j, l, y*), Example C. (*o*), by *Chromatic alteration*, Example B. (*aa*), Example C. (*a, c, d, e, f, g, h, i*), Example D. (*f, i, k*), by *remaining* to be a consonant note of the next chord, Example B. (*m, q, z*), Example C. (*e, g*), Example D. (*c, f, g, h, i, m, o*), are manifest departures from, or elastic enlargements of, the old rule in § 121. Moreover, with the notation as in Fig. 58, and as exemplified in many of these Examples, the directions in §§ 231, 236, respecting the progression of Chromatic notes, do not hold good. But the *notation* of many of these Chords will often be different from that here given, either from *expediency*—the economising of accidentals, &c.—or from a different theoretical view.

Appendix I.

Thus, in Example B. (*aa*), the C♮ would often be written B♯; in Example C. (*h, i*), the F♮ would be written E♯, &c. On the principles here expounded, the notation, and consequent nomenclature, of several chords in Exercises 76, 77, 79, would be changed. Such progressions as that in Example B. (*f*), &c., would, by many musicians, be regarded as *implied* resolutions.

The Chord of the *Augmented* 6th, on the Minor 6th of the Scale (Fig. 189), is now regarded as a combination of the *Minor* 9th on the *Dominant* with the 3rd and 7th on the *Super-tonic,* as shown in Example E.;

and as being, therefore, a double-rooted chord. This chord may also be taken on the *Minor* 2nd of the Scale. Of this chord, the *Tonic* and the *Dominant* are the roots.

This work being explanatory, not polemical, the theory is briefly stated, without argument.

According to this theory and notation, the harmonizing of the Chromatic Scale might be as indicated in Examples F. G. and other ways.

Example G.

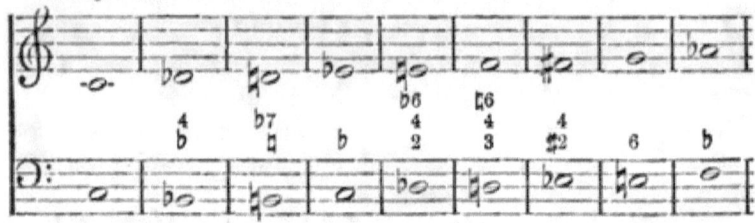
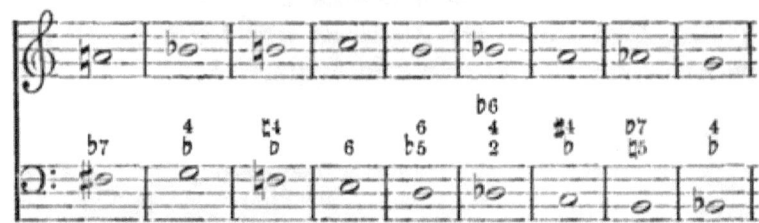
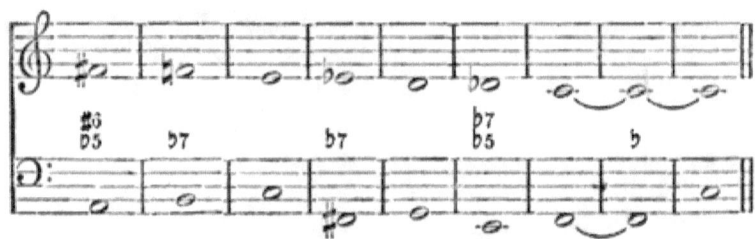

The following Example may serve as an Exercise on some of the progressions just explained.

Example H.

APPENDIX II.

EXAMINATION QUESTIONS, WITH ANSWERS.

THE *materials* for replying to these Questions are amply furnished in the body of this work. The following Answers are given as specimens of the general manner in which an Examination paper should be filled up.

OXFORD UNIVERSITY MIDDLE CLASS EXAMINATION.
Junior, 1858.

1. What do you mean by the following terms *flat, sharp, natural, signature, accidental?*

A *flat* ♭ is a character used to *lower* a note one semitone, without changing its position on the Stave. A *sharp* ♯, on the contrary, *raises* a note one semitone, in like manner. A *natural* ♮ is used to *contradict* a sharp or a flat. The *signature* of a key consists of the sharps or flats proper to it, taken collectively, and placed at the beginning of a piece. An *accidental* is a sharp, flat, natural, double-sharp, or double-flat, applied to a note, but not belonging to the key.

2. What is a *semitone*, and how many semitones make an octave?

A semitone is the smallest interval in practical music, represented by two *proximate* keys upon the Pianoforte. There are twelve semitones in an octave.

3. How many *tones* [or tones & semitones] does a *Major third* contain? and how many does a *Minor third?*

A *Major third* contains two tones; and a *Minor third,* one tone and one semitone.

4. Distinguish between the various kinds of time:—duple, triple, simple, and compound.

Duple time has two beats in a bar: triple time, three beats. Simple time is divisible into undotted notes: in compound time, each beat represents a dotted note. Thus:—

Duple.
Simple, $\frac{2}{4}$, two crotchets.
Compound, $\frac{6}{8}$, two dotted crotchets.

Triple.
Simple, $\frac{3}{4}$, three crotchets.
Compound, $\frac{9}{8}$, three dotted crotchets.

5. How many flats are there in the Major Scale of E flat?

Three: B, E, and A.

6. How many in the scale of E flat Minor?

Six: B, E, A, D, G, and C.

7. What other key has the same signature as E flat? and as E flat Minor?

C Minor has the same signature as E flat; and G flat Major the same as E flat Minor.

8. What is a *Scale*?

A series of tones and semitones (as in the *Diatonic* scale), or of semitones only (as in the *Chromatic* scale), from any note to its octave.

9. How many kinds of Scale are there in common use?

There are two *Genera* in use: the *Diatonic* and the *Chromatic*. Of the former, there are two *Modes*, the *Major* and the *Minor*.

10. How can you tell a *Major* key from a *Minor* key?

In the Minor mode certain accidentals are introduced, raising the 7th, and, in many cases, the 6th notes of the Scale. These 6th and 7th notes of the Minor Scale are the 4th and 5th, respectively, of the relative Major Scale. If these are raised, early in a piece, the presumption is that it is in the Minor mode. Thus, if the signature be two flats, and the F is accidentally sharpened, and the E accidentally naturalized, (though the latter is not always the case,) this accidental alteration would indicate the key of G Minor, the relative to B flat Major. Some acquaintance with Harmony, however, is necessary to determine the point definitely.

11. Explain the words *tonic*, *dominant*, and *sub-dominant*.

The *tonic*, or *key-note*, is the first note of a Diatonic Scale. The *dominant* is its fifth note, and is so termed because of the *governing* character of the harmony of which it is the root. The *sub-dominant* is the fourth note of the scale, being *under* the dominant.

12. What is the difference between C time and ₵ time?

C time is *quadruple*, with two accents in the bar. ₵ time is *duple*, with only one accent. It is termed *alla breve* time, because obtained by the division of a *breve bar* into two bars.

Appendix II. 311

CAMBRIDGE UNIVERSITY MIDDLE CLASS EXAMINATION.
Senior, 1868.

1. Put the *time-signature* to the following extract.[1] (Example 1.)

2. **Name** the leading-note in the key of **G sharp Minor**.
F Double-sharp.
3. In what key is the **following extract?** (Ex. 2.)

In C Minor, as indicated by B♮, the leading-note.
4. Put three upper parts (in pianoforte score) to the following bass, using triads or common chords only. (Ex. 3.)

5. Supply (in pianoforte score) the two vacant parts in the following example, using common chords or triads only where no figures are given. (Ex. 4.)

[[1] It will be understood that **the Example is given** *without* the time-signature **in the** original paper. Examples 3 and **7 are given** without the harmonics. In Example 4, the Bass and Melody only are given, **except** in the **first** two chords. In Example 5, the first chord **only is given**.]

Ex. 4.

N.B. The two middle voices are given in the first two chords.

6. Explain the following harmony and resolve it; also point out the discordant notes to the bass. (Ex. 5.)

Ex. 5.

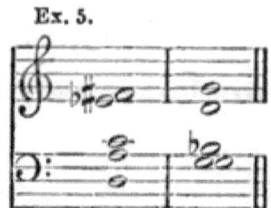

This is the Dominant $\frac{9}{7}$ in the key of G Minor: C and E flat are the dissonances.

7. Explain the following. (Ex. 6.)

Ex. 6.

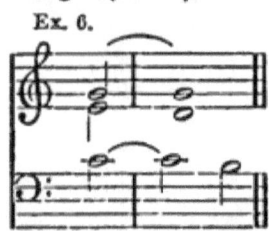

This is a suspension in the bass (prepared and resolved) of a chord of the sixth on B.

8. Supply the absent parts in the following score, and give the roots to those notes in the lower line which are figured. (Ex. 7.)

9. Give an example of a full close or cadence. (Ex. 8.)

10. Give a short description of the following forms of composition: Fugue; Canon: Round; Chant; and Ground-Bass.

(1.) *Fugue:* a composition in which a short phrase, termed the *Subject*, appears successively in all the parts, with various imitational and contrapuntal devices.

(2.) *Canon:* a composition in which the strict imitation of one or more parts is continued throughout.

Appendix II. 313

* The treble or G clef to be used if more convenient to the candidate, but credit will be given for the use of the soprano or C clef.

(3.) *Round:* a kind of Canon in which all the parts are successively sung by all the voices.

(4.) *Chant:* a short composition, adapted for the choral recitation of un-metrical Psalms, &c.

(5.) *Ground-Bass:* a passage in the bass, several times repeated, with different harmonies, or different forms of the same harmony.

COLLEGE OF PRECEPTORS.

Pupil's Examination, Midsummer, 1862.

1. Transpose the following two 8ves higher into the Treble clef.
Example 1.

Transposition.

2. Divide the following into Bars, each of the length of a Semibreve :—
Ex. 2.

Barred.

3. At what distance from each other are Notes placed on each successive line of the Stave, and on each successive space between these lines?

A third.

4. How many Semitones are contained in an Octave?

Twelve.

5. Describe the movements indicated by the following terms: *Adagio, Adagio assai, Adagio cantabile e sostenuto, Allegretto Scherzando, Allegro con fuoco, Allegro ma non troppo.*

Adagio : Slowly (*lit.* leisurely).

Adagio assai : Very (or *decidedly*) slowly.

Adagio cantabile e sostenuto : Slowly, and in a singing and sustained manner.

Allegretto Scherzando : Moderately fast, and playfully.

Allegro con fuoco : Fast, and with fire.

Allegro ma non troppo : Fast, but not too much so.

6. How many sounds may a note of the same name be made to represent by the application of the sharp, flat, &c. &c.?

Appendix II. 315

Five, thus :—

Ex. 3.

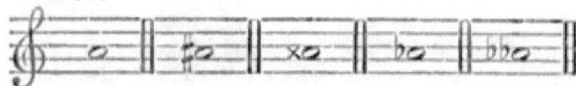

7. What is the difference between a Major and a Minor Scale?

In the Major Scale (so termed from its having a Major 3rd from the Tonic) the Semitones occur between the 3rd and 4th, and between the 7th and 8th notes. In the Minor Scale (so termed from its having a Minor 3rd from the Tonic) the Semitones occur between the 2nd and 3rd, and between the 7th and 8th notes in *ascending* (as usually altered); and between the 6th and 5th, and between the 3rd and 2nd notes, in *descending*. There are, however, other forms of the Minor Scale.

8. What is the *Leading-note* of the key of A (*La*)?
G sharp.

9. Form an Arpeggio on the Chord of C♯ (*Do♯*) Minor.

Ex. 4.

10. Write on the Stave the Chord of the Minor 9th, with its Inversions, in the key of C (*Do*) Major, and resolve them.

Ex. 5.

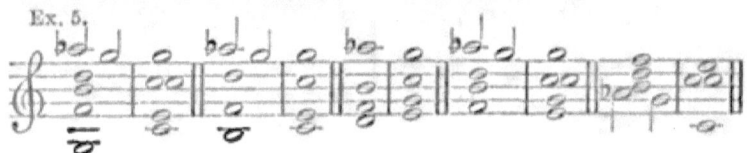

11. Prepare and resolve the Suspensions of the 3rd on the Dominant, and the 6th on the Supertonic, in the key of G (*Sol*).

Ex. 6.

INDEX.

The references in this Index are not to the *Pages*, but to the NUM-
BERED SECTIONS, except where otherwise indicated.

For terms not found herein, reference should be made to the *Glossary*.

Abbreviation, marks of .. 32	Antecedent 366
Accented beats .. 25, 26, 27	Anticipations 228
,, syllables .. 360	Antiphonal effects .. 316
Accents, different kinds of 362	Antithesis 356
Acciaccatura .. 38, 226	Apotome, *note*, p. 34.
Accidentals 50	Appoggiatura .. 38, 226
,, in Figured Bass 125	Arpeggio 34, 157, 244—246
Acuteness of Sound .. 2	Arsis 367
Adagio 39	Assai 39
Added Discords.. 97, 189	Attacco 394
Æolian Mode 62	Attendant keys, modulation to 338
Æsthetic accent .. 362	
Alla Breve time .. 24	Augmentation, answer by 384
Allegro, Allegramente, Allegretto, Allegrino .. 39	,, imitation by 369
	Augmented 6th, chord of 232
Al Rovescio 368	,, Triad 113 (3). 231
Al Segno 30	,, Unison .. 66
Alto Stave 7	Authentic Cadence .. 128
,, Instrument .. 415	,, modes 62
,, Voice .. 408	,, subject in Fugue.. 380
Ambiguous Chord .. 195	Auxiliary-notes, 50, 217, 225-227
Ambrose, St. .. 40, 62	
Amphibrach 358	ß or Si 263
Anapest 358	,, Mollis. See *Bémol*.
Ancient Modes.. .. 62	Bach, C. P. E., *Versuch:* examples from, pp. 285, 296, 297.
,, Style 249	
Andante, Andantino .. 39	
Answer 366	Bach, J. S., Art of Fugue: 373, 385, 397. Examples of Fugue Subjects and Answers from, Figs. 317, 325, 326,
,, in Fugue 379—385	
,, not always in 5th or 4th 393	

Index. 317

328, 329, 330, 332, 333, 336, 341, 342, 346, 349, 350, 351, 352. Examples of Double Counterpoint from, Figs. 278, 280. Fugue on his name, *note*, p. 2. Fugue pour les commençans, 389. Fugues (48) referred to, 237, 346, 381, 389, 390, 395, 397. Motet referred to, 316. Ornaments in Music of, 38. 30 Variations, 373, 406, 411.
Bad Intervals .. 108, 119, 262
Banister, H. C., Round by, Fig. 324.
Bar 18
Baritone (Viola) .. 415
   „ Voice 408
Barring of Compositions   360
Bass, Figured 80
   „ Fundamental 98, 141
   „ Note not synonymous with *Root* .. 141
   „ Radical 141
Basset Horn 423
Basso Cifrato & Continuo   80
Bassoon, & Basson Quinte 424
Bass-Tuba 430
Bass-Viol 416
Bass Voice 408
Beats 19
   „ accented and unaccented 25
Beethoven, Analysis of Rondo by 404
   „ Preludes referred to 353
   „ Sonatas referred to, *note*, p. 29; §§ 39, 237, 400, 401, 403, 404, 405.
   „ Symphonies referred to .. 237, 359, 401
Bémol, B mollis .. 263
Bennett, Fugue Subject and Answer by, Fig. 347.
Binary Time 20
Bind 33
Bis 29
Breve 15
Breve measure 24

Cadence defined, 126; different kinds of, 127; Imperfect, or Half-cadence, 130; Interrupted or Broken, 131; Inverted, 132; Perfect, 128; Plagal, or Church, 129.
Cadences, management of   133
Cancrizans imitation .. 368
Canon 365, 370
   „ different kinds of 371—373
Canonical Imitation .. 365
Canti Fermi, p. 293
Canto Fermo 250
Capriccio 407
Catch 375
Cathedral Music .. 316
Cembalo 411
Changing-note 275
Chants, Ecclesiastical .. 250
Chest Voice 409
Choral writing 408
Chord, defined 79
Chords in succession 106, 124
Chromatic alteration, 64, 230—236; chords, 230—236; genus, 346; scale, 63—65.
Cithara, or Zither .. 411
Clarichord, Clavecin, &c. 411
Clarini 426
Clarionet 423
Clef, Old Mezzo-Soprano, *note*, p. 258.
Clefs, 7; use of, p. 257.
Coda 401, 404
Codetta .. 392, 402, 404
Col Cello 417
Combination of Species in Counterpoint 300, 306, 307, 313
Comes 379
Common Chord. See *Triad*.
Common Time 20
Composers, Young, mistakes and dangers of .. 348, 360, 407
Composition, Form in 398, &c.
Compositions, Early Contrapuntal 248
Compound Intervals subject to same laws as Simple, 103; Modulation, 342; Time, 23.
Compressed Score .. 82
Concertante 398
Concerted music, *note*, p. 209.
Concerto 398
Concords, or Consonances defined, 83; list of, 85; Perfect and Imperfect, 88

Condensed Score .. 82
Conduit 404
Conjunct Movement 103, 104
Con Moto 39
Connection of Chords 106, 107
Consecutive 4ths without 6ths harsh, 210; Perfect Concords, 103, 257, 267, 273; between alternate notes, 273, 296; when permitted, 267; not disguised by Suspensions, 280; broken by Suspensions in Counterpoint, 304; by Contrary Motion, 308, 314; covered, or hidden, 104, 257, 292.
Consequent 366
Consonances. See *Concords.*
Consonant Chords 95, 114
Contra-Basso 417
Contraction in Rhythm .. 359
Contra-Fagotto .. 424
Contralto Voice .. 408
Contrary Motion 102, 261, 292
Cornet-à-pistons .. 426
Corno 425
Corno di Bassetto .. 423
Corno Inglese 422
Correction of Exercises, p. 259.
Counter-Exposition .. 392
Counterpoint defined, 81; described, 248, &c.; Simple or Plain, 249; in two parts, 251, &c.; in three parts, 290, &c.; in four parts, 308, &c.; in more than four parts, 314, &c.; Figurate or Florid, 284, &c.; Mixed, 250, &c.; Free, 317; Double, 318, &c; Triple, Quadruple, &c., 330, 335, 336; Subjects for, p. 293.
Counter-proposition .. 356
Counter-subject .. 386
Counter-Tenor .. 408
Couperin, music of .. 38
Coussemaker referred to, *note,* p. 41.
Cramer's *Studio* referred to, *note,* p. 11.
Crescendo 35
Crossing of parts 264, 294 p. 264
Crotchet 15
Cymbals 431

Da Capo, D. C. 30
Dactyle 358
Dal Segno 30
Dashes 33
Deceptive Cadences .. 131
Decrescendo 35
Deferred Resolution, 139, 168, 214.
Demisemiquaver .. 15
Descant 81
Design .. 139, 407
Devices of Harmony, &c., 247, 248.
Diapason 8
Diaphony 81
Diatessaron, *note,* p. 22.
Diatonic, 43 (see *Scale*).
Diatonic genus 346
Diesis 346
Diminished Intervals, 76; Seventh, chord of, 190, 191, 192; change of notation of, 195; Modulation by Enharmonic, change of, 348; on Chromatically raised Subdominant, 235; Triad, 231 (see *Imperfect Triad*). Unison, 66.
Diminuendo 35
Diminution, Imitation by 369
,, Answer by (Fugue) 384
Direct motion 102
Discords defined, 84, 88; added, or Essential, 97, 189; Fundamental, 88; by prolongation, or Suspension, 169, 198—216; by Supposition, 275; by Transition, 169, 218, &c.; Unessential, 217—230; preparation of, 169, 181; resolution of, 121.
Dissonances. See *Discords.*
Dissonant Chords 96, 114
Dissonant Interval in Melody 262
Distribution of parts 101, 309
Division of Octave, old .. 380
Dominant, 52; bears Major Triad, 113, 122; 7th, 161—168; first use of, 249; Chromatic alterations of, 234; $\frac{9}{7}$, 182—189; derivatives of, 190—195.

Index. 319

Dorian Mode 62
D'Ortigue, referred to, *note*, p. 31.
Dots, 16, 17; where to write, p. 260; over or under a note, 33.
Double-Bar 18
" Bass 417
" Counterpoint. See *Counterpoint.*
" Flat 12
" Fugue 386
" Pedal 237
" Sharp, 11; contradiction of, 13.
Doubling, 292, 297; in Triad, 115—119; of Leading-note, 118; of note on which dissonance resolves, 167; of note on which Suspension resolves, 315; in an Orchestra, 414.
Driving Notes 229
Drum 431
Duple Time .. 20, 360
Dux 378

Eberlin, examples from, Fig. 337, and p. 298-9.
Ecclesiastical Modes .. 62
Eight notes to one 277, 300
Eight-part writing .. 316
Eleventh, sometimes a compound 4th 70
" Chord of the 92, 196, 197
Embellishments .. 38
Emphasis .. 36, 362
Encyclopædia Britannica referred to, *notes*, pp. 6 & 44, § 88; Metropolitana referred to, *notes*, pp. 2 & 42, § 88.
Enharmonic Chord, 195; Modulation, 346, &c.; Notation, sometimes simply a convenience, 347.
Episodes in Fugues, 388, 393, 397 (2.); keys of, in movements, 404.
Episodical form 399, 403—405
es 14
Euphonium 430
Exercises, general directions respecting, p. 255; correction of, p. 259; transposition of, p. 260; on Rudiments, p. 261;

on Triad, p. 262; on Cadences, p. 265; on Sequences, p. 265; on Inversions of Triad, p. 266; on Chords of 7th, p. 268; on Inversions of 7th, p. 270; on Leading and Diminished 7ths, p. 274; on 11th and 13th, p. 276; on Suspensions, p. 276; on Unessential Discords, p. 281; on Chromatic Chords, &c., p. 282.
Exposition (Fugue) .. 391
Extreme Intervals .. 76
" Parts 100
" Triad 231

Fagotto, Fagottone .. 424
False Cadence, 131; Relation, 110, 252, 263.
Falsetto 409
Fantasia 407
Faults in part-writing, most frequent, p. 259; in performance, 17, 31.
Faux-bourdon 81
Fétis' *Traité de l'harmonie*, referred to, *note*, p. 40.
Fifth, Imperfect, how followed in Melody, 108; Perfect followed by Imperfect, 314.
Fifths, Consecutive. See *Consecutive.*
Figured Bass .. 80, 144, 154
Figuring of 3rd in a chord, when inflected, 125; of accidentally raised intervals, 125.
Final 44, 45, 52
Fine 30
Flat, 10, 13; in old music, 14.
Flügel 411
Flute 421
Foot 358
Force of Musical Sounds 3
Form essential to art .. 407
Forms of Movement 399, &c.
Forte 37
Fourth. Perfect, a Concord 85
Free parts added to Double Counterpoint 326
Free style .. 249, 317
Frets 415
Fuga Legata, or Obbligata 370
Fugue defined, 376; Constitu-

ents of, 377; Subject of, 378;
Answer of, 379; Real, 379;
Tonal, 380; Double, 386;
Perpetual, 370; Counter-Subject of, 386; Stretto of, 387;
Episodes of, 388; order of
entry, 390; rules in constructing, 397; number of parts,
389; Exposition, 391; by
Imitation, 394; Second Subject in, 395.
Full Close 128
Fundamental, 86; note, p. 44.
" Bass .. 98, 141
" Chords .. 122
" Harmonies .. 87
" note of Harmonic
Chord 4, 86
Fux, examples from, Figs. 210,
211, 217, 218, 225, 226, 233,
234, 236, 237, 240, 241, 244,
245, 246, 259, 260, 267; and
p. 293.

G, Gamut 62
Genera, the three Greek.. 346
Generator 86
Gran Tamburo .. 431
Grave 39
Gravicembalo 411
Gravity of Musical Sounds,
upon what dependant .. 2
Great Octave 8
Greek Genera 346
Gregory, St., and Gregorian Tones .. 40, 62
Grosse-Caisse 431
Ground Bass 247
Grouping .. 15, 26, 28

H 5, 263
Half-Cadence 130
Handel, Choruses referred to,
248; examples of Fugue Subject and Answer from, Figs.
334, 348; of Imitation from,
Fig. 318; Fugues referred to,
§§ 393, 394; *Israel in Egypt*,
316.
Harmonic Chord, and Harmonics, 4, 86—88, 101, 115.
Harmony defined, 79, 80; and
Counterpoint, 248; and Harmonics, 88.

Harmony-Music, *note*, p. 40.
Harp 418
Harpsichord 411
Hautboy 422
Haydn, Symphonies referred to 359
Head-Voice 409
Herschel, Sir J. F. W., referred
to, *notes*, pp. 2 and 42.
Hexachords .. 62, 263
Hidden Consecutives, 104, 257,
292.
Horn, English, 422; French,
425; open and shut notes on
French, 86.
Hopkins and Rimbault on
Organ, *note*, p. 223.
Hullah's Lectures referred to,
note, p. 41.
Hyper-Ionian, &c. .. 62

Iambus 358
Imitation, 363; Strict, 364;
Canonical, 365; by Contrary
Motion, 367; Retrograde,
368; by Augmentation and
by Diminution, 369.
Imperfect Cadence, 130; Time,
24; Triad, 113, 121, 122, 123,
231; Fifth, 125, 174.
In Alt, In Altissimo .. 8
Increase of tone, sign for 35
Indirect Movement .. 102
Infinite Canon 371
Inflexion, signs of 9—14
Inganno 431
Inner parts 100
Instrumentation .. 432
Instruments .. 410—432
Intervals defined, 67; how
named, 68, 71, 73; Compound
and Simple, 70; Diatonic and
Chromatic, 72; List of Diatonic, 73; different names of
certain, 73, 76; Chromatic,
how obtained, 74; List of
Chromatic, 76; Table of, Fig.
59; Inversion of, 77, 322;
bad, avoidance of, in Melody,
108, 119, 262; Woolhouse on,
note, p. 1; § 88.
Inverse Movement, 318; Fugue,
answer by, 385.

Inversion of Chords, 140; of Fugue, 392; of Intervals, 77, 322; of parts, 318; of Seventh, 173—181; of Triad, 142, 143; sometimes means *Inverse Movement*, 318.
Inverted Pedal 243
Ionian Mode 62
Irregular Passing-notes .. 219
is 14
Italian 6th 232

Kettle-drum 431
Key 50
Key-note .. 45, 52
Key-signature .. 14, 51, 60
Kieswetter, referred to, *note*, p. 41.

Large 15
Largo, Larghetto .. 39
Leading-note, 52; in Minor Scale, 57, &c.; not doubled, 118, 145, 146; progression of, 109, 167, 264.
Leading 7th .. 190—194
Ledger lines, 7; **how to** write, p. 260.
Legato 33
Lento 39
Leslie, Professor, on Harmonics, quoted, *note*, p. 44.
Licenees 168
Ligature 33
Line of Continuation 157, 180
Locke, Matthew, Canon by, Fig. 319.
Loco 32
Long 15
Loudness of Sounds .. 3
Lydian Mode 62

Macfarren's *Lectures* **referred to,** *note***, p.** 22.
„ *Rudiments* referred to, *note*, p. 33.
Major Mode and Scale, 46, 47, &c. .. **Triad**, 113; basis of all Chords, **122**.
Manner of performance .. 33
Manuals (Organ) .. 419
Marshall's *Physiology* referred to, *note*, p. 218.

Martini's *Esemplare,* **Canon from,** Fig. 321.
Measures 18
Mediant 52
Melodies for harmonizing, p. 290.
Melody defined, 78; former **use** of term, 79; bad intervals in, 108, 119; progressions in, 262, 272; variety in, 268.
Mendelssohn's *Elijah*, example from, Fig. 301; *Rivulet* referred to, 24; Fugue Subject and Answer by, Fig. 326.
Metronome 39
Mezzo-Soprano Voice .. 408
„ „ Stave (old), *note*, p. 258.
Mezzo-Staccato .. 33
Mi contra Fa 263
Mi, Fa 62
Military Bands, **Instruments** used in, 421, 426, **430.**
Minim 15
Minor Scale, 55; Relative, 56, 59, 60, 61; Leading-note in, 57, &c.; different forms of, 59.
Minor Triad 113
Minuet and Trio .. 405
Mixed Counterpoint 250, 284
Mixo-Lydian Mode .. 62
Mode, former and **present** meaning of 46
Modern Style .. 249, 317
Modes, Ancient 62
Modulation, 337; Natural, 338—341; Extraneous, 338, 342, &c.; Compound, 342; Enharmonic, 346, &c.; by Double Counterpoint, 351; keys into which made, 338, 343, 344, 352; to Double Dominant deprecated, 345; not twice to same key, 353; in Fugue, 393.
Monotony avoided .. 268, 285
Monteverde, *note*, p. 119.
Mordent 38
Morley's *Introd.*, *note*, p. 23.
Motion of parts .. 102, 104, 105
Mottos to Old Canons .. 373
Movement, defined, 398; forms of, 399; of Development, 400

—402; of Episode, 403—405; free forms of, 407.

Mozart, Analysis of Movement by, 402; Fugue Subjects and Answers by, Figs. 331, 340; Examples of Imitation from, Figs. 309, 312, **316**; of Rhythm, Figs. 307, 308; Fantasia referred to, § 407; Sonata for Pianoforte and Violin referred to, 359; Symphony in G Minor referred to, 359.

Musical Sounds, how produced, 1; pitch of, 2; force of, 3; quality of, 4.

Mutes, Pianoforte. See *Sordini*.

National Anthem, Rhythm of, 357, Fig. 302 (*c.*)
Natural .. 13, 14
Neapolitan 6th 233
Niedermeyer referred to, *note*, p. 31.
Ninth, not inverted or contracted 187
 „ sometimes a compound 2nd 70
 „ Chord of 91, **182**, &c.
 „ non-dominant .. 189
Non-dominant discords, 163, 169, &c., 181.
Non tanto, Non troppo .. 39
Nota cambiata 275
Notation, changeable .. 49
Note sensible, La. See *Leading-note*.
Notes, names of, 5; duration and forms of, 15.

Oblique marks in figured bass 125, 174, 209
 „ Motion 102, 261
Oboe 422
Octave, 8; to Bass always perfect 125
Octave avoided in two-part Counterpoint 259
Octave Flute 421
 „ Rule of the, p. 286.
Octaves, Consecutive. See *Consecutive*.
Omission of note from a Chord 120
Once-marked 8ve .. 8

Open-notes .. 86, 425, 426
Ophicleide 429
Organ 419
Organ Points 237
Organ Score 82
Organum 81
Ornaments 38
Ottava (8va) 32
Ottava Battuta 258
Ouseley on *Counterpoint*, referred to, *note*, p. 41.
 „ on *Harmony*, referred to 88
Overtones 86

Pace, how indicated .. 39
Parallel Motion .. 102
Partita 398
Partition, Partitur .. 82
Parts, Distribution of, 101, 309; real, 314.
Part-writing .. 99, &c.
Passing-notes, 169, 217-224, 227, 265, 267, 295, &c.; figuring of, 224. Passing Shake, 38
Pause 31
Pedal-Chords, 242; notes, 237; Dominant, in Counterpoint, 303; Inverted, **243**; Pedal-points, 237—241, 396.
Pedals, Harp, 418; Organ, **419**; Pianoforte (use of), 412.
Per Arsin et Thesin .. 367
Percussion, Instruments of, 410, 431.
Perfect Cadence. See *Cadence*.
Perfect Time 21
Period 355
Perpetual Canon .. 371
Per rectè et retrò .. 368
Phrase 357
Phrasing 361
Phrygian Mode .. 62
Piano 37
Pianoforte, 411, **412**; origin of its name, 37.
Pianoforte Score .. 82
Piatti 431
Piccolo 421
Pincé simple, Pincé double 38
Pitch, upon what dependent 2
 „ of Middle C .. 8
Pizzicato 410

Plagal, 62; Modes, *note*, p. 31.
Subject in Fugue, 380. See
Cadence.
Plain Song 250
Plectra .. 410, 411
Plectral Instruments 410, 418
Point d'Orgue 126
Portamento 38
Position of Chords .. 101
(See *Distribution of parts*.)
Pots-pourris 407
Preparation of Discords, 169,
181; of Suspensions, 201.
Presto, Prestissimo .. 39
Prime, 86, 141; superfluous, 66
Prolongation, discords by 199
„ in Rhythm 359
Proposition (Imitation) .. 366
„ (Rhythm) .. 356
Purcell, H., Canons by, Figs.
322, 323.

Quadruple Counterpoint. See
Counterpoint.
Quadruple Time 20, 360
Quadruplet 28
Quality of Sound .. 4
Quartet 398
Quaver 15
Quintuple Counterpoint. See
Counterpoint.
Quintuple Time .. 24
Quintuplet 28

Radical Bass 141
Recapitulation in Movement 401
Redundant Intervals .. 76
Reed, Free 420
Reed Instruments, 410, 422-424.
Registers of Organ pipes 419
„ of the Voice .. 409
Relative Keys, Modulation
to 338
„ Scales 53, 54, 56, 59—61
Relaxation of Rules in
Counterpoint .. 308, 317
Repeats 29
Repercussion (Fugue) .. 391
Repetition, signs of 29, 30
Resolution of Discords, 84, 121;
deferred, 139, 168, 214; ornamental, 215; of Canons, 373.
Rests 17

Retardations 229
Retrograde Imitation .. 368
Rhythm, 354, &c.; Broken or
Varied, 359.
Ricercari, Ricercati .. 369
Rinforzando 36
Rivolto 392
Rondo 404
Root 98, 141
Round defined, 375; Example
of, Fig. 324.
Rule of the Octave, p. 286.

Scale, Diatonic, 43, &c.; Major,
46, &c.; Minor, 55, &c.; Degrees of, 52; Chromatic, 63,
&c.; accompaniment of, p.
286.
Scale-signature .. 51
Scarlatti, D., *Lessons* referred to 7
Scherzo 405
Schumann, Concerto referred to 359
Score, short, &c. .. 82
„ writing in, p. 257.
Scoring 432
Second, Compound .. 187
Secondary Sevenths. See *Sevenths*.
Second Subject in Fugue,
395; in Movement of
Continuity 401
Section 356
Semibreve 15
Semidemisemiquaver .. 15
Semiquaver 15
Semitone, 9, 40; Chromatic,
Diatonic, Major, Minor, 66.
Sensitive note. See *Leading-note*.
Sequence defined, 134; Real,
135; Tonal, 136; extent of,
137; accompaniment of, 138;
exceptional progressions, &c.,
in, 118, 122, 139, 171.
Serpent 428
Seventh, Chords of the, 90, 160,
&c.; Dominant, 162, 166—
168; Diminished, 190—192,
195 (see *Modulation*); Non-Dominant or Secondary, 163,
169, &c.; Leading, 190, 194;

Resolution of, 164, 167, 168; figuring of, 165.
Seventh, Minor, how followed in Melody .. 108
Sforzato 36
Shake .. 38, 226
Sharp, 9, 13; in old Music, 14.
Sharp Intervals .. 76
Sharps and Flats, why needed in Scales .. 49, 58, 59
Short Score, 82; how to write in, p. 257.
Shut notes .. 425, 426
Side-Drum 431
Signature, Figured-Bass 144
" Key, 14; of Major Scales, 51; of Minor Scales, 60.
Signature, Time .. 24
Similar motion, 102, 292; danger of, 103; by Skip discommended, 261; to a Perfect Concord, 104, 308.
Simili 32
Simple Time 22
Sinfonia, Symphony .. 398
Six or Eight notes to one 300
Sixth, Chord of the, 142, &c.; figuring of, 144; doubling in, 145, 150; from Imperfect Triad, 146—148; on what notes of the Scale taken, 149; series of Chords of the, 148; Augmented, French, &c., 232; Neapolitan, 233.
Sixth and Fourth, Chord of the, 143, 151, &c.
Skips, two wide, in same direction unadvisable .. 107
Slur 33
Small Octave 8
Smorzatori 412
Sol 62
Sonata, 398; first movement of, 401.
Soprano Voice 408
Sordini 412
Sotto 32
Species of Counterpoint, Five .. 249, 250
Spencer, C. C., on *Modes* referred to, *note*, p. 31.
Spinet 411

Spreading of Chords .. 34
Squareness, how avoided 359
Staccato 33
Staff or Stave 6, 7
Stems, which way to turn, p. 256.
Stopping a string .. 414
Stops, Organ 419
Strain or Period .. 355
Stretto 387
Strict Imitation, 364, 365; style, 249.
Stringed Instruments, 410, 413 —418.
Styles, Free and Strict .. 249
Sub-Dominant 52
Subject of Fugue .. 378
Subjects, varied treatment of, 247, 248, 250.
Sub-mediant, 52; Triad on, 122.
Sub-semitone, Sub-Tonic. See *Leading-note*.
Suite de pièces 398
Superfluous Intervals, 76. See *Prime*.
Super-Tonic 52
" Triad 122, 123
Supposition, Discord by .. 275
Suspensions, 169, 198—216, 278 —280, 302; double, triple, &c., 206, 214; in lowest part, 209 —212, 302; at accent, 202; do not disguise consecutives, 280; use of, 216; delayed resolution of, 214; ornamental resolution of, 215; difference from Retardations, 200, 229.
Syllables, accented .. 360
Symphony. See *Sinfonia*.
Syncopated Counterpoint, 278, &c., 301, &c.
Syncopation, 27; in Rhythm, 359.

Tameness, how averted .. 359
Tasto Solo 241
Temperament 346
Tempo a Cappella .. 24
" Ordinario .. 24
Tenor, 250; Voice, 408.
Ternary Measure .. 21
Tetrachords .. 41, 53, 263
Theme with Variations .. 406

Index.   325

Thesis 356, 367
Thorough-Bass .. 80
Third, doubling of, when
  expedient .. 117, 119
Thirds, successive .. 310
Thirteenth, sometimes a compound 6th, 70; Chord of, 92, 196, 197.
Three notes against one .. 270
Tie 33
Tierce coulée 38
  ,, de Picardie 128, 294
Timbre of Sound .. 4
Time .. .. 20, &c.
Time-Signatures .. 24
Tone, different meanings
  of 40
Tones, Gregorian .. 40
Tonic 45, 50, 52
Transition 337
Transposition, p. 260.
Treble Voice 408
Triad, 89, 95, 112; three kinds of, 113; consonant and dissonant, 114; doubling in, 115—119; omission of note in, 120; figuring of, 125; basis of all chords, 97; resolution of Imperfect, 121; on 3rd and 7th of Scale, little used, 122; on Tonic, Dominant, and Subdominant, &c., 122; in Minor Scale, 123; Augmented and Diminished, 231; Successions of Triads, 124; Inversions of, 142, &c.
Triangle 431
Trill 38
Trio 398, 405
Triple Counterpoint. See *Counterpoint*.
Triple-dot 16
Triple Time .. 21, 360
Triplet, or Triolet .. 28
Tritone, 73; in Melody, 274; when allowed, 139; False Relation of, 263.
Trochee 358
Trombone 427

Trumpet, Tromba .. 426
Tuning 346
Turini, Canon by, Fig. 320.
Turn 38, 226
Twice-marked Octave .. 8
Two parts represent complete harmony .. 152
Tyndall on *Sound* referred to, pp. 1, 2, 44, 219, 223.

Unaccented beats .. 25
Unessential notes 217—229
Unfigured Basses, p. 286.
Unfigured Bass-notes .. 125
Unison, 69; Augmented and Diminished, 66; avoided in Two-part Counterpoint, 259; permitted at unaccented beat. 265, 297.
Unisons, Consecutive .. 103
Ut 5, 62

Variations 406
Vibrations of the air, 1—4; number of, for middle C, 8; of a string, 4, 86, *note* to chap. X., p. 44.
Viola di Braccio .. 415
Viola di Gamba .. 416
Violin 414
Violoncello 415
Violone 417
Virginal 411
Voce di petto, and voce di testa 409
Voices .. 408, 409
Vox Humana 422

Waits 422
Wechsel-noten 275
Wesley and Horn's edition of Bach's Fugues recommended 397
Working of ideas 401, 402
Woolhouse on *Musical Intervals* referred to, *notes*, pp. 1, 6, 46; § 346.

Zither 410

RICHARD CLAY & SONS, LIMITED,
LONDON & BUNGAY.

By the same Author.

Third Edition, revised, crown 8vo, 5s.

LECTURES ON MUSICAL ANALYSIS

EMBRACING SONATA-FORM, FUGUE, ETC.;

ILLUSTRATED BY THE WORKS OF THE CLASSICAL MASTERS.

"It is beyond comparison the best work on the subject in our language."—*Athenæum.*

"The subject of musical form, as exemplified in the works of the composers whose claim to the title of 'classical' has long since been established, is treated with the clearness and comprehensiveness of detail that would be expected from the author of the well-known 'Text-book of Music.'"—*Musical World.*

UNIFORM WITH BANISTER'S "MUSIC."

Sixteenth Edition, 55th—64th thousand, revised to date (1902), fcp. 8vo, 3s. 6d.

CONCISE HISTORY OF MUSIC

FROM THE COMMENCEMENT OF THE CHRISTIAN ERA TO THE PRESENT TIME. FOR THE USE OF STUDENTS.

BY THE

Rev. H. G. BONAVIA HUNT, Mus. Doc., F.R.S.E.,

Warden of Trinity College, London; late Lecturer on Musical History in the same College. Honorary Fellow of the Philharmonic Society of London.

"Mr. Hunt has produced a well-arranged and really concise history of the subject with which he deals. The book is divided into three sections, the first of which is a general review of musical epochs and events, while the second presents a series of chronometrical tables, and the third summarizes a history of the art. The student 'is warned' in the preface 'that he is not to expect what is called a readable book,' but we feel bound to say that Mr. Hunt's work is, in the proper sense of the word, far more readable than books which attempt to combine valuable information with attractiveness by tricks to which Mr. Hunt has not condescended."—*Saturday Review.*

LONDON: GEORGE BELL & SONS,
YORK STREET, COVENT GARDEN.

September, 1901.

A SELECTED LIST
OF
EDUCATIONAL WORKS
PUBLISHED BY
GEORGE BELL & SONS LONDON
AND
DEIGHTON BELL & CO. CAMBRIDGE

CAMBRIDGE MATHEMATICAL SERIES.

ARITHMETIC, with 8,000 Examples. By C. PENDLEBURY, M.A. Thirteenth Edition, with or without Answers. 4*s*. 6*d*.
 In Two PARTS, 2*s*. 6*d*. each. A Key to Part 2, 7*s*. 6*d*. net.
 The EXAMPLES, in a separate volume. Eleventh Edition. 3*s*., or in Two Parts, 1*s*. 6*d*. and 2*s*.

COMMERCIAL ARITHMETIC. By C. PENDLEBURY, M.A., and W. S. BEARD, F.R.G.S. 2nd Edition. 2*s*. 6*d*. Part I, separately 1*s*.

ARITHMETIC FOR INDIAN SCHOOLS. By C. PENDLEBURY, M.A., and S. TAIT, M.A., B.Sc. 3rd Edition. 3*s*.

ELEMENTARY ALGEBRA FOR USE IN INDIAN SCHOOLS. By J. T. HATHORNTHWAITE, M.A. **2*s*.**

CHOICE AND CHANCE. An Elementary Treatise on Permutations, Combinations, and Probability, with 640 Exercises. By W. A. WHITWORTH, M.A. 5th Edition, revised, with additional Examples and Exercises. 7*s*. 6*d*.

——— DCC EXERCISES, including Hints for the Solution of all the Questions in "Choice and Chance." By W. A. WHITWORTH, M.A. Crown 8vo. 6*s*.

EUCLID. Books I.—VI., and part of Book XI. By HORACE DEIGHTON, M.A. Sixth Edition. 4*s*. 6*d*., or Book I. 1*s*. Books I. and II. 1*s*. 6*d*. Books I.—III. 2*s*. 6*d*. Books I.—IV. 3*s*. Books III. and IV. 1*s*. **6*d*.** Books V.—XII. 2*s*. 6*d*. Key 5*s*. *net*.

INTRODUCTION TO EUCLID, including Euclid I., 1—26, with Explanations and numerous Easy Exercises. By HORACE DEIGHTON, M.A., and O. EMTAGE, B.A. 1*s*. 6*d*.

EUCLID. Exercises on Euclid and in Modern Geometry. By the late J. MCDOWELL, M.A. 4th Edition. 6*s*.

ELEMENTARY TRIGONOMETRY. By CHARLES PENDLEBURY, M.A., F.R.A.S. 2nd Edition. 4s. 6d.

SHORT COURSE OF ELEMENTARY PLANE TRIGONOMETRY. By CHARLES PENDLEBURY, M.A. 2s. 6d.

ELEMENTARY TRIGONOMETRY. By J. M. DYER, M.A., and the Rev. R. H. WHITCOMBE M.A. 3rd Edition, revised. 4s. 6d.

TRIGONOMETRY. Introduction to Plane Trigonometry. By the Rev. T. G. VYVYAN, M.A. 3rd Edition. 3s. 6d.

ELEMENTARY MENSURATION. By B. T. MOORE, M.A., 2nd Edition, revised. 3s. 6d.

CONIC SECTIONS, treated Geometrically. By W. H. BESANT, Sc.D., F.R.S. 9th Edition, revised. 4s. 6d. Key, 5th Edition, 5s. net.

ELEMENTARY CONICS, being the first 8 chapters of the above. 2nd Edition. 2s. 6d.

EXAMPLES IN ANALYTICAL CONICS FOR BEGINNERS. By W. M. BAKER, M.A. 2s. 6d.

CONICS, THE ELEMENTARY GEOMETRY OF. By Rev. C. TAYLOR, D.D. 7th Edition. 4s. 6d.

CONIC SECTIONS. An Elementary Treatise. By H. G. WILLIS, M.A. 5s.

ROULETTES AND GLISSETTES. By W. H. BESANT, Sc.D., F.R.S. 2nd Edition, enlarged. 5s.

SOLID GEOMETRY, An Elementary Treatise on. By W. S. ALDIS, M.A. 4th Edition, revised. 6s.

ANALYTICAL GEOMETRY FOR BEGINNERS. By Rev. T. G. VYVYAN, M.A. Part I. The Straight Line and Circle. Second Edition. 2s. 6d.

GEOMETRICAL OPTICS. An Elementary Treatise by Prof. W. S. ALDIS. 5th Edition. 4s.

HYDROMECHANICS. By W. H. BESANT, Sc.D., F.R.S. 5th Edition, revised. Part I. Hydrostatics. 5s.

ELEMENTARY DIFFERENTIAL CALCULUS. By Prof. A. LODGE, M.A. With an Introduction by OLIVER J. LODGE, D.Sc., F.R.S. [In the Press.

ELEMENTARY HYDROSTATICS. By W. H. BESANT, Sc.D. 17th Edition. 4s. 6d. Solutions, 5s. net

THE ELEMENTS OF APPLIED MATHEMATICS. Including Kinetics, Statics, and Hydrostatics. By C. M. JESSOP, M.A. Second Edition. 4s. 6d.

RIGID DYNAMICS. An Introductory Treatise. By W. S. ALDIS, M.A. 4s.

ELEMENTARY DYNAMICS. By W. M. BAKER, M.A. 3s. 6d.

ELEMENTARY DYNAMICS for the use of Colleges and Schools. By W. GARNETT, M.A., D.C.L. 5th Edition, revised. 6s.

DYNAMICS, A Treatise on. By W. H. BESANT, Sc.D., F.R.S. Crown 8vo. 2nd Edition. 10s. 6d.

HEAT, An Elementary Treatise on. By W. GARNETT, M.A., D.C.L. 6th Edition, revised. 4s. 6d.

ELEMENTARY PHYSICS, Examples and Examination Papers in. By W. GALLATLY, M.A. Crown 8vo. 4s.

MECHANICS, A Collection of Problems in Elementary. By W. WALTON, M.A. 2nd Edition. 6s.

MATHEMATICAL EXAMPLES. For Army and Indian Civil Service Candidates. By J. M. DYER, M.A., and R. PROWDE SMITH, M.A. 6s.

Uniform Volume.

GEOMETRICAL DRAWING. For Army and other Examinations. By R. HARRIS. New Edition, enlarged. 3s. 6d.

OTHER MATHEMATICAL WORKS.

A SHILLING ARITHMETIC. By CHARLES PENDLEBURY, M.A., and W. S. BEARD, F.R.G.S. 3rd Edition. Crown 8vo. 1s. With Answers, 1s. 4d.

ELEMENTARY ARITHMETIC. By the same Authors. Crown 8vo. 4th Edition. 1s. 6d. With or without Answers.

GRADUATED ARITHMETIC, for Junior and Private Schools. By the same Authors. In seven parts, in stiff canvas covers. Parts I., II., and III., 3d. each; Parts IV., V., and VI., 4d. each; Part VII., 6d.
    Answers to Parts I. and II., 4d.; Parts III.-VII., 4d. each.

ARITHMETIC, Examination Papers in. By C. PENDLEBURY, M.A. 4th Edition. 2s. 6d. Key 5s. net.

GRADUATED EXERCISES IN ADDITION (Simple and Compound). By W. S. BEARD, F.R.G.S. Third Edition. Fcap. 4to. 1s.

ARITHMETIC PAPERS. Set at the Higher Local Examinations, Cambridge, 1869 to 1887. With Notes by S. J. D. SHAW. 2s. 6d. Solutions to the above, 4s. 6d.

ALGEBRA, LESSONS IN ELEMENTARY. By L. J. POPE, B.A. 1s. 6d.

BOOK-KEEPING BY DOUBLE ENTRY, THEORETICAL and Practical, including a Society of Arts Examination Paper fully worked out. By J. T. MEDHURST, A.K.C., F.S.S. Crown 8vo. 1s.

BOOK-KEEPING, Examination Papers in. Compiled by JOHN T. MEDHURST, A.K.C., F.S.S. 5th Edition. 3s. Key 2s. 6d. net.

BOOK-KEEPING, Graduated Exercises and Examination Papers in. Compiled by P. MURRAY, F.S.S.S., F.Sc.S. (Lond.). 2s. 6d.

TRIGONOMETRY, Examination Papers in. By G. H. WARD, M.A. 2s. 6d. Key 5s. net.

A COLLECTION OF EXAMPLES AND PROBLEMS IN Arithmetic, Algebra, Geometry, Logarithms, Trigonometry, Conic Sections, Mechanics, &c., with Answers and Occasional Hints. By the Rev. A. WRIGLEY. 10th Edition. 20th Thousand. Demy 8vo. 3s. 6d. KEY or COMPANION, 5s. net.

PURE MATHEMATICS AND NATURAL PHILOSOPHY, A Compendium of Facts and Formulæ in. By G. R. SMALLEY, F.R.A.S. New Edition, revised by J. McDOWELL, M.A., F.R.A.S. Fcap. 8vo. 2s.

EUCLID, THE ELEMENTS OF. The Enunciations and Figures. By the late J. BRASSE, D.D. Fcap. 8vo. 1s. Without the Figures, 6d.

MECHANICS (THEORETICAL), Problems in. By W. WALTON, M.A. 3rd Edition. 8vo. 16s.

HYDRODYNAMICS, A Treatise on. By A. B. BASSET, M.A., F.R.S. Vol. I. Demy 8vo. 10s. 6d. Vol. II. 12s. 6d.

HYDRODYNAMICS AND SOUND, An Elementary Treatise on. By A. B. BASSET, M.A., F.R.S. For Students in Universities. 8vo. Second Edition, revised and enlarged. 8s.

PHYSICAL OPTICS, A Treatise on. By A. B. BASSET, M.A., F.R.S. 8vo. 16s.

AN ELEMENTARY TREATISE ON CUBIC AND QUARTIC Curves. By A. B. BASSET, M.A., F.R.S. [*In the Press.*

ANCIENT AND MODERN GEOMETRY OF CONICS, An Introduction to the, with Historical Notes and Prolegomena. By C. TAYLOR, D.D. 8vo. 15s.

THE FOUNDATIONS OF GEOMETRY. By E. T. DIXON, M.A. 8vo. 6s.

ANALYTICAL GEOMETRY. By T. G. VYVYAN, M.A. 6th Edition. Fcap. 8vo. 4s. 6d.

TRILINEAR CO-ORDINATES, and other methods of Modern Analytical Geometry of Two Dimensions. By W. A. WHITWORTH, M.A. 8vo. 16s.

LENSES AND SYSTEMS OF LENSES. Treated after the manner of Gauss. By CHARLES PENDLEBURY, M.A. 8vo. 5s.

ELLIPTIC FUNCTIONS, An Elementary Treatise on. By the late ARTHUR CAYLEY, Sc.D. 2nd Edition. 8vo. 7s. 6d.

PURE AND APPLIED CALCULATION, Notes on the Principles of. By the late J. CHALLIS, M.A., F.R.S., &c. 8vo. 15s.

PHYSICS, The Mathematical Principle of. By the late JAMES CHALLIS, M.A., F.R.S. 8vo. 5s.

PRACTICAL ASTRONOMY, Lectures on. By the late J. CHALLIS, M.A., F.R.S. Demy 8vo. 10s.

THEORY OF NUMBERS, Part I. By G. B. MATHEWS, M.A. 8vo. 12s.

BELL'S ILLUSTRATED CLASSICS.

Edited by E. C. Marchant, M.A.

Elementary Series.

With Introductions and Notes, Exercises on the Text and Numerous Illustrations. Pott 8vo. With or without Vocabularies, price 1s. 6d. *each.*

LATIN AUTHORS.

CAESAR. Book I. By A. C. LIDDELL, M.A.

—— Book II. By A. C. LIDDELL, M.A.

—— Book III. By F. H. COLSON, M.A. and G. M. GWYTHER, M.A.

—— Book IV. By Rev. A. W. UPCOTT, M.A.

—— Book V. By A. REYNOLDS, M.A.

—— Book VI. By J. T. PHILLIPSON, M.A.

CICERO. SPEECHES AGAINST CATILINE. I and II (1 vol.). By F. HERRING, M.A.

—— DE SENECTUTE. By A. S. WARMAN, B.A.

—— DE AMICITIA. By H. J. L. J. MASSÉ, M.A.

—— SELECTIONS. By J. F. CHARLES, B.A.

CORNELIUS NEPOS. EPAMINONDAS, HANNIBAL, CATO. By H. L. EARL, M.A.

EUTROPIUS. Books I and II (1 vol.). By J. G. SPENCER, B.A.

HORACE'S ODES. Book I. By C. G. BOTTING, B.A.

—— Book II. By C. G. BOTTING, B.A.
 [*Preparing.*

—— Book III. By H. LATTER, M.A.

—— Book IV. By H. LATTER, M.A.

LIVY. Book IX, cc. i–xix. By W. C. FLAMSTEAD WALTERS, M.A.
—— HANNIBAL'S FIRST CAMPAIGN IN ITALY. (Selected from Book XXI.) By F. E. A. TRAYES, M.A.
OVID'S METAMORPHOSES. Book I. By G. H. WELLS, M.A.
—— SELECTION FROM THE METAMORPHOSES. By J. W. E. PEARCE, M.A.
—— ELEGIAC SELECTIONS. By F. COVERLEY SMITH, B.A.
—— TRISTIA. Book III. By H. R. WOOLRYCH, M.A.
PHAEDRUS. A SELECTION. By Rev. R. H. CHAMBERS, M.A.
STORIES OF GREAT MEN. By Rev. F. CONWAY, M.A.
VERGIL'S AENEID. Book I. By Rev. E. H. S. ESCOTT, M.A.
—— Book II. By L. D. WAINWRIGHT, M.A.
—— Book III. By L. D. WAINWRIGHT, M.A.
—— Book IV. By A. S. WARMAN, B.A.
—— Book V. By J. T. PHILLIPSON, M.A.
—— Book VI. By J. T. PHILLIPSON, M.A.
—— SELECTION from Books VII to XII. By W. G. COAST, B.A.

XENOPHON'S ANABASIS. Book I. By E. C. MARCHANT, M.A.
—— Book II. By E. C. MARCHANT, M.A.

GREEK PLAYS. 2s. each.

AESCHYLUS' PROMETHEUS VINCTUS. By C. E. LAURENCE, M.A.
EURIPIDES' ALCESTIS. By E. H. BLAKENEY, M.A.
—— BACCHAE. By G. M. GWYTHER, M.A.
—— HECUBA. By Rev. A. W. UPCOTT, M.A.
—— MEDEA. By Rev. T. NICKLIN, M.A.

Intermediate Series.

With numerous Illustrations and Maps. Crown 8vo.

CAESAR'S SEVENTH CAMPAIGN IN GAUL, B.C. 52. DE BELLO GALLICO. Lib. VII. Edited, with Notes, Excursus, and Tables of Idioms, by the Rev. W. COOKWORTHY COMPTON, M.A. Third Edition. 2s. 6d. net.

SOPHOCLES' ANTIGONE. Edited by G. H. WELLS, M.A. 3s. 6d.

THE ATHENIANS IN SICILY. Being portions of Thucydides, Books VI and VII. Edited by the Rev. W. COOKWORTHY COMPTON, M.A. 3s. 6d.

HOMER'S ODYSSEY. Book I. Edited by E. C. MARCHANT, M.A. 2s.

LIVY. Book XXI. Edited by F. E. A. TRAYES, M.A. 2s. 6d. net.

TACITUS : AGRICOLA. Edited by J. W. E. PEARCE, M.A. 2s.

PUBLIC SCHOOL SERIES OF CLASSICAL AUTHORS.

Crown 8vo.

ARISTOPHANES. THE PEACE. By F. A. PALEY, M.A., LL.D. 2s. 6d.

ARISTOPHANES. THE ACHARNIANS. By F. A. PALEY, M.A., LL.D. 2s. 6d.

ARISTOPHANES. THE FROGS. By F. A. PALEY, M.A., LL.D. 2s. 6d.

ARISTOPHANES. THE PLUTUS. By M. T. QUINN, M.A. 3s. 6d.

CICERO. THE LETTERS OF CICERO TO ATTICUS. Book I. By A. PRETOR, M.A. Third Edition. 4s. 6d.

DEMOSTHENES. THE ORATION AGAINST THE LAW OF LEPTINES. By B. W. BEATSON, M.A. 3rd Edition. 3s. 6d.

DEMOSTHENES. DE FALSA LEGATIONE. By the late R. SHILLETO, M.A. 9th Edition. 6s.

LIVY. Book VI. Edited by E. S. WEYMOUTH, M.A., and G. F. HAMILTON, B.A. 2s. 6d.

LIVY. Book XXI. By Rev. L. D. DOWDALL, M.A., B.D., Ch. Ch. Oxon. 2s.

LIVY. Book XXII. By Rev. L. D. DOWDALL. 2s.

PLATO. THE PROTAGORAS. By W. WAYTE, M.A. 7th Edition. 4s. 6d.

PLATO. THE APOLOGY OF SOCRATES AND CRITO. 12th Edition. By W. WAGNER, Ph.D. 2s. 6d.

PLATO. THE PHAEDO. By W. WAGNER, Ph.D. 13th Edition. 5s. 6d.

PLATO. THE GORGIAS. By the late W. H. THOMPSON, D.D. New Edition. 6s.

PLATO. THE EUTHYPHRO. By G. H. WELLS, M.A. 3rd Edition, revised. 3s.

PLATO. THE EUTHYDEMUS. Edited by G. H. WELLS, M.A. 4s.

PLATO. THE REPUBLIC. Books I. & II. Edited by G. H. WELLS, M.A. 5th Edition. 5s.

PLAUTUS. MENAECHMEI. With Notes, Critical and Exegetical, and an Introduction. By WILHELM WAGNER, Ph.D. 3rd Edition. 4s. 6d.

PLAUTUS. TRINUMMUS. With Notes, Critical and Exegetical. By W. WAGNER, Ph.D. 6th Edition. 4s. 6d.

PLAUTUS. AULULARIA. With Notes, Critical and Exegetical. By W. WAGNER, Ph.D. 5th Edition. 4s. 6d.

PLAUTUS. THE MOSTELLARIA. By E. A. SONNENSCHEIN, M.A. 5s.

SOPHOCLES. THE TRACHINIAE. By ALFRED PRETOR, M.A. 4s. 6d.

SOPHOCLES. THE OEDIPUS TYRANNUS. Edited by the late B. H. KENNEDY, D.D. 2s. 6d.

TERENCE. With Notes, Critical and Explanatory. By W. WAGNER, Ph.D. 3rd Edition. 7s. 6d.

THUCYDIDES. Book VI. Edited by T. W. DOUGAN, M.A. 2s.

GRAMMAR-SCHOOL CLASSICS.

Fcap. 8vo.

CAESAR. DE BELLO GALLICO. Books I.—III. Edited by G. LONG, M.A. 1s. 6d. Books IV., V. 1s. 6d. Books VI., VII. 1s. 6d.

CATULLUS, TIBULLUS, and PROPERTIUS. Selected Poems. By the Rev. A. H. WRATISLAW and F. N. SUTTON, B.A. 2s. 6d.

CICERO. DE SENECTUTE, DE AMICITIA, AND SELECT EPISTLES. By G. LONG, M.A. 3s.

CORNELIUS NEPOS. By the late J. F. MACMICHAEL, M.A. 2s.

HOMER. ILIAD. Books I.-XII. By F. A. PALEY, M.A., LL.D. 4s. Books I.-VI. 2s. 6d. Books VII.-XII. 2s. 6d.

HORACE. By A. J. MACLEANE, M.A. With a short Life. Revised Edition. 3s. 6d. Or, Part I., Odes, 2s.; Part II., Satires and Epistles, 2s.

JUVENAL. SIXTEEN SATIRES (expurgated). By HERMAN PRIOR, M.A. 3s. 6d.

MARTIAL. SELECT EPIGRAMS. By F. A. PALEY, M.A., LL.D., and the late W. H. STONE. With a Life of the Poet. 4s. 6d.

OVID. The SIX BOOKS OF THE FASTI. By F. A. PALEY, M.A., LL.D. New Edition. 3s. 6d. Or Books I. and II. 1s. 6d., Books III. and IV. 1s. 6d., Books V. and VI., 1s. 6d.

SALLUST. CATILINA AND JUGURTHA. With a Life. By G. LONG, M.A., and J. G. FRAZER, M.A. 3s. 6d. Or, separately, 2s. each.

TACITUS. GERMANIA AND AGRICOLA. By P. FROST, M.A. 2s. 6d.

VIRGIL. BUCOLICS, GEORGICS, AND AENEID, Books I.-IV. By J. G. SHEPPARD, D.C.L. Abridged from Professor Conington's Edition. 4s. 6d.

VIRGIL. **AENEID**, Books V.-XII. Abridged from Prof. Conington's edition, by H. NETTLESHIP, and W. WAGNER, Ph.D. 4s. 6d. Or in 9 separate volumes, price 1s. 6d. each.

XENOPHON. THE ANABASIS. With Life, Itinerary, Index, and Three Maps. By the late J. F. MACMICHAEL. Revised edition. 3s. 6d.
 Or in 4 separate volumes, price 1s. 6d. each.

XENOPHON. THE CYROPAEDIA. By G. M. GORHAM, M.A. 3s. 6d. Books I. and II. 1s. 6d. Books V. and VI. 1s. 6d.

XENOPHON. THE MEMORABILIA. By P. FROST, M.A. 3s.

CAMBRIDGE TEXTS WITH NOTES.

Price 1s. 6d. each, with exceptions.

AESCHYLUS. 6 Vols. PROMETHEUS **VINCTUS**—SEPTEM CONTRA THEBAS—AGAMEMNON—PERSAE—EUMENIDES—CHOEPHOROE. By F. A. PALEY, M.A., LL.D.

EURIPIDES. 13 Vols. ALCESTIS—MEDEA—HIPPOLYTUS—HECUBA—BACCHAE—ION (2s.)—ORESTES—PHOENISSAE—TROADES—HERCULES FURENS—ANDROMACHE—IPHIGENIA IN TAURIS—SUPPLICES. By F. A. PALEY, M.A., LL.D.

HOMER. ILIAD, Book I. By F. A. PALEY, M.A., LL.D. (1s.)

SOPHOCLES. 5 Vols. OEDIPUS TYRANNUS—OEDIPUS COLONEUS—ANTIGONE—ELECTRA—AJAX. By F. A. PALEY, M.A., LL.D.

XENOPHON'S ANABASIS. 6 Vols. With Life, Itinerary, Index, and Three Maps. MACMICHAEL's Edition, revised by J. E. MELHUISH, M.A., Assistant Master at St Paul's School. In separate Books.
Book I. (with Life, Introduction, Itinerary, and 3 Maps.)—Books II. and III.—Book IV.—Book V.—Book VI.—Book VII.

XENOPHON'S HELLENICA. Book I. and Book II. By the Rev. L. D. DOWDALL, M.A. 2s. each.

CICERO. 3 Vols. DE AMICITIA—DE SENECTUTE—
EPISTOLAE SELECTAE. By GEORGE LONG, M.A.

OVID'S FASTI. 3 Vols. By F. A. PALEY, M.A.,
LL.D. 2s. each. Books I. and II.—Books III. and IV.
—Books V. and VI.

OVID. SELECTIONS FROM THE AMORES, TRISTIA,
HEROIDES, AND METAMORPHOSES. By A. J. MACLEANE, M.A.

TERENCE. 4 Vols. ANDRIA—HAUTON TIMORUME-
NOS—PHORMIO—ADELPHOE. By Prof. WAGNER.

VIRGIL'S WORKS. 12 Vols. Abridged from Prof.
CONINGTON'S Edition by Professors NETTLESHIP and WAG-
NER and Rev. J. G. SHEPPARD.
BUCOLICS—GEORGICS, I. and II.—GEORGICS, III. and IV.
—AENEID, I. and II.—AENEID, III. and IV.—AENEID, V.
and VI. (2s.)—AENEID, VII.—AENEID, VIII.—AENEID, IX.
—AENEID, X.—AENEID, XI.—AENEID, XII.

CAMBRIDGE TEXTS.

AESCHYLUS. By F. A. PALEY, M.A., LL.D. 2s.

CAESAR DE BELLO GALLICO. By G. LONG, M.A. 1s. 6d.

CICERO DE SENECTUTE ET DE AMICITIA ET
EPISTOLAE SELECTAE. By G. LONG, M.A. 1s. 6d.

CICERONIS ORATIONES IN VERREM. By G. LONG, M.A.
2s. 6d.

EURIPIDES. By F. A. PALEY, M.A., LL.D. 3 vols.
2s. each.

HERODOTUS. By J. W. BLAKESLEY, B.D. 2 vols.
2s. 6d. each.

HOMERI ILIAS. Lib. I.—XII. By F. A. PALEY,
M.A., LL.D. 1s. 6d.

HORATIUS. By A. J. MACLEANE, M.A. Price
1s. 6d.

JUVENALIS ET PERSIUS. By A. J. MACLEANE,
M.A. 1s. 6d.

LUCRETIUS. By H. A. J. MUNRO, M.A. 2s.

OVIDIUS. By A. PALMER, M.A., G. M. EDWARDS, M.A., G. A. DAVIES, M.A., S. G. OWEN, M.A., A. E. HOUSMAN, M.A., and J. P. POSTGATE, M.A., Litt.D. 3 Vols. 2s. each.

SALLUSTI CATILINA ET JUGURTHA. By G. LONG, M.A. 1s. 6d.

SOPHOCLES. By F. A. PALEY, M.A., LL.D. 2s. 6d.

TERENTIUS. By W. WAGNER, Ph.D. 2s.

THUCYDIDES. By J. W. DONALDSON, B.D. 2 vols. 2s. each.

VERGILIUS. By J. CONINGTON, M.A. 2s.

XENOPHONTIS EXPEDITIO CYRI. By J. F. MAC-MICHAEL, M.A. 1s. 6d.

NOVUM TESTAMENTUM Graece, Textus Stephanici, 1550. Accedunt variae lectiones editionum Bezae, Elzeviri, Lachmanni, Tischendorfii, Tregellesii. Curante F. H. SCRIVENER, M.A. New Edition. 4s. 6d.

EDITIO MAJOR. Containing the readings approved by Bp. Westcott and Dr. Hort, and those adopted by the revisers. Also the Eusebian Canons and the Capitula and additional references. Small post 8vo. 7s. 6d.

An Edition with wide margins. Half-bound, price 12s.

CRITICAL EDITIONS AND TEXTS.

AETNA. Revised, emended, and explained by the late H. A. J. MUNRO, M.A., Litt.D. Demy 8vo. 3s. 6d.

ARISTOPHANES' COMEDIES. By H. A. HOLDEN, LL.D. Demy 8vo. Vol. I. Text and Notes. 18s. Vol. II. Indices. 5s. 6d. The plays sold separately.

CALPURNIUS SICULUS AND M. AURELIUS OLYMPIUS NEMESIANUS. The Eclogues, with Introduction, Commentary, and Appendix. By CH. HAINES KEENE, M.A. Crown 8vo. 6s.

CATULLUS. Edited by J. P. POSTGATE, M.A., Litt. D. Fcap. 8vo. 3s.

EURIPIDES, ELECTRA. Edited with Introduction and Notes by C. H. KEENE, M.A. Demy 8vo. 10s. 6d.

HYPERIDES, THE ORATIONS OF. Edited with Notes and a Translation by F. G. KENYON, M.A. 5s. net.

Livy. The first five Books. Prendeville's edition revised throughout and the notes in great part rewritten, by J. H. Freese, M.A. Books I, II, III, IV, V. With Maps and Introductions. 1s. 6d. each.

Lucan. The Pharsalia. By C. E. Haskins, M.A. With an Introduction by W. E. Heitland, M.A. Demy 8vo. 14s.

Lucretius. Titi Lucreti Cari de rerum natura libri sex. With Notes, Introduction, and Translation by the late H. A. J. Munro. 4th Edition finally Revised. 3 vols. 8vo. Vols. I. and II. Introduction, Text and Notes, 18s. Vol. III. Translation, 6s.

Ovid. P. Ovidii Nasonis Heroides XIV. Edited by Arthur Palmer, M.A. Demy 8vo. 6s.

——— Ars Amatoria et Amores. A School Edition, by the Rev. J. H. Williams, M.A. Fcap. 8vo. 3s. 6d.

——— The Metamorphoses. Book XIII. With Introduction and Notes by C. H. Keene, M.A. 2s. 6d.

——— The Metamorphoses. Book XIV. With Introduction and Notes by C. H. Keene, M.A. 2s. 6d.
 ⁂ Books XIII. and XIV. together. 3s. 6d.

——— Epistolarum ex Ponto Liber Primus. With Introduction and Notes. By C. H. Keene, M.A. Crown 8vo. 3s.

Plato. The Proem to the Republic of Plato. (Book I and Book II, chaps. 1—10). Edited, with Introduction, Critical Notes, and Commentary, by T. G. Tucker, Litt.D. 6s.

Propertius. Sexti Propertii Carmina recognovit J. P. Postgate, Litt.D. 4to. 3s. net.

Propertius. Sex. Aurelii Propertii Carmina. The Elegies of Propertius, with English Notes. By the late F. A. Paley, M.A., LL.D. 2nd Edition. 8vo. cloth. 5s.

Sophocles. The Oedipus Tyrannus of Sophocles. By B. H. Kennedy, D.D. Crown 8vo. 8s.

Theocritus. Edited, with Introduction and Notes, by R. J. Cholmeley, M.A. Post 8vo. 7s. 6d.

THUCYDIDES. THE HISTORY OF THE PELOPONNE-
SIAN WAR. With Notes and a Collation of the MSS.
By the late R. SHILLETO, M.A. Book I. 8vo. 6s. 6d.
Book II. 5s. 6d.

CORPUS POETARUM LATINORUM, a se aliisque denuo
recognitorum et brevi lectionum varietate instructorum,
edidit JOHANNES PERCIVAL POSTGATE, Litt.D. Tom. I.
quo continentur Ennius, Lucretius, Catullus, Horatius,
Vergilius, Tibullus, Propertius, Ovidius. Large post 4to.
21s. net. Or in Two Parts sewed, 9s. each net.
 Part III. containing Grattius, Manilius, Phaedrus,
Aetna, Persius, Lucan, Valerius Flaccus. 9s. net.
 Part IV. completing the work, *in the press.*

CORPUS POETARUM LATINORUM. Edited by WALKER.
1 thick vol. 8vo. Cloth, 18s.
 Containing:—Catullus, Lucretius, Virgilius, Tibullus,
Propertius, Ovidius, Horatius, Phaedrus, Lucanus, Persius,
Juvenalis, Martialis, Sulpicia, Statius, Silius Italicus, Vale-
rius Flaccus, Calpurnius Siculus, Ausonius, and Claudianus.

TRANSLATIONS, &c.

AESCHYLUS. Translated by ANNA SWANWICK.
With Introduction and Notes. 5th Edition, revised. 5s.

ARISTOTLE ON THE CONSTITUTION OF ATHENS.
Translated, with Introduction and Notes, by F. G. KENYON,
M.A. Pott 8vo. buckram. Third Edition. 4s. 6d.

HORACE. Translated into English Verse by the
late Professor CONINGTON, M.A. The Odes and Carmen
Saeculare. 12th Edition. Fcap. 8vo. 3s. 6d. The
Satires and Epistles. 8th Edition. 3s. 6d.

HORACE, ODES AND EPODES. Translated with
Introduction and Notes, by Sir STEPHEN E. DE VERE,
Bart. 3rd Edition. 7s. 6d. net.

LUCRETIUS. Translated by late H. A. J. MUNRO,
Litt.D. 6s. *See page* 14.

PLATO. GORGIAS, literally translated. By the late
E. M. COPE, M.A. 2nd Edition. 8vo. 7s.

—— AN ANALYSIS AND INDEX OF THE DIALOGUES.
With References to the Translation in Bohn's Classical
Library. By Dr DAY. Post 8vo. 5s.

SABRINÆ COROLLA In Hortulis Regiæ Scholæ
Salopiensis contexuerunt tres viri floribus legendis. 4th
Edition, revised and re-arranged. By the late BENJAMIN
HALL KENNEDY, D.D. Large post 8vo. 10s. 6d.

SOPHOCLES, THE DRAMAS OF. Rendered in English
Verse, Dramatic and Lyric, by Sir GEORGE YOUNG, Bart.,
M.A. 12s. 6d.

SOPHOCLES. THE ŒDIPUS TYRANNUS. Translated
by the late B. H. KENNEDY, D.D. In paper cover. 1s.

THEOCRITUS. Translated into English Verse by
the late C. S. CALVERLEY, M.A. Crown 8vo. 2nd Edition,
revised. 5s.

TRANSLATIONS INTO ENGLISH AND LATIN. By the
late C. S. CALVERLEY, M.A. 4th Edition. Post 8vo. 5s.

TRANSLATIONS FROM AND INTO LATIN, GREEK, AND
ENGLISH. By Sir R. C. JEBB, M.P., Litt.D., LL.D.,
H. JACKSON, Litt.D., and W. E. CURREY, M.A. Third
Edition. Crown 8vo. 5s.

BELL'S CLASSICAL TRANSLATIONS.

*A Series of Translations from the Classics. With Memoirs,
Introductions, &c. Crown 8vo. 1s. each.*

ÆSCHYLUS. THE SUPPLIANTS. Translated by
WALTER HEADLAM, M.A.

ARISTOPHANES. THE ACHARNIANS. Translated
by W. H. COVINGTON, B.A.

ARISTOPHANES. THE PLUTUS. Translated by M. T.
QUINN, M.A.

CÆSAR'S GALLIC WAR. Translated by W. A.
M'DEVITTE, B.A. With Map. 2 vols. Books I.—IV.—
Books V.—VII.

CICERO. FRIENDSHIP AND OLD AGE. Translated
by G. H. WELLS, M.A.

DEMOSTHENES ON THE CROWN. Translated by C.
RANN KENNEDY.

EURIPIDES. Translated by E. P. COLERIDGE, M.A.
14 vols.
MEDEA—ALCESTIS—HERACLEIDÆ—HIPPOLYTUS—SUP-
PLICES — TROADES — ION — ANDROMACHE — BACCHÆ —
HECUBA—HERCULES FURENS—PHŒNISSÆ—ORESTES—
IPHIGENIA IN TAURIS.

HORACE. Translated by A. H. BRYCE, LL.D. 4 vols.
  ODES I. and II.—ODES III. and IV. with the CARMEN SECULARE and EPODES—SATIRES—EPISTLES and ARS POETICA.
LIVY. Books I., II., III., IV. A Revised Translation by J. H. FREESE, M.A. With Maps. 4 vols.
LIVY. Book V. and Book VI. A Revised Translation by E. S. WEYMOUTH, M.A., Lond. With Maps. 2 vols.
LIVY. BOOK IX. Translated by F. STORR, B.A.
LIVY. Books XXI., XXII., XXIII. Translated by J. Bernard Baker, M.A. 3 vols.
LUCAN. THE PHARSALIA. Book I. Translated by FREDERICK CONWAY, M.A.
OVID'S FASTI. Translated by H. T. RILEY, M.A. 3 vols. Books I. and II.—III. and IV.—V. and VI.
OVID'S TRISTIA. Translated by H. T. RILEY, M.A.
PLATO. APOLOGY OF SOCRATES AND CRITO (1 vol.), PHÆDO, AND PROTAGORAS. Translated by H. CARY, M.A. 3 vols.
PLAUTUS. TRINUMMUS, AULULARIA, MENÆCHMI, AND CAPTIVI. Translated by HENRY T. RILEY, M.A. 4 vols.
SOPHOCLES. Translated by E. P. COLERIDGE, M.A. 7 vols.
  ANTIGONE — PHILOCTETES — ŒDIPUS REX — ŒDIPUS COLONEUS—TRACHINIÆ—ELECTRA—AJAX.
THUCYDIDES. Books VI., VII. Translated by E. C. MARCHANT, M.A. 2 vols.
VIRGIL. Translated by A. HAMILTON BRYCE, LL.D. 6 vols.
  GEORGICS—BUCOLICS—ÆNEID I.-III.—ÆNEID IV.-VI.—ÆNEID VII.-IX.—ÆNEID X.-XII.
XENOPHON'S ANABASIS. Translated by the Rev. J. S. WATSON, M.A. 3 vols. Books I. and II.—Books III., IV. and V.—Books VI. and VII.
XENOPHON'S HELLENICS. Books I. and II. Translated by the Rev. H. DALE, M.A.

LATIN AND GREEK CLASS BOOKS.

Bell's Illustrated Latin Readers.
Edited by E. C. MARCHANT, M.A.

I. SCALAE PRIMAE. A SELECTION OF SIMPLE STORIES FOR TRANSLATION INTO ENGLISH. With Vocabulary. By J. G. SPENCER, B.A. Pott 8vo. with 29 Illustrations. 1s.

II. SCALAE MEDIAE. SHORT EXTRACTS FROM EUTROPIUS AND CAESAR, GRADUATED IN DIFFICULTY. With Vocabulary. By PERCY A. UNDERHILL, M.A. Pott 8vo. with 20 Illustrations. 1s.

III. SCALAE TERTIAE. SELECTIONS IN VERSE AND PROSE FROM PHAEDRUS, OVID, NEPOS, AND CICERO, GRADUATED IN DIFFICULTY. With Vocabulary. By E. C. MARCHANT, M.A. Pott 8vo., with 28 Illustrations. 1s.

BELL'S LATIN COURSE, for the First Year. In three Parts. By E. C. MARCHANT, M.A., and J. G. SPENCER, B.A. With numerous Illustrations. 1s. 6d. each.

BADDELEY. AUXILIA LATINA. A Series of Progressive Latin Exercises. By M. J. B. BADDELEY, M.A. Fcap. 8vo. Part I., Accidence. 5th Edition. 2s. Part II. 5th Edition. 2s. Key to Part II. 2s. 6d.

BAIRD. GREEK VERBS. By J. S. BAIRD, T.C.D. New Edition, revised. 2s. 6d.

—— HOMERIC DIALECT. Revised by the Rev. W. GUNION RUTHERFORD, LL.D. 1s.

BAKER. LATIN PROSE FOR LONDON STUDENTS. By ARTHUR BAKER, M.A. Wide Fcap. 8vo. 2s.

BARRY. NOTES ON GREEK ACCENTS. By the Rt Rev. A. BARRY, D.D. New Edition. 1s.

CHURCH. LATIN PROSE LESSONS. By A. J. CHURCH, M.A. 9th Edition. Fcap. 8vo. 2s. 6d.

CLAPIN. LATIN PRIMER. By the Rev. A. C. CLAPIN, M.A. 4th Edition. Fcap. 8vo. 1s.

COLERIDGE. RES ROMANAE, being brief Aids to the History, Geography, Literature and Antiquities of Ancient Rome for less advanced students. By E. P. COLERIDGE, B.A. With 3 maps. Crown 8vo. 2nd Edition. 2s. 6d.

COLERIDGE. RES GRAECAE. Being Aids to the study of the History, Geography, Archæology, and Literature of Ancient Athens. By E. P. COLERIDGE, B.A. With 5 Maps, 7 Plans, and 17 other illustrations. Crown 8vo. 5s.

COLLINS. LATIN EXERCISES AND GRAMMAR PAPERS. By T. COLLINS, M.A. 7th Edition. Fcap. 8vo. 2s. 6d.

—— UNSEEN PAPERS in Latin Prose and Verse. 8th Edition. Fcap. 8vo. 2s. 6d.

—— UNSEEN PAPERS in Greek Prose and Verse. 5th Edition. Fcap. 8vo. 3s.

—— EASY TRANSLATIONS from Nepos, Caesar, Cicero, Livy, &c., for Retranslation into Latin. With Notes. 2s.

COMPTON. RUDIMENTS OF ATTIC CONSTRUCTION AND IDIOM. By the Rev. W. COOKWORTHY COMPTON, M.A. Crown 8vo. 3s.

FROST. ECLOGÆ LATINÆ; or, First Latin Reading Book. With Notes and Vocabulary by the late Rev. P. FROST, M.A. New Edition. Fcap. 8vo. 1s. 6d.

—— ANALECTA GRÆCA MINORA. With Notes and Dictionary. New Edition. Fcap. 8vo. 2s.

—— MATERIALS FOR LATIN PROSE COMPOSITION. By the late Rev. P. FROST, M.A. New Edition. Fcap. 8vo. 2s. Key, 4s. net.

—— A LATIN VERSE BOOK. New Edition. Fcap. 8vo. 2s. Key, 5s. net.

—— MATERIALS FOR GREEK PROSE COMPOSITION. New Edition. Fcap. 8vo. 2s. 6d. Key, 5s. net.

HOLDEN. FOLIORUM SILVULA. Part I. Passages for Translation into Latin Elegiac and Heroic Verse. By H. A. HOLDEN, LL.D. 12th Edition. Post 8vo. 7s. 6d.

—— FOLIORUM SILVULA. Part II. Select Passages for Translation into Latin Lyric and Comic Iambic Verse. 3rd Edition. Post 8vo. 5s.

—— FOLIORUM CENTURIAE. Select Passages for Translation into Latin and Greek Prose. 10th Edition. Post 8vo. 8s.

JEBB, JACKSON and CURREY. EXTRACTS FOR TRANSLATION IN GREEK, LATIN, AND ENGLISH. By Sir R. C. JEBB, M.P., Litt.D., LL.D.; H. JACKSON, Litt.D.; and W. E. CURREY, M.A. 2s. 6d.

NETTLESHIP. PASSAGES FOR TRANSLATION INTO LATIN PROSE. By H. NETTLESHIP, M.A. Crown 8vo. 3s.

A KEY. Crown 8vo. 4s. 6d. net.

NOTABILIA QUAEDAM: OR THE PRINCIPAL TENSES OF THE IRREGULAR GREEK VERBS, AND ELEMENTARY GREEK, LATIN AND FRENCH CONSTRUCTIONS. 1s.

PENROSE. LATIN ELEGIAC VERSE, Easy Exercises in. By the Rev. J. PENROSE. New Edition. 12mo. 2s. Key, 3s. 6d. net.

PRESTON. GREEK VERSE COMPOSITION. By G. PRESTON, M.A. 5th Edition. Crown 8vo. 4s. 6d.

THACKERAY. ANTHOLOGIA GRAECA. A Selection of Greek Poetry, with Notes. By F. ST JOHN THACKERAY. 6th Edition. 16mo. 4s. 6d.

—— ANTHOLOGIA LATINA. A Selection of Latin Poetry, from Naevius to Boëthius, with Notes. By Rev. F. ST JOHN THACKERAY. 8th Edition. 16mo. 4s. 6d.

WAINWRIGHT. EXERCISES IN LATIN SYNTAX. By L. D. WAINWRIGHT, M.A. In Five Parts. 8d. each.

Part I. The 'Ut' book, with Ne, Quominus, Quin.
Part II. Conditional Sentences, with Dum and Dummodo.
Part III. The 'Cum' book. Part IV. Oratio Obliqua.
Part V. The 'Qui' book, with Utinam, Quasi, &c.

WELLS. FIRST EXERCISES IN LATIN PROSE COMPOSITION. By E. A. WELLS, M.A. Pott 8vo. With Vocabulary. 2nd Edition, revised. 1s.

TEUFFEL'S HISTORY OF ROMAN LITERATURE. 5th Edition, revised by Dr SCHWABE, translated by Prof. G. C. W. WARR, M.A. Medium 8vo. 2 vols. 15s.

DONALDSON'S THEATRE OF THE GREEKS. 10th Edition. 5s.

KEIGHTLEY'S (T.) MYTHOLOGY OF ANCIENT GREECE AND ITALY. 4th Edition, revised by L. SCHMITZ, Ph.D., LL.D. With 12 Plates. 5s.

FRENCH AND GERMAN CLASS BOOKS.

GASC (F. E. A.). FIRST FRENCH BOOK. Crown 8vo. 128th—132nd Thousand. 1s.

—— SECOND FRENCH BOOK. 57th Thousand. Fcap. 8vo. 1s. 6d.

—— KEY TO FIRST AND SECOND FRENCH BOOKS 7th Edition. Fcap. 8vo. 3s. 6d. net.

—— FRENCH FABLES FOR BEGINNERS, in Prose. 17th Thousand. 12mo. 1s. 6d.

—— SELECT FABLES OF LA FONTAINE. 19th Thousand. Fcap. 8vo. 1s. 6d.

—— HISTOIRES AMUSANTES ET INSTRUCTIVES. With Notes. 17th Thousand. Fcap. 8vo. 2s.

—— PRACTICAL GUIDE TO MODERN FRENCH CONVERSATION. 19th Edition. Fcap. 8vo. 1s. 6d.

—— FRENCH POETRY FOR THE YOUNG. With Notes. 5th Edition. Fcap. 8vo. 1s. 6d.

—— MATERIALS FOR FRENCH PROSE COMPOSITION; or, Selections from the best English Prose Writers. 23rd Thousand. Fcap. 8vo. 3s. KEY, 6s.

—— PROSATEURS CONTEMPORAINS. With Notes. 11th Edition, revised. 12mo. 3s. 6d.

—— LE PETIT COMPAGNON; a French Talk-Book for Little Children. 16th Edition. 16mo. 1s. 6d.

—— AN IMPROVED MODERN POCKET DICTIONARY of the French and English Languages. 63rd Thousand. 16mo. 2s. 6d.

—— FRENCH-ENGLISH AND ENGLISH-FRENCH DICTIONARY. 8th Edition, reset and enlarged. Large 8vo. 12s. 6d.

—— CONCISE DICTIONARY OF THE FRENCH AND ENGLISH LANGUAGES. Medium 16mo. 3s. 6d.

GASC (F. E. A.). THE A B C TOURIST'S FRENCH INTERPRETER of all Immediate Wants. 1s.

CLAPIN (A. C.). FRENCH GRAMMAR for Public Schools. By the Rev. A. C. CLAPIN, M.A., B.-ès-L. Fcap. 8vo. 14th Edition. 2s. 6d. KEY, 3s. 6d. net.

—— FRENCH PRIMER. Fcap. 8vo. 11th Edition. 1s.

—— PRIMER OF FRENCH PHILOLOGY, with Exercises for Public Schools. 10th Edition. Fcap. 8vo. 1s.

—— ENGLISH PASSAGES FOR TRANSLATION INTO FRENCH. 2s. 6d. KEY, 4s. net.

GOSSET (A.). MANUAL OF FRENCH PROSODY. By A. GOSSET, M.A. Fcap. 8vo. 3s.

BUCHHEIM (C. A.). GERMAN PROSE COMPOSITION, Materials for. By DR C. A. BUCHHEIM. 15th Edition. Fcap. 8vo. 4s. 6d. A KEY to Pts. I. & II., 3s. net. Pts. III. & IV., 4s. net.

—— FIRST BOOK OF GERMAN PROSE. Being Parts I. and II. of the above, with Vocabulary. Second Edition. 1s. 6d.

CLAPIN (A. C.). A GERMAN GRAMMAR for Public Schools. By the Rev. A. C. CLAPIN, and F. HOLL-MÜLLER. 6th Edition. Fcap. 8vo. 2s. 6d.

—— A GERMAN PRIMER. 2nd Edition. Fcap. 8vo. 1s.

FRANCKE (KUNO). HISTORY OF GERMAN LITERATURE. By KUNO FRANCKE. 4th Edition. 8vo. 10s. net.

PHILLIPS (M. E.). HANDBOOK OF GERMAN LITERATURE. By MARY E. PHILLIPS, L.L.A. With Introduction by Dr A. WEISS. 3s. 6d.

FOREIGN CLASSICS.

Edited for use in Schools, with Introductions, Notes, &c. Fcap. 8vo.

CHARLES XII. par VOLTAIRE. By L. DIREY. 8th Edition. 1s. 6d.

GERMAN BALLADS FROM UHLAND, GOETHE, AND SCHILLER. By C. L. BIELEFELD. 7th Edition. 1s. 6d.

Cambridge: Deighton, Bell and Co. 23

AVENTURES DE TÉLÉMAQUE, par FÉNELON. By C. J. DELILLE. 6th Edition. 2s. 6d.

SELECT FABLES OF LA FONTAINE. By F. E. A. GASC. 19th Edition. 1s. 6d.

PICCIOLA, **by** X. B. SAINTINE. By DR DUBUC. **16th** Thousand. 1s. 6d.

LAMARTINE'S LE TAILLEUR DE PIERRES DE SAINT-POINT. By J. BOÏELLE, B.-ès-L. 7th Edition. 1s. 6d.

GOETHE'S HERMANN UND DOROTHEA. By E. BELL, M.A., and E. WÖLFEL. New Edition. 1s. 6d.

SCHILLER'S WALLENSTEIN. Complete Text. By Dr BUCHHEIM. 6th Edition. 5s. Or the LAGER and PICCOLOMINI, 2s. 6d. WALLENSTEIN'S TOD, 2s. 6d.

MAID OF ORLEANS; with English Notes by Dr W. WAGNER. 3rd Edition. 1s. 6d.

MARIA STUART. By V. KASTNER, Lecturer at Victoria University, Manchester. 4th Edition. 1s. 6d.

GOMBERT'S FRENCH DRAMA. Re-edited, with Notes, by F. E. A. GASC. Sewed, 6d. each.

List of Plays in the Series.

By MOLIÈRE.—LE MISANTHROPE. L'AVARE. LE BOURGEOIS GENTILHOMME. LE TARTUFFE. LE MALADE IMAGINAIRE. LES FEMMES SAVANTES. LES FOURBERIES DE SCAPIN. LES PRÉCIEUSES RIDICULES. L'ECOLE DES FEMMES, L'ECOLE DES MARIS. LE MÉDECIN MALGRÉ LUI.

By **RACINE**.—LA THÉBAÏDE, OU LES FRÈRES ENNEMIS. ANDROMAQUE. LES PLAIDEURS. IPHIGÉNIE. BRITANNICUS. PHÈDRE. ESTHER. ATHALIE.

By CORNEILLE.—LE CID. HORACE. **CINNA.** POLYEUCTE.

By VOLTAIRE.—ZAÏRE.

BELL'S MODERN TRANSLATIONS.

A Series of Translations from Modern Languages, with Memoirs, Introductions, etc. Crown 8vo. 1s. each.

DANTE. Translated by the Rev. H. F. CARY, M.A. With Notes. 3 Vols.
    INFERNO—PURGATORIO—PARADISO.

GOETHE. EGMONT. Translated by ANNA SWANWICK.

GOETHE. IPHIGENIA IN TAURIS. Translated by ANNA SWANWICK.

GOETHE. GOETZ VON BERLICHINGEN. Translated by SIR WALTER SCOTT.

GOETHE. HERMANN AND DOROTHEA. Translated by E. A. BOWRING, C.B.

HAUFF. THE CARAVAN. Translated by S. MENDEL.

HAUFF. THE INN IN THE SPESSART. Translated by S. MENDEL.

LESSING. LAOKOON. Translated by E. C. BEASLEY.

LESSING. NATHAN THE WISE. Translated by R. DILLON BOYLAN.

LESSING. MINNA VON BARNHELM. Translated by ERNEST BELL, M.A.

MOLIÈRE'S PLAYS. Translated by C. HERON WALL. 8 Vols.
    THE MISANTHROPE—THE DOCTOR IN SPITE OF HIMSELF—TARTUFFE—THE MISER—THE SHOPKEEPER TURNED GENTLEMAN—THE AFFECTED LADIES—THE LEARNED WOMEN—THE IMPOSTURES OF SCAPIN.

RACINE'S TRAGEDIES. Translated by R. BRUCE BOSWELL, M.A. 5 Vols.
    ATHALIE—ESTHER—ANDROMACHE—BRITANNICUS—IPHIGENIA.

SCHILLER. WILLIAM TELL. Translated by Sir THEODORE MARTIN, K.C.B., LL.D.

SCHILLER. THE MAID OF ORLEANS. Translated by ANNA SWANWICK.

SCHILLER. MARY STUART. Translated by MELLISH.

SCHILLER. WALLENSTEIN'S CAMP AND THE PICCOLOMINI. Translated by JAMES CHURCHILL and S. T. COLERIDGE.

SCHILLER. THE DEATH OF WALLENSTEIN. Translated by S. T. COLERIDGE.

ENGLISH CLASS BOOKS.

ADAMS (Dr E.). THE ELEMENTS OF THE ENGLISH LANGUAGE. By ERNEST ADAMS, Ph.D. 26th Edition. Revised by J. F. DAVIS, D.Lit. Post 8vo. 4s. 6d.

—— THE RUDIMENTS OF ENGLISH GRAMMAR AND ANALYSIS. 20th Thousand. Fcap. 8vo. 1s.

BARNETT (T. DUFF). NOTES ON SHAKESPEARE'S PLAYS. With Introduction, Summary, Notes (Etymological and Explanatory), Prosody, Grammatical Peculiarities, &c. By T. DUFF BARNETT, B.A. Lond. Crown 8vo. 1s. each.
MIDSUMMER NIGHT'S DREAM.—JULIUS CÆSAR.—THE TEMPEST.—MACBETH.—HENRY THE FIFTH.—HAMLET.—MERCHANT OF VENICE.—KING RICHARD II.—KING JOHN.—KING RICHARD III.—KING LEAR.—CORIOLANUS.—AS YOU LIKE IT.—TWELFTH NIGHT.—MUCH ADO ABOUT NOTHING.

TEN BRINK (B.). EARLY ENGLISH LITERATURE. By BERNHARD TEN BRINK. Vol. I. (to Wyclif). Vol. II. (Wyclif, Chaucer, Earliest Drama, Renaissance). Vol. III. (to Surrey's Death). Post 8vo. 3s. 6d. each.

—— LECTURES ON SHAKESPEARE. Translated by JULIA FRANKLIN. Post 8vo. 3s. 6d.

EDWARDS (F.). EXAMPLES FOR GRAMMATICAL ANALYSIS IN VERSE AND PROSE. By F. EDWARDS. 1s.

LOUNSBURY (PROF.). HISTORY OF THE ENGLISH LANGUAGE. By T. R. LOUNSBURY. Crown 8vo. 5s.

PANCOAST (H. S.). INTRODUCTION TO ENGLISH LITERATURE. By HENRY S. PANCOAST. 556 pages. Crown 8vo. 5s.

READY (A. W.). ESSAYS AND ESSAY WRITING FOR PUBLIC EXAMINATIONS. By A. W. READY, B.A. Crown 8vo. 3s. 6d.

PRÉCIS AND PRÉCIS-WRITING. Crown 8vo. 3s. 6d.

SKEAT (Prof.). QUESTIONS FOR EXAMINATION IN ENGLISH LITERATURE. By Prof. SKEAT, Litt.D., LL.D. 3rd Edition, revised. Crown 8vo. 2s. 6d.

GRAMMARS

By C. P. Mason.

FIRST NOTIONS OF GRAMMAR FOR YOUNG LEARNERS. Fcap. 8vo. 135th—144th Thousand. Revised. 1s.

FIRST STEPS IN ENGLISH GRAMMAR FOR JUNIOR CLASSES. Demy 18mo. 64th—68th Thousand. 1s.

OUTLINES OF ENGLISH GRAMMAR FOR THE USE OF JUNIOR CLASSES. 117th—126th Thousand. Crown 8vo. 2s.

ENGLISH GRAMMAR, including the Principles of Grammatical Analysis. 40th Edition. Crown 8vo. 3s. 6d.

A SHORTER ENGLISH GRAMMAR, with copious Exercises. 57th to 61st Thousand. Crown 8vo. 3s. 6d.

PRACTICE AND HELP IN THE ANALYSIS OF SENTENCES. 2s.

ENGLISH GRAMMAR PRACTICE, being the Exercises separately. 3rd Edition. 1s.

CODE STANDARD GRAMMARS. Parts I. and II., 2d. each. Parts III., IV. and V., 3d. each.

HANDBOOKS OF ENGLISH LITERATURE.

Edited by Professor Hales. Crown 8vo. 3s. 6d. each.

THE AGE OF SHAKESPEARE. By THOMAS SECCOMBE and J. W. ALLEN. [*In the Press.*

THE AGE OF CHAUCER. By F. J. SNELL, M.A. With an Introduction by Prof. HALES.

THE AGE OF MILTON. By J. BASS MULLINGER, M.A., and the Rev. J. H. B. MASTERMAN.

THE AGE OF DRYDEN. By RICHARD GARNETT, LL.D., C.B. Second Edition.

THE AGE OF POPE. By JOHN DENNIS. 3rd Edition.

THE AGE OF JOHNSON. By THOMAS SECCOMBE.

THE AGE OF WORDSWORTH. By Professor C. H. HERFORD, Litt.D. Third Edition.

THE AGE OF TENNYSON. By Professor HUGH WALKER. Second Edition.

BELL'S ENGLISH CLASSICS.

Edited for use in Schools, with Introduction and Notes.

Crown 8vo.

BROWNING, SELECTIONS FROM. Edited by F. RYLAND, M.A. 2s. 6d.

BROWNING'S STRAFFORD. Edited by E. H. HICKEY. With Introduction by S. R. GARDINER, LL.D. 2s. 6d.

BURKE'S LETTERS ON A REGICIDE PEACE. I. and II. Edited by H. G. KEENE, M.A., C.I.E. 3s.; sewed, 2s.

BYRON'S CHILDE HAROLD. Edited by H. G. KEENE, M.A., C.I.E., &c. 3s. 6d. Also Cantos I. and II., sewed, 1s. 9d.; Cantos III. and IV., sewed, 1s. 9d.

—— SIEGE OF CORINTH. Edited by P. HORDERN. 1s. 6d.; sewed, 1s.

CARLYLE'S HERO AS MAN OF LETTERS. Edited with Introduction by MARK HUNTER, M.A. 2s. Sewed, 1s. 6d.

—— HERO AS DIVINITY. By the same Editor. 2s.; sewed, 1s. 6d.

CHAUCER'S MINOR POEMS, SELECTIONS FROM. Edited by J. B. BILDERBECK, B.A. 2s. 6d.; sewed, 1s. 9d.

DE QUINCEY'S REVOLT OF THE TARTARS and ENGLISH MAIL COACH. Edited by CECIL M. BARROW, M.A., and MARK HUNTER, M.A. 3s.; sewed, 2s.
.*. The REVOLT OF THE TARTARS. Separately. Sewed. 1s. 3d.

DE QUINCEY'S OPIUM EATER. Edited by MARK HUNTER, M.A. 4s. 6d.; sewed, 3s. 6d.

GOLDSMITH'S GOOD-NATURED MAN. Edited by K. DEIGHTON. 2s.; sewed, 1s. 6d.

GOLDSMITH'S SHE STOOPS TO CONQUER. Edited by K. DEIGHTON. 2s.; sewed, 1s. 6d.

*** THE GOOD-NATURED MAN and SHE STOOPS TO CONQUER may also be had in one volume. Sewed, 2s. 6d.

GOLDSMITH'S TRAVELLER AND DESERTED VILLAGE. Edited with Introduction and Notes by the Rev. A. E. WOODWARD, M.A. 2s.

*** THE TRAVELLER and THE DESERTED VILLAGE may also be had separately, sewed, 10d. each.

IRVING'S SKETCH BOOK. Edited by R. G. OXENHAM, M.A. Sewed, 1s. 6d.

JOHNSON'S LIFE OF ADDISON. Edited by F. RYLAND. 2s. 6d.

—— LIFE OF SWIFT. Edited by F. RYLAND, M.A. 2s.

—— LIFE OF POPE. Edited by F. RYLAND, M.A. 2s. 6d.

*** THE LIVES OF SWIFT AND POPE, together. Sewed, 2s. 6d.

—— LIFE OF MILTON. Edited by F. RYLAND, M.A. 2s. 6d.

—— LIFE OF DRYDEN. Edited by F. RYLAND, M.A. 2s. 6d.

*** THE LIVES OF MILTON AND DRYDEN, together. Sewed, 2s. 6d.

—— LIVES OF PRIOR AND CONGREVE. Edited by F. RYLAND, M.A. 2s.

LAMB'S ESSAYS. Selected and Edited by K. DEIGHTON. 3rd Edition, 3s.; sewed, 2s.

LONGFELLOW, SELECTIONS FROM, including EVANGELINE. Edited by M. T. QUINN, M.A. 2s. 6d.; sewed, 1s. 9d. Also EVANGELINE separately, sewed, 1s. 3d.

MACAULAY'S LAYS OF ANCIENT ROME. Edited by P. HORDERN. 2s. 6d.; sewed, 1s. 9d.

—— ESSAY ON CLIVE. Edited by CECIL M. BARROW, M.A. 2s.; sewed, 1s. 6d.

MASSINGER'S A NEW WAY TO PAY OLD DEBTS. Edited by K. DEIGHTON. 3s.; sewed, 2s.

MILTON'S PARADISE LOST. Books III. and IV. Edited by R. G. OXENHAM, M.A. 2s.; sewed, 1s. 6d., or separately, sewed, 10d. each.

—— PARADISE REGAINED. Edited by K. DEIGHTON. 2s. 6d.; sewed, 1s. 9d.

POPE'S ESSAY ON MAN. Edited by F. RYLAND, M.A. 1s. 6d.; sewed, 1s.

POPE, SELECTIONS FROM. Containing Essay on Criticism, Rape of the Lock, Temple of Fame, Windsor Forest. Edited by K. DEIGHTON. 2s. 6d.; sewed, 1s. 9d.

SCOTT'S LADY OF THE LAKE. Edited by the Rev. A. E. WOODWARD, M.A. 3s. 6d., or each Canto separately, sewed, 8d.

SHAKESPEARE'S JULIUS CÆSAR. Edited by T. DUFF BARNETT, B.A., London. 2s.

—— MERCHANT OF VENICE. Edited by T. DUFF BARNETT, B.A., Lond. 2s.

—— TEMPEST. Edited by T. DUFF BARNETT, B.A., Lond. 2s.

WORDSWORTH'S EXCURSION. Book I. Edited by M. T. QUINN, M.A. Sewed, 1s. 3d.

PHILOSOPHY, PSYCHOLOGY, &c.

HANDBOOK OF THE HISTORY OF PHILOSOPHY. By E. BELFORT BAX. 2nd Edition, revised. 5s.

HEGEL'S PHILOSOPHY OF RIGHT (Grundlinien der Philosophie des Rechts). Translated by Samuel W. DYDE, M.A., D.Sc. Crown 8vo. 7s. 6d.

HISTORY OF MODERN PHILOSOPHY. By R. FALCKENBERG. Trans. by Prof. A. C. ARMSTRONG. Demy 8vo. 16s.

PSYCHOLOGY: An Introductory Manual for the use of University Students, designed chiefly for the London B.A. and B.Sc. By F. RYLAND, M.A. 7th Edition, re-written. Crown 8vo. 4s. 6d.

ETHICS: An Introductory Manual for the use of University Students. By F. RYLAND, M.A. 2nd Edition, revised. 3s. 6d.

LOGIC. An Introductory Manual by F. RYLAND, M.A. Crown 8vo. 4s. 6d.

POLITICAL ECONOMY. By M. PROTHERO, M.A. Crown 8vo. 4s. 6d.

BELL'S SCIENCE SERIES.

Edited by Percy Groom, D.Sc., F.L.S., Lecturer on Botany, and G. M. Minchin, M.A., F.R.S., Professor of Applied Mathematics in the Royal Indian Engineering College, Cooper's Hill.

ELEMENTARY BOTANY. By PERCY GROOM, D.Sc., F.L.S. Second Edition. With 275 Illustrations. Crown 8vo. 3s. 6d.

THE STUDENT'S DYNAMICS: COMPRISING STATICS AND KINETICS. By Professor G. M. MINCHIN, M.A., F.R.S. 3s. 6d.

ELEMENTARY INORGANIC CHEMISTRY. By JAMES WALKER, D.Sc., Ph.D., F.R.S.

AN INTRODUCTION TO THE STUDY OF THE COMPARATIVE ANATOMY OF ANIMALS. By G. C. BOURNE, M.A. With numerous Illustrations.
    Vol. I. Animal Organization. The Protozoa and Cœlenterata. 4s. 6d.
    Vol. II. The Cœlomata. 4s. 6d.

ELEMENTARY GENERAL SCIENCE. By D. E. JONES, D.Sc., and D. S. McNair, Ph.D., B.Sc. [*In the Press.*

PHYSIOGRAPHY. By H. N. DICKSON, F.R.S.E., F.R.Met.Soc., F.R.G.S. [*In the Press.*

ELECTRICITY AND MAGNETISM. By OLIVER J. LODGE, D.Sc., F.R.S. [*In Preparation.*

ZOOLOGY.

A TEXT-BOOK OF VERTEBRATE ZOOLOGY. By Prof. J. S. KINGSLEY. With 378 Diagrams. 8vo. 12s. *net.*

MUSIC.

MUSIC. A complete Text-Book of Theoretical Music, with Glossary of Musical Terms, Exercises on Harmony, and an Appendix of Examination Papers. By H. C. BANISTER. 17th Edition. 5s.

MUSIC, A CONCISE HISTORY OF, from the Commencement of the Christian Era to the present time. By Rev. H. G. BONAVIA HUNT, Mus. Doc. 15th Edition, revised. 3s. 6d.

HISTORY.

A HISTORY OF MODERN EUROPE. From the Fall of Constantinople to the present time. By the late THOMAS HENRY DYER, LL.D. A new edition, **revised and brought up to date by** ARTHUR HASSALL, M.A. **In 6 vols.** Crown 8vo. with Maps. 6s. *net* each.

HISTORY OF THE CITY OF ROME IN THE MIDDLE AGES. By FERDINAND GREGOROVIUS. Translated by Mrs HAMILTON. 8 vols. £3. 3s. *net.* Or Vols. I—III, 6s. *net* each. **Vols IV—VIII,** 9s. *net* each.

HISTORY OF GERMANY IN THE MIDDLE AGES. By E. F. HENDERSON, Ph.D. Post 8vo. **7s. 6d.** *net.*

SELECT HISTORICAL DOCUMENTS OF THE MIDDLE AGES. Collected and translated by ERNEST F. HENDERSON, Ph.D. Small post 8vo. 5s.

SIDELIGHTS ON ENGLISH HISTORY. Being Extracts from Letters, Papers, and Diaries of the past three centuries. Collected and arranged by E. F. HENDERSON, Ph.D. With 83 Portraits and other Illustrations. Impl. **8vo.** 21s. *net.*

LEADING DOCUMENTS OF ENGLISH HISTORY. Edited by Dr GUY CARLETON LEE, of John Hopkins University. 8vo. 7s. 6d. **net.**

THE INTERMEDIATE HISTORY OF ENGLAND. For Army and Civil Service Candidates. By H. F. WRIGHT, M.A., LL.M. Crown 8vo. 6s.

HISTORY OF ENGLAND, 1800—46. By HARRIET MARTINEAU. 5 vols. 3s. 6d. each.

A PRACTICAL SYNOPSIS OF ENGLISH HISTORY. By A. BOWES. 9th Edition, revised. 8vo. 1s.

LIVES OF THE QUEENS OF ENGLAND. By A. STRICKLAND. 6 vols. 5s. each. Abridged Edition, 1 vol. 6s. 6d.

For other Historical Books, see Catalogue of Bohn's Libraries, sent free on application.

Price 7s. 6d. net. Published Annually.
The Cambridge University Calendar.

The Student's Guide to the University of Cambridge.

Fifth Edition, 1893, Fcap. 8vo. 6s. 6d. *or in separate Parts*, 1s. *each.*

Part I. Introduction. By Bp. of BRISTOL. University Expenses and Non-Collegiate Students. By T. F. C. HUDDLESTON, M.A. Part II. The Mathematical Tripos. By Dr BESANT. Part III. The Classical Tripos. By Rev. R. BURN. Part IV. The Theological Examinations. By Rev. Dr SINKER. Part V. The Law Tripos. By Prof. CLARK. Part VI. Degrees in Medicine and Surgery. By Prof. Sir G. M. HUMPHRY. Part VII. The Natural Sciences Tripos. By W. N. SHAW, M.A. Part VIII. The Moral Sciences Tripos. By Prof. J. WARD. Part IX. The Historical Tripos. By Prof. G. W. PROTHERO. Part X. The Previous Examination and the Ordinary or Poll Degree, and Local Examinations, Lectures, etc. By Rev. J. T. WARD, M.A., and Bp. of BRISTOL. Part XI. The Mediæval and Modern Languages Tripos. By E. G. W. BRAUNHOLTZ, M.A. The Oriental Triposes. By Dr J. PEILE.

WEBSTER'S INTERNATIONAL DICTIONARY
OF THE
ENGLISH LANGUAGE.

Medium 4to. 2118 pp., 3500 Illustrations. Prices: cloth, £1. 11s. 6d.; half-calf, £2. 2s. ; half-**russia**, £2. 5s.; calf, £2. 8s.; **also in two vols.**, **cloth**, **£1. 14s.**, and in various bindings.

In addition to the Dictionary of Words, with their pronunciation, etymology, alternative spellings, and various meanings, illustrated by quotations and numerous woodcuts, there are several valuable appendices, comprising a Pronouncing Gazetteer of the World; Vocabularies of Scripture, Greek, Latin, and English Proper Names ; a Dictionary of the noted Names of Fiction ; a Brief History of **the** English Language ; a Dictionary of Foreign Quotations, Words, Phrases, Proverbs, &c.; a Biographical Dictionary with 10,000 Names, &c.

Prospectuses, with Specimen Pages, on application.

LONDON:
GEORGE BELL & SONS, YORK ST. COVENT GARDEN.
CAMBRIDGE: DEIGHTON, BELL AND CO.

Cambridge: at the University Press.

www.ingramcontent.com/pod-product-compliance
Lightning Source LLC
Chambersburg PA
CBHW030401230426
43664CB00007BB/688